School for Cool

SCHOOL FOR COOL

The Academic Jazz Program and the Paradox of
Institutionalized Creativity

Eitan Y. Wilf

The University of Chicago Press
Chicago and London

Eitan Wilf is assistant professor of anthropology at the Hebrew University of Jerusalem.

The University of Chicago Press, Chicago 60637
The University of Chicago Press, Ltd., London
© 2014 by The University of Chicago
All rights reserved. Published 2014.
Printed in the United States of America

23 22 21 20 19 18 17 16 15 14   1 2 3 4 5

ISBN-13: 978-0-226-12505-3 (cloth)
ISBN-13: 978-0-226-12519-0 (paper)
ISBN-13: 978-0-226-12522-0 (e-book)
DOI: 10.7208/chicago/ 9780226125220.001.0001

Library of Congress Cataloging-in-Publication Data

Wilf, Eitan Y., author.
    School for cool : the academic jazz program and the paradox of institutionalized creativity / Eitan Y. Wilf.
        pages cm
    Includes bibliographical references and index.
    ISBN 978-0-226-12505-3 (cloth : alkaline paper) — ISBN 978-0-226-12519-0 (paperback : alkaline paper) — ISBN 978-0-226-12522-0 (e-book)   1. Jazz—United States—Instruction and study.   2. Jazz musicians.   3. Berklee College of Music.   4. New School for Jazz and Contemporary Music.   I. Title.
    ML3508.W54 2014
    781.65071′073—dc23

                                                        2013029154

♾ This paper meets the requirements of ANSI/NISO Z39.48–1992 (Permanence of Paper).

This book is dedicated to my family—
a somewhat cacophonous, but always swingin', group.

CONTENTS

ACKNOWLEDGMENTS

First and foremost, my deepest gratitude is to the educators, administrators, and students at Berklee College of Music and the New School for Jazz and Contemporary Music, who shared with me their time, insights, and sounds. The joy of the many memorable conversations, educational lessons, and playing sessions I experienced while conducting fieldwork in these two remarkable places sustained me during the long months of the writing-up phase, when sounds had to be converted into theory. In a field often characterized by either purely celebratory or denunciatory accounts of the academic jazz program, I have worked hard to reflect my interlocutors' complex perspectives and practices, as well as to account for the tremendous challenges and social forces that structure these perspectives, practices, and their outcomes.

Jean Comaroff, Karin Knorr Cetina, and Michael Silverstein in the Department of Anthropology at the University of Chicago, as well as Ingrid Monson at Harvard, have been immensely generous with their feedback and guidance throughout the various stages of the project.

Working closely with scholars of their caliber convinced me that the long trip from Tel-Aviv to Chicago was well worth it.

Alessandro Duranti must be thanked for being a generous interlocutor for many years. Asif Agha, Laura Ahearn, Don Brenneis, Summerson Carr, Susan Gal, Nicholas Harkness, John Kelly, Bruce Mannheim, Robert Moore, and Greg Urban provided insightful feedback on various portions of the manuscript when it was presented at various venues both within and outside the University of Chicago. Travis Jackson was helpful in orienting me early on in the vast field of jazz studies. I thank the Department of Anthropology and the Center for Gender Studies at the University of Chicago for giving me the opportunity to teach courses of my own design about jazz and American culture, from which portions of this book emerged. Additionally, the University of Chicago's workshop culture, especially the Semiotics—Culture in Context Workshop, and the Medicine, Body, and Practice Workshop, has been a great incubator for many of the ideas developed in this book. Special thanks are due to Eva Illouz, first as my teacher and then as my colleague, whose level of scholarship and intellectual creativity have provided me with inspiration.

I am grateful to my editor at the University of Chicago Press, Elizabeth Branch Dyson, for her encouragement and support throughout the long process of the project's maturation; to Carol Fisher Saller for her copyediting of the manuscript; and to Russell Damian, also at the Press, for his editorial assistance. I thank the three anonymous reviewers for the Press, who provided much needed feedback. Nurit Stadler was encouraging at the earlier stages of the manuscript's preparation. Anne Ch'ien was immensely helpful during the little more than six years I spent in the Department of Anthropology at the University of Chicago. Elayne Oliphant and Catherine Rhodes read and commented on earlier versions of the project. Lainie Goldwert must be thanked for being herself.

Related versions of certain portions of this work have been published elsewhere, as follows: portions of chapter 5 in "Rituals of Creativity: Tradition, Modernity, and the 'Acoustic Unconscious' in a U.S. Collegiate Jazz Music Program," in *American Anthropologist* 114(1): 32–44; portions of chapter 7 in "Swinging in the Iron Cage: Modernity, Creativity, and Embodied Practice in American Postsecondary Jazz Education," in *American Ethnologist* 37(3): 563–582; and portions of chapter 8 in "Modernity, Cultural Anesthesia, and Sensory Agency: Technologies of the Listening Self in a U.S. Collegiate Jazz Music Program," in *Ethnos* (forthcoming). I am grateful to the editors and reviewers involved in the production of these publications and the arguments developed therein.

It is a pleasure to acknowledge the financial support awarded by the following funding agencies for the research and write-up phases: a University of Chicago Century Fellowship, a Dan David Prize, a Lichtstern Grant from the Department of Anthropology at the University of Chicago, the Josephine de Kármán Fellowship, a Mellon Foundation Dissertation Year Fellowship, a Marie Curie Career Integration Grant from the European Research Council, and a Faculty Matching Grant from the Hebrew University.

INTRODUCTION

The Academic Jazz Program as a Hybrid

The Practice of Creativity and the Creativity of Practice

It is a cold, mid-February Friday night. Pierre and I are preparing to begin our weekly playing session in the deserted main office of Berklee's guitar department, where Pierre works part-time as part of his student fellowship. I suggest we begin with a Miles Davis tune titled "Four," but Pierre is not sure he knows all the chords. He plucks the chords hesitantly on his guitar, one by one. When he arrives at the thirteenth bar of the B section of the tune, Pierre repeats the same chords he played at bars thirteen through sixteen of the A section and in the same harmonic rhythm. Suddenly, a deep, irritated voice thunders at us from another part of the office: "No, no, no! G minor 7, then immediately F-sharp minor 7 to B7, then F minor 7 to B-flat 7, then E-flat major 7!" Pierre is confused. "What?" he asks loudly. Pierre tries to play the chords of the B section again and stops at the thirteenth bar. The voice thunders again, spelling out the chords: "No, no! Listen: G minor 7, then immediately F-sharp minor 7 to B7, F minor 7 to B-flat 7, then E-flat major 7!" Pierre, discouraged, gives up.

"Who is it?" I ask Pierre. I cannot see the person talking to us, because he sits behind a partition that divides the office into two sections. I didn't even know there was another person in the office until I heard his voice. Pierre, still focused on his guitar, says: "That's T.K. He's a piano teacher at the school. He often hangs around in the department." I hear footsteps and then T.K., a tall black man in his midfifties, appears. He nods to me quickly and then speaks to Pierre: "Man, how come you don't know the chord changes to this tune? You consider yourself a jazz player, but you don't know this tune?" Pierre gives an embarrassed half-smile. T.K. stands silently for a minute and continues: "Can you tell me how the relationship between Miles [Davis] and Herbie [Hancock] changed by listening to their recordings?[1] Can you tell me how Trane's [saxophone player John Coltrane] thought evolved by listening to his music?" Pierre and I remain silent. "Man, this is ridiculous. Everything here in the school is ridiculous. They teach you nothing. Do you think that in the past a player would not know that in his later recordings Miles asked Herbie to play fewer chords? If you want to play a tune you have to know everything about it! In the old days a player would play with Art Taylor [a legendary drummer], and when the player would mess up the tune A.T. would tell him "Stop that bullshit" and then he would tell a story and that's how you'd learn! But here, there's nothing like that. It's all sterile. And this is why you can't play this tune!" Pierre and I remain silent while T.K. walks away and disappears in the other part of the office. After a brief moment, Pierre begins again, hesitatingly, to outline the chords to the tune. This time he incorporates the chords that T.K. suggested. It sounds good. Everything starts to fall into place. Pierre repeats the chord sequence faster, each time more fluently than before. At a certain point, T.K.'s voice thunders at us again from behind the partition. This time it is much more encouraging: "Now you got it!"

As I was walking back home after our long playing session, I kept thinking about this incident. T.K.'s criticism of the academic jazz program brought to my mind Walter Benjamin's well-known essay, "The Storyteller" (Benjamin 1969a), which is illustrative of the Frankfurt School's concern with the crisis of experience in modernity (Jay 2005). In this essay, Benjamin argues that the ability to transmit experience via the art of storytelling has disappeared in modernity because experience itself has been devalued. According to Benjamin, a story can transmit experience only if the storyteller grounds herself in the life-world and living praxis of her audience. This art necessitates face-to-face interaction between storyteller and audience. It requires the audience to adopt a certain disinterestedness that verges on boredom, a stance that allows it to assimilate the story more deeply. Benjamin argues that with the advent of modernity, storytelling has been gradually replaced with "information"—knowledge that is decontextualized from the life-world of those who consume it, disseminated in printed form as in newspapers and novels, and produced and consumed in isolation by authors and audiences who are endowed with an instrumental and goal-oriented approach to knowledge.

On the surface, T.K.'s words resonate with Benjamin's diagnosis of the crisis of experience in modernity. T.K. argues that in the past, novice jazz musicians would learn their craft by playing with seasoned musicians who had experiential knowledge of the music and its history. He invokes legendary drummer Art Taylor—A.T.—as an example of a person who had firsthand experience of the living reality of jazz. Taylor understood jazz tunes not only in terms of abstract melodies and chord changes but also as musical entities embedded in specific histories that he himself had lived. Taylor could transmit this experience to neophyte musicians through stories and anecdotes about legendary musicians, performance situations, and notable recordings that are the building blocks of a tune's meaning. As I soon realized, T.K.'s criticism represented a general malaise about academic jazz education both within and outside of the jazz programs I worked in. Many of the educators I encountered had little doubt that jazz training has suffered from its introduction into the academic program. They argued that knowledge has become increasingly abstract, disseminated through method books and other pedagogical aids that transmit standardized information about jazz, and inculcated by professional educators who lack the experiential authority of an Art Taylor because most of them acquired most of their knowledge by attending the same colleges and schools in which they now teach rather than through extensive firsthand experience with the past masters. This has been compounded by the fact that today's students have fewer opportunities to implement this knowledge in real-time performance because of the decline in jazz's popularity and the subsequent disappearance of venues where jazz is performed.[2]

Yet something in the incident that involved T.K. and Pierre did not fit well into this scheme. As I was approaching my apartment, it became clear to me that this incident had another dimension. T.K.'s mode of reprimanding Pierre was at odds with the content of his criticism. While T.K. argued that jazz knowledge is no longer transmitted in the form of stories told by seasoned musicians about their lived experience as performers, he conveyed this argument in the form of a story that relied precisely on his own lived experience as a performer. In other words, T.K.'s mode of imparting knowledge mirrored what he himself experienced when he played with Art Taylor in a nonacademic setting a few decades ago. Now it is T.K. who orders the junior musicians in his presence to "stop that bullshit" and who uses stories as a pedagogical tool for teaching jazz.

It took me many months of data collection and analysis to realize that this apparent contradiction at the heart of T.K.'s criticism epitomizes the complexity, challenges, and potentialities of the institutionalization of creativity, which are reflective of a key problematic in the cultural code of Western modernity. This book builds upon a tightly focused, two-year ethnographic study of two US academic jazz programs—Berklee College of Music in Boston and the New School for Jazz and Contemporary Music in NYC—not only to clarify this problematic in the specific context of the academic jazz program but also to tease out its implications (filtered mainly through anthropological theory) with respect to modern individuals' attempts to engage in creative practice within modernity's rational institutions in general.

An Academic Jazz Program?

Not limited anymore to classical music, the plastic arts, and dance, the socialization into a growing number of art forms—from poetry writing (McGurl 2011; Myers 1993; Wilf 2011) to turntable technique (Muther 2004)—now takes place within the institutions of higher education. Today, for most neophyte and aspiring artists in the United States and elsewhere, becoming an artist means enrolling in one of the hundreds of specialized art programs that confer degrees (from BA to PhD) and certificates in art (Elkins 2009; Singerman 1999).

The dramatic rise of academic jazz training in the United States over the last few decades has been one of the most visible aspects of this institutionalization of artistic practices.[3] Although throughout most of the first half of the twentieth century jazz was mostly excluded from American institutions of higher education due to its basis in African American communities and presumed lack of artistic value (Ake 2002; Caswell and Smith 2000; Lopes 2002; Ogren 1992; Prouty 2008), in 2010 *JazzTimes*'s *Jazz Education Guide* listed hundreds of collegiate jazz programs in the United States alone, in which thousands of students enroll annually. A recent *New York Times* article addressed the expansion of academic jazz education as it found expression at the thirty-fourth annual conference of the International Association for Jazz Education in New York City. The article, significantly titled "Jazz Is Alive and Well; In the Classroom, Anyway" (Chinen 2007), marvels at the eight thousand conference attendees and the numerous panels, concerts, and merchandise booths in which hundreds of jazz pedagogy books and audio and video materials were sold. Its author concludes that the health of jazz education seems to be in inverse proportion to the music's popularity outside of school.[4]

The expansion of academic jazz education has generated much ambivalence in different circles. Many veteran jazz musicians who received their training by prolonged apprenticeship with master musicians prior to the full-blown academization of jazz training have been dismissive of the very idea of the jazz program. The late drummer Max Roach argued that

> we wouldn't have the Duke Ellingtons and the Charlie Parkers if we had gone to the universities and got doctorates because our minds would have been locked into something else. . . . [Academia is] okay if you want to get a job and be like everybody else. But if you want to go outside and above all that and be like Charlie Parker, Bud Powell, Chick Webb, and these people, academia can't teach you. (Monson 2007, 285)

Similar views abound in the jazz world. The ethnomusicologist Paul Berliner quotes pianist Walter Bishop Jr. as saying, "I was a high school dropout, but I graduated from Art Blakey College, the Miles Davis Conservatory of Music, and Charlie Parker University" (Berliner 1994, 36). With these words, Bishop invokes the opposition between the institutionalized jazz school and apprenticeship with the great jazz masters. Bishop suggests that of the two, the latter rather than the former mode of learning is conducive to great jazz. Similarly, on the Lower East Side in Manhattan operates the nonprofit organization the University of the Streets, which offers various educational activities to young people. Jazz plays a key role in the identity of this institution. Its name invokes the same distinction between the university and the supposedly "real"—meaning noncodified and informal—learning environment that is presumably the basis for great jazz. When I attended one of the Friday-night jam sessions hosted in this organization and described my research to some of the activists there, one of them commented that "all those students sound the same. This is not where you go and learn jazz." Presumably, great jazz emanates from the "street," a trope denoting an informal learning environment that is closer to jazz's humble origins in the earlier decades of the twentieth century.

These views have been rampant within academia, too. In her piece, "Jazz

Goes to College: Has Academic Status Served the Art?" scholar Alice Marquis quotes a former editor of *DownBeat* magazine who argues that "the gravest danger facing jazz may lie in . . . comfortable acclimation to the academic world. . . . It will leach the individuality out of the art" (Marquis 1998, 122). Marquis ends her article,

> Yet, jazz deserves all the respect, scholarship, and training that its presence in academe suggests. It deserves to be taken seriously. But, unlike the classical music created for society's stratosphere (elite), jazz erupted from the lowest levels of society, to capture the hearts and bodies of exuberant masses. Despised and persecuted, jazz won a place for itself at the center of American culture. . . . Now, swaddled inside the velvet cage of academic music, can real jazz survive? (Marquis 1998, 122)

Thus, jazz's entrance into academia signals for many commentators its inevitable abstraction and divorce from affect, the body, individuality, and social marginality—all, presumably, loci of creativity. Although academia provides stable employment and prestige, it is also assumed to be stifling in its rational rigidity—a combination Marquis figures with the notion of the "velvet cage."[5] Something "real," which is never fully defined (and whose rhetorical force lies precisely in this lack of definition), is thereby lost (see also Nicholson 2005). Such skeptical and pessimistically one-sided scholarly commentary on academic jazz education has been prevalent.[6]

The dismissive stance toward the jazz program reflects a deep-seated suspicion in relation to the academic art program in general. Scholars of artistic practice have often considered the academic art program as a contradiction in terms because, so they argue, art cannot be cultivated in the institutional environment of modern schooling (Adler 1979). Indeed, one author titled his book on art education, "Why Art Cannot Be Taught" (Elkins 2001). These reactions resurfaced whenever I disclosed the subject of my study to laypeople involved neither in academia nor in the jazz world. Many of them responded with surprise, saying "An academic jazz program? I didn't know you can teach jazz at school!" and then adding "The music probably sounds really bad!"

Different versions of the ambivalence toward the academic art program have played a key role in anthropological theory too, especially in the form of the entrenched opposition between rule-governed behavior and creative practice. A number of foundational scholars located creativity—whether individual or cultural—on the margins of social reality, that is, away from society's normative center and its codified norms of conduct. For example, Franz Boas, writing on the Native American art of the north Pacific Coast, argued that the emergence of pattern books signals the decadence of folk art (Boas 1955, 157). Boas thus associated codified behavior with the demise of creative practice. Max Weber instituted a similar distinction between creative (charismatic) and rule-governed (instrumentally rational) social action, arguing at one point that "genuine charismatic education is the radical opposite of specialized professional training as it is espoused by bureaucracy" in that the latter retains hardly any of "the original irrational means of charismatic education" (Weber 1978b, 1144). Decades later, Victor Turner developed the notions of *communitas* and *liminality* to designate the potentially creative state in which society's members step outside of and reflect upon taken-for-granted social norms. Significantly, Turner argued that this state takes place away from society's normative centers and routine work, for example, in initiation rites in premodern societies, and in leisure and art in modern societies (Turner 1967). Similarly, in an edited volume dedicated specifically to the anthropological study of creativity (Lavie, Narayan, and Rosaldo 1993), the editors begin by qualifying Turner's view of creativity as located on the margins of social reality by arguing that creative practices are "integrated into the mundane arenas of everyday life." However, they also add that "creativity (not unlike laughter) often erupts at unpredictable times and on unexpected occasions" (5). They thus continue to relegate creativity to the realm of the unpredictable that is set apart from rule-governed behavior. More recently, the view of Western schooling as a site of abstract formalization that cannot be conducive to creativity has been given expression in an anthropological study of apprenticeship into a specific form of an improvised musical practice in Turkey (Bryant 2005). After surveying the specific mode of socialization into this art form, which includes immersion in the social context within which this art form is practiced, Rebecca Bryant adds: "Hence, the contradiction of trying to teach [this improvisational form] in lessons modeled after what is considered to be 'modern,' that is, 'Western' music learning: Doing so would be very much like teaching someone how to think by offering him or her a set of instructions" (Bryant 2005, 228). In all these accounts, then, formalized or rule-governed social behavior is consistently viewed as the opposite of creative agency.

These pessimistic accounts notwithstanding, academic jazz programs are thriving all across the United States, offering professional training in the form of a rationalized and formalized curriculum that is implemented through teaching aids such as instruction booklets and audio and video materials that have reconfigured the mode of the cultural reproduction of jazz. These programs address numerous topics such as arranging, jazz composition, ear training, harmony, and ensemble playing. They offer instrumental labs and classes that focus on different stylistic, instrumental, and performance-related considerations, as well as private classes, classes in music technology, and improvisation classes. How can the ambivalence generated by the academic jazz program in particular, and the academic art program in general, be explained? Why has this ambivalence persisted despite the proliferation of such programs, and why has this proliferation continued despite this ambivalence?

The Two Faces of Modernity

Two key narratives about modernity are often understood to be in conflict with one another: The first narrative views modernity and its institutions as sites of increased rationalization associated with the Enlightenment. This narrative was formulated and endorsed by a number of founding figures in sociology and anthropology. For example, it received an influential formulation in Max Weber's writings about modernity as disenchantment, that is, the gradual eradication of religion from a number of spheres, and the increasingly impersonal, formalized, and rational nature of modernity's institutions, most notably bureaucracy (Weber 1978a; Weber 2001). As William Mazzarella puts it:

> The just-so story we too often tell ourselves about the origins of modernity takes disenchantment as its central theme. In this denuded fairy-tale, affect is progressively evacuated from an increasingly rationalized bourgeois world . . . The legitimacy of bourgeois modernity seems here to depend upon processes of abstraction that are at once universalizing and vampiric. The inevitable end point is Max Weber's "iron cage," an arrogantly soulless bureaucratic "nullity" ruled by "specialists without spirit, sensualists without heart." (Mazzarella 2009, 294)

This first narrative, then, views modernity as increased rationalization and disenchantment that take place in formalized institutions, of which the modern school is an example, which promote rule-governed behavior and universal, predictable, decontextualized, and standardized knowledge. This narrative has been a key defining feature in modernity's identity. In the context that concerns us here, it has structured the alarm about the supposedly noncreative nature of the American school system, which has been a constant fixture in the American public imagination. For example, A *New York Times* article from 1983, titled "About Education; New Study Finds Lack of Creativity," quotes scholars who describe school curriculum as "sterile," homogenizing, conservative, inflexible, and reinforcing "the status quo" (Hechinger 1983). In 2010, the situation seems to have changed only slightly, if not deteriorated. In a *Newsweek* article titled "The Creativity Crisis," scholars argue that "American creativity is declining" and that one of the reasons for this decline is "the lack of creativity development in our schools," which focus instead on "standardized curriculum, rote memorization, and nationalized testing" (Bronson and Merryman 2010).

If the first narrative about modernity views it in terms of increased universal rationality divorced from emotions, the second narrative frames modernity via normative ideals of creative agency and expressivity that received their crystallized form with the rise of Romanticism and that have continued to inform our notions of art and creativity ever since. Romanticism emerged at the end of the eighteenth century as a reaction to Enlightenment ideas that emphasized rationality and the search for universal principles of action (Berlin 1999). Romanticism instituted the notion that individuals have their own unique nature or voice with which they must be in touch and to which they must remain faithful. Crucially, it also stipulated that this nature cannot be known prior to its articulation and hence cannot rely on external principles and models of action (Wilf 2011). As Charles Taylor explains (1989), this stipulation was based on a fundamental distinction between the mimetic and the creative types of imagination. Whereas mimetic imagination is concerned with an accurate articulation of a reality that exists prior to such articulation, creative imagination is about making something manifest: "But to talk about 'making manifest' doesn't imply that what is so revealed was already fully formulated beforehand. Sometimes that can be the case, as when I finally reveal my feelings that I had already put in words for myself long ago. But in the case of the novel or play, the expression will also involve a formulation of what I have to say. I am taking something, a vision, a sense of things, which was inchoate and only partly formed, and giving it a specific shape" (Taylor 1989, 374). Although such notions emerged in the sphere of art, they have subsequently come to define normative ideals of the modern subject in general, especially ideals of self-expression and creative agency, as highly personal attributes that develop independently of outside strictures: "A human life is seen as manifesting a potential which is also being shaped by this manifestation; it is not just a matter of copying an external model or carrying out an already determinate formulation. . . . What the voice of nature calls us to cannot be fully known outside of and prior to our articulation/definition of it" (Taylor 1989, 375, 376). Taylor concludes: "[Expressivism] has been a tremendously influential idea. Expressive individuation has become one of the cornerstones of modern culture. So much so that we barely notice it" (Taylor 1989, 376).

Thus, on the one hand, we take institutionalized schooling to represent modern rationality, the search for universal and standardized knowledge, and the formalization of rules of action and cognitive schemata that all students ought to follow. On the other hand, we understand modern normative ideals of expressive individualism and creative agency as epitomizing the demand that each and every one of us explore, discover, and follow our singular nature and voice. This voice cannot be known in advance and hence should not be trapped within and modeled according to external strictures. One key thesis that this book advances is that the academic art program in general generates so much ambivalence because it is a hybrid of these two presumably irreconcilable narratives about modernity. The figure of the academically accredited artist generates anxiety and ambivalence because it is neither here nor there; it is a boundary figure that threatens the integrity of both narratives.

The clash between these two narratives is the reason criticisms of the schooled jazz musician have been so similar in form to one another over a number of decades. Consider the following two vignettes. The first commentary is taken from a 1958 interview with jazz giant Lester Young:

> [Interviewer:] Are there any tenor sax men nowadays, newcomers, that you like especially?
> [Young:] Well, I imagine I'll say I like them all. They all sound the same to me, because almost all of them went to Juilliard and whoever that teacher was, he taught them all the same thing. This one will start playing it, this one will pick it up and start playing it, the same thing. In my mind, the individual is going to come out and play for himself. Like, if you have thirteen people and the teacher teach [sic] all thirteen of them, you mean to tell me out of the thirteen he can't get *one* individual? That's the way *I* think. (Dance 1980, 31; emphasis in the original)

The second commentary is taken from an interview I conducted almost fifty years later, in 2007, with Greg, a Berklee educator in his late thirties:

> Today more and more cookie-cutter players come out. They learn from their teachers to become teachers, and they kind of sound like teachers. Berklee— they call it "the factory" for a reason. It sounds like a factory. Cats come out [from the school] and you go to New York [and people say] "Oh man, a Berklee cat," because they all sound the same. You know, a little bit of [Greg names a specific Berklee teacher], little bit of [Greg names another Berklee teacher], whoever, you know. And that's good and bad. It's good if they learn to get past that. But if they don't—and many don't—they're gonna just be what they are. And there are tons of decent players out there that aren't nearly—there's not the level of innovators that there was because back in the day cats had to go out and be in the scene.

The two commentaries very much overlap, and their speakers employ the same words and phrases, despite their historical distance from one another. Both argue that many musicians attend schools where they study with the same educators and hence "sound the same." That Lester Young refers to jazz players who studied at Juilliard in the 1950s rather than in a jazz program specifically,[7] whereas Greg refers to a program with a strong focus on jazz, makes the alignment of their criticisms all the more significant. It suggests that fears about the possible standardization and demise of jazz as a result of its academization are not a new phenomenon and that there is something about institutionalized art education that invokes these fears, namely the clash between the two narratives of modernity I have outlined above.[8]

In a sense, none of this is new. In his book, *The Cultural Contradictions of Capitalism*, Daniel Bell (1978) pointed up a principal contradiction in modern polities (one among a number of contradictions) between, on the one hand, the sector of culture organized around the idea of the expression of the self and the rejection of any limits posed upon it and, on the other hand, the techno-economic sector with its emphasis on specialization, bureaucratization, and social compartmentalization of the self. This tension results in social conflicts expressed ideologically as alienation and the attack on authority.

What is new, however, is the fact that whereas Bell discussed a contradiction between normative ideals that are anchored in different sectors of society, the academic art program condenses this contradiction in a single site. This contradiction is no longer between one's leisure and one's work, to take one of the often-cited examples for the kind of cultural contradictions with which Bell and his followers were concerned, but rather between jazz and the modes in which it is cultivated in a specific site at the present historical moment, for example. The academic art program is a site in which the presumably conflicting modern normative ideals of rationality and creative agency are intertwined with one another as never before. It is precisely for this reason that it constitutes a fascinating site in which to explore the intricacies of this intertwining, the ways in which individuals attempt to negotiate it, and the unintended consequences of such negotiation.

If the academic art program in general provides a good entry point to clarify these issues, the academic jazz program in particular provides perhaps the best site to do so from among the different academic art programs, because more than any other modern art form, jazz has come to epitomize the ethos of Western modernistic creativity. Because of its improvisatory nature, a number of key figures in different branches of twentieth-century artistic modernism such as abstract expressionism (e.g., Jackson Pollock), surrealism (e.g., René Magritte), and the new wave cinema (e.g., Jean-Luc Godard), as well as in the existential philosophical school (e.g., Jean-Paul Sartre), embraced jazz as a model of radical creative freedom and spontaneity (Belgrad 1998; Nettelbeck 2005, 95–188). Although some of modernism's borrowing from jazz was based in misunderstandings about the nature of improvisation (as if it were creation ex nihilo) and in various appropriations of blackness as a locus of authenticity (Gioia 1988a; Monson 1995; Ramshaw 2006), it suggests that the academic jazz program can serve as a productive site in which to explore the relationship between institutionalized rationality, or rule-governed behavior, and creative agency in the context of a purportedly modern creative practice.

Taking up the interrogation of the relation between institutionalized rationality and creative agency in two academic jazz programs, I will answer the following questions: How could artistic creativity, which, according to the Romantic ethos, depends on being in touch with one's unique inner nature and voice rather than conforming to outside models of being, be cultivated within the rational, bureaucratic, organizational structure of the university, with its institutional paraphernalia of standardization such as curricula, syllabuses, and tests? How could neophyte jazz musicians be trained in creativity by formalized procedural means? What would modern forms of "routinization of charisma" through "charismatic education" look like (Weber 1978b)? And what would be the implications of such forms of routinization for how we understand schooling, creative practice, and the possibility of their reconciliation?

Beyond the general level of the academic art program and the relation between creative practice and institutionalized rationality, I will unpack the specific challenges, potentialities, and contradictions that have resulted from the academization of jazz training. Although some of them are similar to those of academic training in other art forms, the case of academic jazz training possesses its own specificity. Most important, perhaps, is that whereas many musicians of previous generations could rely on long apprenticeship with seasoned musicians in live performance situations, the training of today's students is heavily informed by formalized knowledge mediated by printed material and taught in classrooms by professional educators in a broader social environment in which extracurricular performance is rare. On a more specific level, then, this book is about these transformations in modes of training, as well as their impact; educators' and students' attempts to negotiate these transformations; and the unintended consequences of these attempts.

The Book's Argument

Zooming in on the everyday reality in two academic jazz programs, I offer a three-fold argument. First, the socialization into jazz in these two programs does involve numerous challenges and paradoxes for both educators and students who strive to inform their playing and teaching with traditions, ideologies, myths, and ideals that they associate with great jazz, in an institutional environment that often entails highly different traditions, ideologies, and ideals. Indeed, many of these educators and students subscribe to the same powerful associations that circulate in the American public imaginary at large, which hold jazz and institutionalized schooling to be antithetical to one another. And they have good reasons for doing so. On a more general level, normative ideals of rationality and Romantic creativity that, on the surface, seem to conflict with one another find expression in concrete ways in the everyday pedagogical reality of the jazz program. For example, at Berklee, students are assigned a five-digit rating during their audition that is further updated throughout their studies. The curriculum is divided into numerous discrete theoretical topics that are mediated by ever more specialized method books and formalized terminology. At the same time, students are bombarded with messages about the need for them to be "true" to their unique artistic self, to eschew imitation, and to strive to develop a unique style of improvisation. The reason many people view the academic jazz program as an anomaly is that it seems to bring these two presumably irreconcilable forces together under one roof. Beyond this general level, the academic environment of the jazz program often leads to modes of training that are at odds with key aesthetic principles of the cultural order of jazz. For example, many programs' heavy reliance on formalized, abstract, and easily testable knowledge mediated in printed form hinders students from mastering crucial skills such as participating in group creativity, developing a distinct voice or stylistic identity, and swinging.

Second, such challenges notwithstanding, administrators, educators, and students often manage to draw on the resources of the academic environment to cultivate forms of creativity they believe are faithful to jazz's cultural order. They recruit charismatic performers who played with the past masters to serve as teachers; they take advantage of advanced technologies of sound mediation to immerse students in the sounds of the past jazz masters' creative improvisations; they imbue the past masters' improvisations with the institutionalized terminology of the academic jazz program through acts of translation, interpretation, and narration that bring the two closer together; they use rule-governed techniques to reconfigure students' playing bodies and thus to open up new creative horizons in their improvisations; and they devise routinized strategies of sensorial self-fashioning that increase the role played by aurality in students' improvisational competence. Their strategies contest a number of traditional binary oppositions, such as spontaneous/ rule-governed social action, creative practice/institutionalized rationality, and informal/formal learning.

Third, however, the different strategies deployed by the administrators, educators, and students I worked with in their efforts to negotiate what they believe are distinct and oppositional categories frequently *sustain* different dimensions of the basic opposition between creative practice and institutionalized rationality. They reproduce oppositions such as aurality/literacy, blackness/whiteness, intuition/theory, lowbrow/highbrow, and associate creativity in jazz with the terms occupying the left side of these oppositions, and institutionalized rationality with the terms occupying the right side of these oppositions. In doing so, they reconcile creative practice and institutionalized rationality on one level, but keep them polarized on another level.[9]

Returning to the vignette that opens this chapter, which involves T.K. scolding Pierre over the latter's failure to master the contextual knowledge within which the tune "Four" is grounded, note that even as T.K. voices the challenge of reconciling the academic environment and creative practice in jazz, he finds a way to do precisely that. However, he manages to perform such reconciliation through an argument that such reconciliation is impossible and that the academic jazz program is the direct antithesis to "real" jazz training. This vignette exemplifies the unexpected ways in which creative practice and institutionalized rationality are reconciled and at the same time reproduced as antithetical to one another in sites such as the academic jazz program, which bring normative ideals of institutionalized rationality and creative agency together under one roof. When contemporary criticisms of the academic jazz program or advocacy groups whose goal is to foster this type of jazz training do not take this complex dynamics into account, they reduce the enormous complexity of educators' and students' praxis and the ways in which this praxis both reconfigures and reproduces publicly circulating discourses about modern rationality and modern creative agency. Here, I would like to uncover this complexity and tease out its numerous theoretical and practical implications.

The Ethnographic Setting and Fieldwork

Beginning in July 2006, I spent a year at Berklee College of Music in Boston, followed by four months at the New School for Jazz and Contemporary Music in New York City (September–December 2007). Additionally, I spent nine months in the jazz scene of New York City (September 2007–May 2008) during which I followed Berklee graduates who relocated to the city to further their career, and participated in and attended various jazz educational conferences and activities organized by nonprofit groups.[10]

One of the first US colleges to focus on jazz, Berklee has come to be identified with institutionalized jazz education both in and outside of this field. It has had a definitive impact on the jazz education curriculum through the production and dissemination of pedagogical method books and thousands of graduates who have gone on to teach in and establish other schools. For this reason, my main focus will be on Berklee. The school is commonly viewed as close to the epitome of mass jazz education because of its size (annually enrolling approximately four thousand students);[11] its standardization and rationalization of knowledge in the form of pedagogical aids, practices, and curricula; and its eager incorporation of sophisticated media technologies and online courses potentially available to masses of novice players.[12] The New

School's jazz program, in contrast, is commonly regarded as Berklee's antithesis because of its smaller size and reliance on a greater percentage of faculty members with "direct links" to the tradition of the music, as its administrators put it. These are musicians who played with key jazz masters prior to jazz's full-blown academization and who presumably rely on more "traditional" pedagogies that are less mediated by print artifacts and standardized course material.

Juxtaposed, Berklee and the New School offer a good view of the wide spectrum of jazz pedagogical practices and ideologies in academic jazz education. At the same time, it should be clear from the outset that these two do not represent the full spectrum of programs—from the Thelonious Monk Institute, which pairs a very limited number of students with some of the most highly regarded jazz musicians active today, to programs in which jazz training is even more formalized than at Berklee. Thus, although the two programs that stand at the center of this book provide a good vantage point from which to make sense of the field of academic jazz education, I purport neither to represent the entire field nor every aspect of the pedagogical reality within these two programs.[13] Readers with stakes in academic jazz education who do not recognize their own experience in this book should bear this dual-aspect partiality in mind. Throughout the book I have attempted to make sure that the ethnographic specificity of my study remains clear.

During my fieldwork, I observed numerous theoretical and performance-based classes—all jazz-focused, taught by different educators. I also attended concerts, clinics, workshops, and master classes held at the schools.[14] In addition to observing in classrooms, I conducted formal interviews and engaged in countless informal conversations with educators and students. I supplemented this with the collection and analysis of school publications, from brochures to class material. Lastly, during my fieldwork in the jazz scene of New York City, I attended various events related to academic jazz education (broadly defined) such as the annual meeting of the International Association for Jazz Education, the conference organized by the trade magazine *Jazz Improv*, and public forums and concerts organized by other jazz programs and organizations. I deployed these methods of data collection to zone in on key pedagogical strategies in both programs as a way of teasing out a number of implications—filtered through anthropological theory—of the relationship between institutionalized rationality and creative practice, and its negotiation in specific institutional sites. I was not interested in providing a purely descriptive account of these phenomena. At the same time, I was cautious not to impose any theories upon my data where they did not fit. Taking seriously what my interlocutors were telling me, as well as their everyday pedagogical practices, my aim is to present a nuanced picture that is neither celebratory nor outright critical. Indeed, one of my main arguments is that we need to extract ourselves from one-sided views of academic jazz education and approach it as the complex social institution that it is.

Using early twentieth-century arguments made by classical music educators against the introduction of jazz into the university, data gathered in classes at Berklee and the New School, interviews with these schools' administrators, and notes taken in jazz education conferences in New York City, chapter 2 focuses on two social forces (out of many) that have led to the rise of academic jazz education in its present form and that were salient in the commentary and vignettes I collected in the two jazz programs: first, the desire to elevate jazz's traditionally marginal status in the American cultural hierarchy by introducing it into the institutions of high art, including those of music education; and second, the need to create alternative jazz scenes, in lieu of the increasingly nonviable commercial ones, which would provide financial security for mature players and training grounds for neophyte players. Thus market forces and cultural hierarchy emerge as key engines behind the academization of jazz training.

In chapter 3, I highlight the paradoxes and ambivalences that result when cultural legitimacy is no longer a future goal of a marginalized art form but rather a present achievement, and when embeddedness in the market gives way to the search for autonomy from the market. I explore three of these ambivalences and contradictions by zooming in on a number of public events and institutional rituals, mainly at Berklee. First, jazz's academization involved the adoption of the markers of high art and academia that continue to signify elitism for many jazz musicians and educators, a fact that results in heightened ambivalence. Second, although academic jazz education initially emerged from a nonexclusionary agenda that strived to inform music schools' curricula by popular demand, today jazz is no longer popular. Ironically, in their efforts to protect jazz's place in the contemporary music program against the backdrop of this shift in its popularity, many of the administrators and educators I worked with adopt some of the same discourses about the autonomy of high art and its necessary uncoupling from the market that were responsible for the exclusion of jazz from higher education prior to its academization. Finally, although today the efforts to cultivate jazz and grant it cultural legitimacy have borne fruit, and jazz's status is mostly secured, a growing consensus has emerged among many of my interlocutors that the music's creativity is grounded in, and can only be sustained by, interactional norms, behaviors, and epistemologies that are radically at odds with those that characterize the institutional bases of high art and especially the academic environment.

In the second half of the book, I explore the pedagogical strategies that administrators, educators, and students use to resolve the ambivalences, especially those that relate to the jazz program's implications for students' improvisational competence. The strategies are varied, yet they have something in common: they tap into what many in the two jazz programs consider to be the golden age of jazz, namely from its inception to the late 1960s (and hence prior to the music's full-blown academization). These strategies entail more than focusing on the styles associated with this period. They allow students and educators to reconnect with the charisma of the jazz masters who were active at that time, as well as with the epistemologies that are believed to have led to the masters' unsurpassed creative output. Ironically, these strategies mobilize the resources of the academic jazz program with the implicit and sometimes explicit goal of undoing its effects. This irony is productive of a number of unintended consequences.

Chapter 4 explores the institutionalization of creative practice in the two academic jazz programs through the prism of Max Weber's notion of routinization of charisma. It focuses on administrators' efforts to address the *compartmentalization and abstraction of knowledge* in the jazz program, that is, the departmentalization of knowledge into discrete and specialized subjects that become increasingly disconnected from one another and render the overall curriculum somewhat incoherent. They do so by recruiting musicians who played with the past legendary jazz masters at some point in their careers and who can thus introduce the charisma associated with the pre-academic era of jazz into the program. Although they constitute a small share of the body of educators, these musicians play a significant role in the effort to reconcile creativity in jazz and the academic environment. This strategy is inherently contradictory: At the same time that its goal is to mitigate the effects of the academization of jazz training by recruiting musicians who are able to teach "in the old way," it perpetuates the opposition between institutionalized rationality and creative practice by associating these musicians with stereotypes of past creative jazz as anti-institutional, male-centric, lowbrow, and suffused with tropes of "blackness."

Chapters 5–7 are concerned with the ways in which the majority of educators in the two jazz programs—"professional" educators who acquired most of their training within academic jazz education rather than by prolonged apprenticeship with the past masters—tap into a charismatic era with which they have had little to no personal experience. As I explain in chapter 5, against the backdrop of mounting discontent about *the growing role played by print pedagogy* in jazz training, which hinders students from developing crucial stylistic features such as distinct timbre and the ability to swing, educators instruct students to produce precise replications of the recorded improvisations of past jazz masters and then play them in synchrony with the original recordings in the classroom. New digital sound technologies make it possible for students to slow down past legendary jazz masters' recorded improvisations with little distortion of pitch or timbre and thus to produce more precise replications. When they play these replications in synchrony with the original recordings in the classroom, students experience a kind of fusion with the masters that has profound experiential effects. I argue that this strategy of orchestrating ritual transformation complicates long-held assumptions both within and outside of anthropology about the opposition between rule-governed behavior and creative practice. At the same time, I suggest, this practice often frustrates such fusion. The perceptual enhancement produced by these new technologies of sound mediation transforms the ideal of fusing with the masters into a promise that cannot be fully fulfilled. The result is frustration that keeps creative practice and institutionalized rationality distinct despite moments in which they are powerfully reconciled.

If discontent about the increased abstraction of jazz education—most notably symbolized by the ubiquity of print pedagogy—has led educators to instruct their students to inhabit the past echoes of the music, this does not mean that printed artifacts and music notation do not play an important role in educators' attempts to bridge the gap between institutionalized rationality and creative practice. Chapter 6 explores a strategy educators deploy in response to criticisms about *the predominance of chord-scale theory* in academic jazz training. This strategy involves the production and analysis of transcriptions of legendary past masters' recorded improvisations. When educators analyze masters' solos in class, they implicitly construct the masters' decision-making processes as if they were informed by considerations that are grounded in academic jazz education's body of expert knowledge. These interpretative techniques thereby legitimize this knowledge because of the prestige associated with the past masters. However, these techniques are also contradictory. Educators turn to the past masters because they believe they epitomize the creative variety that can revitalize the standardized knowledge produced and transmitted in the academic jazz program. Yet their interpretative techniques inadvertently reduce the plurality of voices and aesthetics, which informed the creativity of these masters, into academic jazz education's body of expert knowledge. Furthermore, given the fact that much of the creative plurality of the past masters emerged from aesthetic sensibilities and social concerns that were specific to the social and cultural experience of African American communities, the reduction of this plurality to the standardized terminology of academic jazz education, which in some contexts today is dominated by a white middle-class majority of educators and students, is political through and through.

Chapter 7 discusses a strategy educators deploy to address *the decline of students' ability to play editorially*. Many of the educators I worked with argued that the masterpieces of the past masters were the result of heavy reliance on aurality as a mode of knowledge production and transmission. Learning was extensively mediated by listening, which prepared the masters to function well in performance situations predicated on improvisation. Today's students, however, incorporate into their playing bodies standardized patterns of improvisation they learn mostly visually, from commercially produced method books and other aids, while having few opportunities to gain experience in live performance. Consequently, when they are required to improvise, students fall back on standardized and predictable embodied patterns of improvisation rather than executing emergent musical ideas and responding to the ongoing musical cues provided by their band members. They lack the ability to play editorially. To counter this predicament, educators reconfigure students' playing bodies by limiting them so that students can no longer play what they were used to playing and instead must intentionally hear what they want to play before playing it. Thus, they teach their students rule-governed techniques of cultivating their creative agency. At the same time, the chapter highlights this strategy's role in reproducing the opposition between aurality and literacy, which has supported the opposition between creativity and institutionalized rationality throughout jazz's history, as well as objections to the introduction of jazz into institutions of higher education.

Chapter 8 shifts the analysis from educators to students. It focuses on a series of competitive games played by students to cultivate different dimensions of aural sensitivity and to address a key challenge they face in their academic setting, namely, *the virtualization and atomization of musical sociality* that impede their ability to participate in and contribute to real-time group creativity and musical interaction. By playing these games with one another, students hone the skills of responding to an external or internal auditory representation by whistling, singing, or playing their instruments; participating in live musical interaction with other musicians; cultivating distinct timbres and improvisational styles; and tapping into tunes' melodies and titles as a basis for meaningful improvisation. I analyze these games as forms of Michel Foucault's notion of "technologies of the self"—that is, as collective practices through which students help one another to hone what they consider to be the key skills that every proficient jazz musician ought to master but that have been neglected by the programs they are enrolled in. However, inasmuch as they are based on a competition between individuals, these games also transform this culturally specific, meaningful sensual experience into a scarce resource over which individuals must compete in order to attain it. Thus, much like the pedagogical strategies discussed in the other chapters, these informal practices embody a contradiction in their very logic: they reconcile institutionalized rationality and creative practice on one level yet keep them distinct on another level.

Anthropology + Trumpet = Trumpology

The days when anthropologists were associated solely with the study of "exotic" cultures in faraway places (from the West, of course) seem to lie in the distant past.[15] Every year a plethora of theoretically rigorous ethnographies are published that are concerned with sites to which one can take "a subway" from one's university base, to use Joanne Passaro's felicitous phrase (Passaro 1997). From an addiction treatment center in a Midwestern city (Carr 2010) to investment banks in New York City's Wall Street (Ho 2009), it is no longer professional suicide to do your fieldwork "at home." Even so, whenever I tell people about my fieldwork, their reactions are fairly consistent. At first, they react with surprised disappointment, for they expected me to tell them Indiana Jones tales about crocodile-infested swamps and hairy-legged tarantulas. However, soon they regroup themselves and ask me to tell them stories about smoky jazz clubs and people of dubious moral character. In other words, they figure that if I can tell them nothing about the Amazonian jungle, at least they can get a taste of the urban jungle connoted by jazz. When I tell them that my work took place mostly in academic jazz programs and upper-scale jazz clubs in Boston and the West Village, they lose all hope and express their surprise and disdain at the very idea of the jazz school. Finally, almost in an accusatory tone, they say that "I had it made": rather than getting mosquito bites and food poisoning, I arranged a "sweet deal" of a fieldwork living in Boston and Manhattan.

I agreed with them wholeheartedly but for entirely different reasons. Sure, I enjoyed living next to Boston's Museum of Fine Arts and then later on Manhattan's Upper West Side in a new, three-bedroom, two-bathroom apartment (with a washer and a drier!) in a doorman building—an apartment normally inhabited by a Columbia University professor who was on sabbatical and in need of someone to take over the place for the year. But I considered my fieldwork to be a "sweet deal" primarily because it allowed me to learn from, interact and even play with some of my musical idols. Suddenly I found myself sitting in classes and clinics taught by musicians to whom, until that point, I had access only via LPs, CDs, and books. Additionally, my fieldwork has contributed to my development as a jazz trumpet player.

This does not mean that conducting this kind of fieldwork was free of challenges. As Stephan Helmreich put it apropos his own fieldwork at the Santa Fe Institute, "Doing anthropology among powerful people is different. Many do not like to be studied and can easily prevent anthropological access to their lives" (Helmreich 1998, 25). This challenge has certainly been compounded in the case of my fieldwork. In the context of jazz's history of marginalization and the fact that it had been the subject of institutional elitism, many jazz educators were highly ambivalent about my attending their classes. This was certainly the case at the New School, many of whose educators are older African Americans. They had good reasons to be suspicious, because jazz musicians, especially African Americans, have often been misrepresented by white critics. What eventually helped me gain access to their classes was the fact that I am not a US citizen and hence am less implicated in this problematic history (although some of the most essentializing depictions of jazz musicians are the product of non American critics—see Gioia 1988a). Even so, I welcomed these challenges, for they reminded me of the imperative to be sensitive to how I represent my informants.

An additional element that eased my fieldwork was the fact that I have experience in the curriculum of US academic jazz education as a trumpet player. This has certainly made it easier for me to gain educators' respect and form friendships with students, which culminated in many hours of shared playing. I accompanied students in their practice routines, parties, and day-to-day informal interactions both in and outside of school. I have maintained contact with a number of these students after their graduation and have continued to play with them in New York City.

My path toward doing this study began even before I embarked on my undergraduate studies in anthropology. Following a long career as a classical violin player, I switched to the trumpet to specialize in jazz. After studying jazz trumpet privately, I enrolled in a jazz school in Israel, which is one of the first non American jazz schools founded by Berklee graduates. The school's curriculum is based on that of Berklee's, and there is an accreditation agreement between the two schools that allows Israeli students to complete their degrees at Berklee. Thus, my experience with Berklee began before I could imagine I would eventually conduct fieldwork on academic jazz education at Berklee. Ten years later, when I decided to do so, my contacts at the Israeli school helped me gain access to Berklee.

To some extent, my connection to the New School also began in Israel. One of the founders of the New School's jazz program was the late saxophonist Arnie Lawrence, who passed away in 2005. In 1997, after a long career in the United States, during which he played with some of the greatest jazz masters, Arnie moved to Israel and opened the International Center for Creative Music in Jerusalem, whose purpose was to connect young Jewish and Arab musicians. I played a few times in the jam sessions organized at that center. I also played regularly in a jam session in a bar at the center of Jerusalem, which Arnie used to frequent. One night in 2004, when I already knew that I was going to pursue my doctoral studies in anthropology at the University of Chicago, I came to this bar with my trumpet. Arnie was there with his alto saxophone. As the rhythm section debated what to play, Arnie asked me what I was doing in life. Trying to overcome the surrounding noise, I answered that I am studying anthropology. Arnie's white bushy eyebrows rose up in surprise. He asked in wonder: "Trumpology?" looking at the trumpet I was holding. I laughed and said again: "Anthropology." "Aha!" Arnie responded, "then let's play it!" Without further ado, he began playing Charlie Parker's tune "Anthropology," and the rhythm section and I immediately joined him.

I have come to believe that Arnie's unintended pun was ingenuously prophetic of the deep coupling of the personal and the professional that would sustain me during fieldwork and the write-up process. More than once, anthropology and jazz became one and the same for me, and I have remained thankful for that. Ultimately, the following account of the complexity involved in administrators', educators', and students' attempts to reconcile their notions of creativity in jazz with the university's institutional infrastructure represents my own attempt to perform the same reconciliation between creative agency and institutionalized rationality, and in that respect my account no doubt encompasses some of the same potentialities and limitations that pervade their attempts. Rather than an analytical shortcoming, I consider this fact to be supportive of my thesis that the academic jazz program epitomizes a widespread predicament that numerous individuals—academics included—need to grapple with. This predicament begs for clarification. This book is an attempt to provide it.

2

CONTEXTS AND HISTORIES

The Search for Cultural Legitimacy and the Reconfiguration of Obsolete Jazz Scenes

"So, how does it feel to play for Harvard students?"

Early in my fieldwork at Berklee, eager to make contact with students, I approached many of them and asked whether they "gigged" somewhere in the city, adding that I would be interested in attending and listening to them play. Such an approach was not very successful. Students had very few performances scheduled to take place outside of school. About two months into the research, however, when I approached Pierre, a guitar player, with the same question, he answered with a hesitant "yes." He quickly added that "this is not really a gig. It's not for money. Someone at Harvard asked John, the sax player, if he can organize a small band to play in this event he is planning at Winthrop House—it's this undergraduate residence house at Harvard. So John called me and a couple of guys. It's kind of an opportunity to play outside of school, you know? If you want, you can come to this event."

A couple of days later, on a Friday evening, I took the subway to Harvard Square and from there made my way in search of Winthrop House according to a map I had, which turned out to be of little help.

After erring between similar-looking buildings for half an hour, I suddenly heard the sound of a saxophone and followed it until I arrived at Winthrop House and entered a large hall where the performance was taking place. The first thing that struck me was the discrepancy between the appearance of the Berklee students playing on stage and the Harvard students standing in small groups, drinks in their hands, talking to one another. While the Berklee students were dressed in plain T-shirts and jeans, the Harvard students were dressed in tuxedos and ballroom dresses. The second thing that struck me was how little the Harvard students seemed to be interested in the music played on stage. They were totally immersed in their own conversations. When the tune ended, there was short and barely audible applause, and John, the band leader, announced that the players are going to take a short break. I approached the band members and walked with them to grab some drinks. We watched the scene around us in silence for a couple of minutes. Suddenly, Pierre, out of the blue, said in a bitter voice: "If we were a string quartet with ties and suits, they would pay us, but we are jazz musicians so they pay us nothing, you know what I mean?" At that precise moment, as if to confirm his worst suspicions, a Harvard student, wearing a beautiful long gray dress and a pearl necklace, left a small group of students and approached us with a glass of wine in her hand. She curiously looked at us for a few seconds and then asked in dead earnestness: "So how does it feel to play for Harvard students?"

Years later, as I was thinking of how to tell the story of the rise and expansion of academic jazz education in the best possible way, I was reminded of this incident. It became clear to me that it epitomizes two factors that played an important role in the rise and transformation of academic jazz education into a key infrastructure for jazz training and performance today: first, jazz musicians' search for cultural legitimacy and for a place in institutions of higher music education against the backdrop of systematic marginalization and unequal access to resources; and second, their need to find alternative sites of employment and training in view of the increasingly disappearing commercial marketplace for jazz. Pierre's suggestion that the band members were not paid because they were jazz musicians rather than a string quartet, as well as the fact that the band members felt ill at ease amid what they perceived to be the visible markers of wealth and the sense of entitlement displayed around them at Harvard are directly related to the first factor. That they were willing to play for free at this event because it provided them with a rare opportunity to perform outside of school is directly related to the second factor.

Although the rise of academic jazz education has been determined by many factors (Ake 2002; Collier 1994; Gennari 2006, 207–225; Prouty 2005), I want to focus on these two, because they were the most salient in the ways in which the administrators, educators, and students I worked with understood the rise of academic jazz education, and because these factors impacted the everyday pedagogical reality at Berklee and the New School at the time of my fieldwork there. In discussing each factor in detail, my purpose is to complicate simplistic arguments that represent the introduction of jazz training into academe as the easy choice made by musicians who did not mind jeopardizing their craft and betraying their presumed vocation or "essence" in pursuit of various forms of institutional comfort.

Cultural Marginalization

In 1993, during his first inauguration, TV viewers from around the world watched president-elect Bill Clinton, in the company of veteran jazz musicians, "jamming" with his tenor saxophone on Duke Ellington's tune "C Jam Blues." This performance was only one marker of the status of jazz as a recognized and respected American tradition. The National Endowment for the Arts has bestowed "lifetime achievement awards" upon master jazz musicians since 1982, designating the musicians and their music "National Treasures." Indeed, jazz is often hailed as "America's classical music" (Sales 1992). The status of jazz as a self-conscious American tradition has also been solidified through the establishment of various museums dedicated to jazz, such as the American Jazz Museum in Kansas City and the National Jazz Museum in Harlem, as well as by the programming of performance and education centers that focus on jazz, such as Jazz at Lincoln Center in New York. The dramatic expansion of academic jazz education in the United States over the last few decades has been perhaps the most significant aspect of the institutionalization of jazz as a firmly recognized and respected American tradition.

Indeed, each morning during my fieldwork at Berklee, I walked from my apartment on Park Drive in Boston's Fenway-Kenmore neighborhood to the school, a fifteen-minute walk that seemed to perfectly symbolize jazz's secured position in the American cultural hierarchy. My studio apartment—a space just big enough for a bed, a table, a little kitchenette, and a bathroom, for which I paid the hefty monthly rent of $1,125 due to Boston's soaring real-estate market (this was in 2006!)—was in an apartment building dating from 1910. It faced Back Bay Fens, the beautiful park designed in the late nineteenth century by Frederick Law Olmsted, the same person who designed New York

City's Central Park. My daily walk to Berklee took me across this park and its Canada geese, past Simmons College, the Isabella Stewart Gardner Museum, Boston's Museum of Fine Arts, the Forsyth Institute, and Boston Conservatory. A few blocks from my apartment were Wheelock College, Emmanuel College, Harvard Medical School, Wentworth Institute of Technology, and Northeastern University. While it was not unusual for me to hear from time to time the thunderous roar of baseball fans coming from Fenway Park, my daily walk to Berklee was mostly a quiet tour along a number of venerable institutions that each and collectively indexed the higher echelons of the American cultural hierarchy. Berklee itself, centrally located at the intersection of Massachusetts Avenue and Boylston Street, is blocks away from the New England Conservatory and the Boston Public Library. Standing outside Berklee, one can see the towering dome of the Massachusetts Institute of Technology just across the Charles River, in Cambridge. And further down Massachusetts Avenue lies the imposing presence of Harvard University, which, though not visible from Berklee's campus buildings, seems to orient to itself all these different tokens of high culture like a powerful magnet.

I elaborate on these details not because they reflect the highly impressionable mind of a non-American anthropologist who was thrilled to be immersed in this abundance of American cultural history—or at least not only because of that (for I was definitely thrilled by this scenery). Rather, I argue that there is a palpable symbolic load to the fact that Berklee—one of the first major academic jazz programs in the United States—was established in the midst of this dense configuration of different tokens of American high culture from which jazz had been systematically excluded throughout most of the twentieth century. By looking only at the present status of jazz in general and academic jazz education in particular, it is hard to imagine that such systematic exclusion played a key role in jazz's history in the US. Academic jazz education's present success reveals very little about its more contentious beginning.[1]

"The joke-smith in the world of tones"

The story of this contentious beginning took place within what the sociologist Pierre Bourdieu has called "a field of cultural production" (Bourdieu 1993). Bourdieu has argued that different fields of cultural production such as music, the plastic arts, and journalism consist of positions relative to one another as well as the propensity of different agents for position-taking. In Bourdieu's words, this is a universe in which "to exist is to differ, i.e. to occupy a distinct, distinctive position" (Bourdieu 1993, 58). Such fields are often, though not always, arenas in which the unequal distribution of economic capital is naturalized through its misrecognized translation into cultural capital. In this way, taste and talent for producing and consuming specific cultural forms are perceived to be natural rather than the products of a certain position within the social structure, often economically determined. It is this kind of naturalization that helps reproduce unequal social formations.

The field of music in the United States in the first half of the twentieth century consisted of many positions. Two of the positions that were often defined in relation to one another were occupied by jazz and classical music. This was not pure abstract difference. Rather, classical music often occupied the higher echelons of the American cultural hierarchy vis-à-vis jazz. The distinction between the two genres naturalized forms of economic inequality and racial ideologies, masked under notions of taste, talent, and aesthetics.[2]

A good entry point into this story and the assumptions that played a key role in it is an article from 1926 titled "'Jazz'—An Educational Problem" and published in the *Musical Quarterly* (Stringham 1926).[3] The author begins with the following sentence: "It may seem a bit strange that Jazz should receive serious attention from musical educators." He then adds: "A thing may be ever so good under certain conditions; but if it be used to excess, the effects will very likely be bad. Conversely, poison, in proper doses, may be used as a helpful agent toward health. . . . So it is with jazz. This form of music, as we shall call it for the time being, at least for sake of argument, has been denounced far and wide as being of immoral character and having within it the means of inducing immorality. Nothing is so absurd" (190). Arguing that jazz has acquired immoral associations because of the contexts in which it was played rather than due to its inherent nature, the author, however, immediately places jazz in its proper position relative to classical music, using interesting metaphors:

Gastronomically speaking, the music of Bach, Beethoven and Brahms may possibly be likened unto beefsteak; but a menu cannot be constructed out of such all the time. We need something to make us grin and laugh once in a while. Jazz certainly can do that much better than music of the finer qualities, and who is there among us that does not crave for musical relaxation now and then? Jazz is the joke-smith in the world of tones, and who would deny us mortals a joke now and then? The musical jokes of the "classical" lore are usually as funny as a hospital. Jazz has no pretensions of being anything other than light and disposed toward levity; at least it has had no other ambitions until recently. But what of future possibilities? (192)

Again, on first impression, this invocation of "future possibilities" suggests that jazz may one day "ascend" into the realms of high art. Yet though the author is reluctant to completely reject jazz as a viable art form, he immediately tempers his sympathy for the genre by subordinating it to classical music: "What we need on the part of serious musicians, is not wholesale denunciation, but succor. Jazz is in need of guidance into true, wholesome channels wherein it may be developed into what we would like to have it" (Stringham 1926, 192). Thus, by the end of the article it is clear that this author views jazz as a mere primer for listeners whose tastes will eventually evolve to appreciate classical music: "In many cases, persons who once knew and appreciated nothing higher than jazz were led onward toward the appreciation of the so-called 'Better music' by being introduced to the tunes of the classical scores by means of the jazz pieces" (1926, 193). The author's closing remarks reverberate with the metaphor of jazz as poison, and are a summary of all that he argued before:

> I share the view that jazz is the most distinctive contribution America has made to the world-literature of music. What we now need is proper guidance of the jazz germ. There are two kinds of germs in the physical world— those that kill and those that preserve human life. Jazz germs are of the same nature. It is for the open-minded American musicians and musical educators to discover, preserve and develop the worthy elements of jazz. Jazz as an end in itself, except for dancing and the like, is to be deplored. Jazz as an idiom for something worthwhile, as a stepping-stone to something better than we now recognize, is, as Shakespeare put it, "a consummation devoutly to be wished." (195)

I quote from this article at length because it succinctly represents the kind of discourses about jazz that were prevalent in the United States in the first half of the twentieth century, especially among nonjazz music educators and various gatekeepers. The article gives expression to a number of ideas and tropes. First, jazz is akin to a poison, a polluting agent that can be dangerous to American culture more generally and to American music more particularly. Hence it must be carefully contained and supervised. Second, jazz is of a lower artistic value relative to Western classical music. Third, jazz has the potential to be elevated into something else; yet for this to happen it needs guidance from classically trained musicians versed in the classical European music tradition. Fourth, if jazz is to have any use whatsoever it would be as a preparatory stage for the appreciation of Western classical music. Jazz should not be practiced as an end in itself except when one needs "musical relaxation" and mindless diversion from the more serious kind of musical activity.

The rise of academic jazz education cannot be understood without taking into account such elaborate ideologies, subtly undergirded by racial and class-based discourses. These were responsible for the active exclusion of jazz from many institutions of higher music education throughout the first half of the twentieth century. They also crucially impacted the cultural logic of academic jazz education, which emerged in response to and in dialogue with such ideologies and discourses.

Strategies of Exclusion

At the time this article was written, jazz had been gaining increased visibility and commercial success. These, however, were not accompanied by unqualified social acceptance but, rather, with deep ambivalence, which found expression in the reluctance to accommodate the music into formal institutions of music education. Middle-class Americans experienced simultaneous fascination with and ambivalence toward jazz, which spoke to its ability to provoke diverse anxieties and identifications. Threatened by its participatory nature, its percussive emphasis, its association with the red-light districts in New Orleans and Chicago, and its association with African American communities, many people thought of jazz as a threat to the moral order and as a lower musical form (Ake 2002; Ogren 1992). The nature of the music and the dangers it represented were topics of much debate in various venues other than scholarly publications. Numerous articles expressed hostility toward the music, like the one appearing in *Ladies Home Journal* in 1921, suggestively titled "Does Jazz Put the Sin in Syncopation?," or a textbook on teaching music in high schools published in the 1940s that associated jazz with "voodoo" practices and "barbaric people" having a "demoralizing effect upon the human brain," and that determined that jazz is "fleshy" rather than "spiritual" and hence an unfit "substitute for serious music" in schools (quoted in Ake 2002, 117–118). The rejection of jazz as unserious, the deep anxieties it evoked, and the racial politics that surrounded it formed the background for its exclusion from many music schools' curricula in this period despite (or due to) its growing commercial success. Hence, till the mid-twentieth century, jazz was allowed into few schools and mostly as an extracurricular activity. Only in rare cases did colleges offer credit-based jazz activities (Gennari 2006; McDaniel 1993).

As the article on jazz as "an educational problem" reveals, the rejection of jazz on racial and class bases was often naturalized by and masked under claims about its lack of artistic value and its threat to those genres of music that presumably do possess such value. "Theory" was often recruited for this purpose, yet racial and class-based ideologies often resurfaced beneath this strategy of naturalization in the form of the trope of pollution. The author's recurring likening of jazz to poison that can harm American music and his advice to educators to take precautions to thin out its dosage are a case in point.

In a classic study, the anthropologist Mary Douglas (2002) has argued that societies the world over often conceptualize as "polluting" elements they consider foreign and dangerous to their normative centers. To ward off this threat, they engage in boundary work and purification rituals. Ethnomusicologist Bruno Nettl, in his mid-1990s study of classical music schools in the Midwest, has argued that jazz and other musical genres are still treated in precisely these terms, that is, as potentially polluting elements that threaten the normative center of these schools as defined by the tradition of Western classical music. Nettl describes the institutional work these schools perform to protect their centers as "purification rituals," as when educators forbid their students to sing jazz because it might harm their voices (Nettl 1995, 82). He argues that these rituals have many forms in addition to explicit rejection. One is taxonomy: whereas educators designate Western classical music composed between 1720 and 1930 with the unmarked labels of "standard music" or "normal music," they mark other musical genres by referring to them as "jazz," "folk music," "popular music," "ethnic music," and the like. Furthermore, schools' librarians often choose to ignore these genres through selective acquisition of pedagogical material. In addition, when schools integrate these genres into their curricula, they do so in a marked way. As Nettl puts it, these "other" genres "usually gained admission via the back door of musicology because faculty and administrators felt, on first application, that one should not teach them as fields of performance, but that it might be all right to teach 'about' them because they could be helpful in fostering an understanding of the evolution of the central repertory or of the cultures of early, recent, and contemporary, foreign, or rural peoples" (Nettl 1995, 84–85). Nettl's observations about contemporary music schools' purification rituals mirror Stringham's admonition to educators to accommodate jazz music not as an end in itself but only as a preparatory stage for the appreciation of the "higher" genre of Western classical music in the context of an evolutionary framework that places the latter at its pinnacle.[4]

Although this evolutionary framework often portrays Western classical music's higher status as a natural consequence of its superior artistic value (which presumably can be proved through "theory"), sociologist Paul Di-Maggio (1982) has argued that, to a large extent, the contemporary cultural hierarchy in the United States is the result of "cultural entrepreneurship," or efforts made by upper-class Americans in the late nineteenth century to distinguish themselves from the masses of immigrants and rural migrants who arrived in urban centers by establishing elite-supported and hence exclusive high-art organizations. The historian Lawrence Levine (1988) has described in detail these major transformations across the various arts. Levine has showed how the distinction between highbrow and lowbrow in the nineteenth-century United States was made possible through the establishment of institutions such as symphony orchestras, opera companies, museums, theaters, and dance companies. In combination with the development of high art appreciation, scholarship, and training in newly expanding universities and conservatories, high art has become a major index of upper-class and genteel culture.

The distinction between highbrow and lowbrow did not exist merely in an abstract symbolic sphere. It had tangible repercussions. In sociological terms, it existed in the form of both symbolic and social boundaries. Whereas symbolic boundaries are "conceptual distinctions made by social actors to categorize objects, people, practices, and even time and space," social boundaries are "objectified forms of social differences manifested in unequal access to and unequal distribution of resources . . . and social opportunities" (Lamont and Molnár 2002, 168). Thus the distinction between highbrow and lowbrow in the United States existed in the form of symbolic boundaries, as when highbrow art was associated with natural sensitivity and lowbrow art with lack of sophistication, but these conceptual distinctions were also translated into social boundaries, as when greater state funding was given to highbrow art, and lowbrow art was excluded from schools' curricula.

Origin Stories

I suggest that this conflicted history has structured the ways in which many of the jazz educators I worked with understand the meaning of academic jazz education and what forms it should and should not take. This became apparent to me when I collected the stories of Berklee's foundation that were available in printed material and when I elicited such stories from a number of the school's senior administrators. These stories can be considered to be what anthropologists call "origin myths," or stories about the origin of the world that explain to the people who believe in them the basic coordinates and forces that structure and operate in it (Eliade 1998). Origin stories are thus extremely useful for scholars who want to understand a specific culture, because they reveal basic themes in this culture's logic.

As told in a celebratory book that chronicles Berklee's first fifty years (Hazell 1995), the school was founded in 1945 by Lawrence Berk, a native Bostonian. Berk worked as a professional pianist and arranger in Boston's music scene during his teenage years. After graduating from high school in 1927, he enrolled in the prelaw program at Boston University. He then pursued a degree in architectural engineering at MIT, graduating in 1932. Since there were not many jobs in the aftermath of the Depression, he resumed his musical career. He worked in Boston for two years and then moved to New York. In New York, Berk worked as an arranger for various bands, such as the NBC studio orchestra. He also studied for three years with the music theorist Joseph Schillinger, who had devised "a system of composition that employed mathematical permutation and combination processes to generate rhythms, harmonies, and melodies" (Hazell 1995, 10).[5] After returning to Boston and during a short stint as an engineer, Berk began giving composition lessons based on Schillinger's ideas and his own practical experience in the music industry. The demand for such lessons was great, partly due to the recently instituted GI Bill, which allowed war veterans to pursue degrees in higher education, including music degrees. In 1945, Berk established the Schillinger House (renamed Berklee in 1966, a combination of the names of Berk and of Berk's son, Lee), a school for contemporary music whose pedagogy was based on Schillinger's ideas. Berk established the school to cater to the growing external demand for jazz training. In addition, "he recalled the difficulties he and his circle of fellow musicians faced in developing their talents because there were no organized sources of information that could help them. He wanted to give his students the opportunity for organized study that he missed as a young man" (Hazell 1995, 12).

Indeed, there were no "organized sources of information" for jazz musicians at that time. The reasons for this lack were subtly alluded to in an interview I conducted with Fred, one of Berklee's high-level administrators, a

man in his midsixties who was a student at Berklee in the 1960s and who has
served in various pedagogical and administrative capacities at Berklee ever
since. When I asked him whether he could identify a consistent philosophy
that has structured Berklee's pedagogy since the school's early days, Fred
responded:

> We at Berklee don't have a philosophy—it's all pragmatic. Berk's idea was
> "get them a job—help them make a living, such things as help them fill out
> their tax forms, teach them to dress in suits—treat it as a trade. Forget about
> theory, I don't want to hear about theory." He distrusted the trappings of
> theory. So that was the philosophy—not to have a philosophy, not to be
> enslaved by classical traps. His idea was that we should teach the people who
> wanted to study the music. Teach them craft, not creativity. Don't be an elit-
> ist: listen to the students, see what they want and also raise their craft level.
> The idea was to derive the pedagogy from the music.

Berklee's origin story as told by Fred receives its meaning from the conflicted history of jazz's own marginalization. The notions of "trappings of
theory," "classical traps," and the rejection of "philosophy," "creativity," and
"elitism" stem from this complicated history of cultural marginalization made
natural through aesthetic theories and ideologies of "high art."[6] It is in this
respect that many educators and students consider Berklee's location in Boston among the multiple tokens of high art and genteel culture to be highly
symbolic: for many of them this location signifies that jazz has finally gained
a place for itself—literally and physically—on the upper echelons of the
American cultural hierarchy. Despite Fred's claim that Berklee does not have
a "philosophy," his insistence on rejecting "the trappings of theory" certainly
constitutes a philosophy, yet it derives its meaning from the negation of what
he and many other educators consider the elitist philosophy of high art most
explicitly associated with Western classical music.

It is against this convoluted backdrop that many of the educators I worked
with understand the advent of jazz into the academy as both personally and
culturally significant. Thus David, one of the New School's most venerable educators, an octogenarian African American saxophone player, told me about
his early days as a music student in Chicago. While studying classical music
in college in the 1940s, he was temporarily suspended from school after he
was caught playing jazz in the practice room. After telling me this anecdote,
he surveyed the empty classroom in which we sat and then said: "Now I am

a professor for jazz at a university—who could have imagined it back then?" Other educators made sure that I understood the potential implications of my own research precisely in this light. Thus when I sent an introductory e-mail to one of the administrators at the New School's jazz program, he wrote back: "It's a study that, if done sensitively and well, could have a huge impact toward bringing this art form and its community into new cultural and scholarly legitimacy and understanding." For many of the administrators, educators, and students I worked with, the battle was indeed far from being over, and they considered my research as a potential resource in affecting its outcomes.

The quest for cultural legitimacy, then, has been one engine behind the rise and expansion of academic jazz education. Yet there was another, equally powerful set of conditions that motivated jazz musicians to introduce jazz training into the institutions of higher music education: the significant changes that took place in the marketplace for jazz in the second half of the twentieth century.

The Disappearance of Extracurricular Jazz Scenes

When discussing the rise of academic jazz education, it is often tempting to frame it as yet another manifestation of the rise of vocational training in American higher education at large (Levine 1986, 23–67; Martin 2004, 1–2). This is so because academic jazz education emerged in the mid twentieth century in part as a response to outside market demands, most notably from army veterans who, thanks to the GI Bill, were able to pursue college education, including music education, and as a response to dance orchestras' need for qualified musicians and arrangers (Ogren 1992; Murphy 1994). Remember that the pedagogical philosophy of Berklee's founder as narrated to me by Fred was "get them a job—help them make a living; such things as help them fill out their tax forms; teach them to dress in suits—treat it as a trade." Fred added that Berk forecasted the booming popular music industry and hence the financial potential of this pedagogical enterprise. Indeed, today academic jazz education is a big business (Chinen 2007), comprising hundreds of programs that grant degrees in jazz studies or offer individual jazz-related courses for credit.

That said, although academic jazz education was indeed originally based in the vocational training model, today it does not easily fit this slot. Unlike some business schools, for example, where students are often offered future jobs before graduating, almost all graduates of jazz programs face dismal job prospects. Many educators and students told me that a graduate of one of the jazz programs would be very lucky to end up earning a living as a performing artist even as a supplementary job to teaching. Thus, in contrast to many forms of vocational training, the full-blown academization of jazz training, as opposed to its initial stages, took place against the backdrop of the gradual disappearance, not the expansion, of an outside market for jazz. To understand the logic of academic jazz education, then, it is necessary to elaborate on the different reasons for this disappearance, because the need to negotiate it, in addition to the search for cultural legitimacy discussed above, has structured the rationale for, and the shape of, the various institutional forms of academic jazz education.

From the late 1950s and increasingly in the following decades, jazz faced growing competition with other musical genres such as rhythm and blues, country, and especially rock music. This competition led to a decline in jazz's popularity even within the urban African American communities that have traditionally been the source of innovation in jazz and the training ground for future musicians (Chevigny 2005, 51–52; Rosenthal 1992, 170–173). At the same time, new jazz styles such as bebop, which were not geared toward dancing, emerged. These styles were less accessible to the average audience. These changes in tastes and styles were accompanied by parallel changes in the actual spaces where jazz was performed, owing to increasing gentrification and the rising urban real estate costs of most jazz venues (Chevigny 2005, 52). Noise complaints were beginning to be a pressing issue. Performance venues were scarcer, and those that survived maintained shorter playing hours. While in the past every major American city had its own local jazz scene of a number of clubs and a dense network of musicians, these scenes have disappeared at an alarming rate. Despite efforts to develop alternative performance venues, as in the case of the so-called "loft scene" in mid-1970s New York City, viable commercial jazz scenes persisted only in a few enclaves (Jackson 2012, 29).[7]

Unfit for Funding

One significant determinant of these changes has been the organizational structure of jazz as an art form performed almost exclusively by for-profit individuals or groups and in for-profit venues. This factor, in addition to jazz's uncertain status in the American cultural hierarchy, has motivated its exclusion from public funding initiatives' criteria.

The first federal agency in US history dedicated to providing support for the arts, the National Endowment for the Arts (NEA), was founded by Congress in 1965. Its mission was formulated as the Public Leveraging Arts (PLA) policy whose assumptions and goals motivated a focus on nonprofit organizations (Cherbo and Wyszomirski 2000, 10). As a result of this structural support, American nonprofit art institutions of various kinds have experienced a dramatic growth. These include dance troops, opera companies, chamber-music groups, art museums, nonprofit theater groups, as well as mixed-arts complexes (Cherbo and Wyszomirski 2000, 6).

The organizational structure of jazz as mainly a for-profit enterprise, together with its cultural marginality, prevented it from benefiting from this public funding. To be sure, the NEA began to support jazz in 1969, yet this support, due to the PLA policy, was narrowly targeted at a handful of specific activities. The funding that the NEA granted jazz is described in one of its brochures:

> NEA assistance to the jazz field began in 1969, with its first grant in jazz
> awarded to pianist/composer George Russell . . . allowing him to work on
> his groundbreaking book, *Lydian Chromatic Concept of Tonal Organization*,
> the first major academic work in jazz. In a decade, jazz funding went from
> $20,000 in 1970 to $1.5 million in 1980 to more than $2.8 million in 2005,
> supporting a wide range of activities, including jazz festivals and concert seasons, special projects such as Dr. Billy Taylor's Jazzmobile in New York and
> the Thelonious Monk Institute of Jazz's Jazz Sports program, educational
> jazz programming on National Public Radio, artists-in-schools programs,
> and research. (NEA 2008, 3–4).

The fact that public funding was given mainly to educational activities is noteworthy. The first financial award funded the writing of "the first major academic work in jazz," and further assistance was directed to educationally oriented organizations such as Jazzmobile, the Thelonious Monk Institute, artist-in-schools programs, and research. These organizations were funded precisely because they are not-for-profit. Very little funding supported the purely commercial performances of jazz. As I will argue in further detail below, this funding strategy has encouraged the academization of jazz as a means of securing funding.

Jazz's for-profit nature is not the only characteristic that has made it unfit for funding. Jazz is often organized around ad hoc and changing combinations of musicians. This often clashes with funding agencies' criteria of eligibility that are based on calculability and predictability. Furthermore, such criteria seem to target art forms in which "the performance can be repeated in exactly the same way as often as might be desirable" (Heilbrun and Gray 2007, 4). Jazz's improvisatory formal traits make it everything but such a performance. This criterion of repeatability reproduces a key distinction in Western modernity that has valued the virtuosic production and performance of fixed texts (such as composing or performing a piece of Western classical music) more than the nonreplicable kinds of virtuosity (such as jazz improvisation that unfolds in real time).[8] Indeed, as Ted Gioia has so aptly argued, the contingency at the heart of jazz improvisation and the bias against this contingency in many circles motivated the framing of jazz as an "imperfect art" with respect to the presumed perfection of Western classical music (Gioia 1988b).

The decline in jazz's popularity, coupled with its exclusion from public funding, had two main repercussions. First, musicians had a difficult time finding jobs, and second, it has become increasingly hard to sustain traditional modes of learning jazz, which involved prolonged apprenticeship with seasoned musicians and amassing ample real-time performance experience in clubs, local scenes, and on tour.

A Gig-Oriented Culture with Few Commercial Gigs

Data published by the National Endowment for the Arts (Jeffri 2003) demonstrate the current tenuous financial position of the average jazz musician. These data suggest that in 2000, approximately 45 percent of jazz musicians held a bachelor's degree or higher, compared to 24.4 percent of the US population over the age of twenty-five. However, on average, jazz musicians earned less than their male, nonjazz musician counterparts. The average nonjazz musician male with a bachelor's degree earned $52,985 in 1999 ($66,243 for men with higher-level degrees), while the annual income of most jazz musicians fell below $40,000.[9]

The low socioeconomic status of the average jazz musician finds expression, for example, in the fact that many lack health coverage. An article in the New York Times titled "Jazz World Confronting Health Care Concerns" (Chinen 2008) featured accounts of jazz musicians who experience sudden serious illness but lack health insurance to make immediate health care a financially viable option. The ubiquity of this problem is given valence in the revelation by the executive director of the Jazz Foundation of America—an organization that supports jazz musicians—that "We get 60 cases a week like this, each having its own urgency and desperation." Some of these cases were brought to public awareness in the pages of the *New York Times* amid a number of high-profile benefit concerts that raised funds for the medical expenses of musicians in urgent need.

Much of jazz musicians' tenuous financial position is related to the absence of viable commercial jazz scenes outside of a few selected urban enclaves. Indeed, during my fieldwork at Berklee, the lack of a viable extracurricular jazz marketplace infiltrated the classroom via subtle and not so subtle messages that educators imparted to their students time and again. Educators often jokingly referenced the lack of gigs available to jazz musicians outside of school. For example, prior to the beginning of one class, Greg, an educator in his early sixties, asked the bass player, "So, you got the gig?" When the student answered, "Yes," Greg replied, "Good—at least one of us has a gig," whereupon everybody present laughed. In the middle of another class, Thomas, an educator in his midsixties who had had ample performance experience in his youth with some of the great masters, told his students: "When I decided that I need to work on this stuff [the material that he had been discussing in class] I designed a few exercises specifically for that and then I worked on that for like six months until I got it and then I didn't have to think about it anymore. [He pauses and stares at the floor.] But on the other hand, if I am so great, how come I still have to teach you guys after fifty years of playing?"

Often, when a phone call was mentioned in class, educators jokingly invoked the trope of "the call," that is, getting a call about a gig. This usually caused laughter because of the paucity of gigging opportunities. Consider the following example, as students prepared their instruments at the beginning of class:

[Student 1:] Sorry, man, for not returning your call yesterday.
[Student 2:] Ah, no, it's cool. Forget about it. It went o.k.
[Student 3:] What was it about?
[Educator, intervening:] Oh, nothing. It was a weekly gig at the Vanguard
    [the Village Vanguard, a NYC jazz club], nothing special. [Everybody
    laughs.]

The lack of gigs was such a significant factor in Berklee's jazz culture that when the school's magazine published a section on jazz jokes in one of its issues, many of them belonged to the genre of "gig jokes" in which the absence of gigs played a key part.

Educators would often recall to their students the vibrant jazz scenes of their youth and contrast them with the difficulty of securing gigs faced by jazz musicians today. For example, when a student's cell phone rang in the middle of class, Hal, an educator in his late sixties, immediately asked, "Is it a gig?" and everyone burst into laughter. He then told us about his own experience as a college student in Detroit in the 1960s:

> I was busy working when I went to college. It was unbelievable: six nights a week, for ten years. Before college, during college, after college. And you could get a gig during the day. But you'll find a way. I mean, you're smart. You just need to find people who will give you money to do this [laughter]. Really, you have to make your own venues now. You got to make your own—do concerts, and you do this club, talk to this club owner. There are not so many gigs like they used to be. [. . .] I guess that's why everyone is going to New York. There used to be a scene like that in every city. Detroit—four bands in one place. I remember Detroit, once, when there were four bands playing in the same hotel. Count Basie's band, Buddy Rich's band, Duke Ellington's band, and Glenn Miller's band, or someone else.

Students often reacted with amazement upon hearing about the historically vibrant jazz scenes in different US cities. They received such testimonies with quasi disbelief, because Boston—a major East Coast city only four hours' driving distance from NYC and home to several music schools and jazz programs—has so few jazz clubs, and even these are eclectic in their programming decisions. Getting a gig in such places is out of the question for the majority of students, and, as some educators told me, for them as well. This situation applies not only to Boston but to New York. Although there are many more jazz venues and opportunities to play in New York than there are in Boston, there are also many more musicians in NYC who compete with one another over these opportunities. A well-known bass player in his seventies who teaches at the New School commented on this situation in an interview:

> It's so hard to get gigs here in New York. There are so many students who graduate—both here and students who come from other places. They graduate and they're going to stay here. But how will they get gigs? There aren't even enough gigs here for folk who have been living here all their lives! And I notice that sometimes they'll take those gigs in the East Village for peanuts, for the door. That's exploitation. But on the other hand, they have

to play to learn the music. It's catch-22. They need to learn how to play, but they are being taken advantage of.

Educators' subtle and not so subtle classroom messages were soon corroborated when students attempted to secure gigs both in Boston and in New York City after they graduated and moved there. I accompanied several students to such gigs. These gigs were usually what are called "restaurant gigs," playing in restaurants and bars. In this kind of gig the music plays a background role, and the pay reflects that. One student was paid $25 for two hours of playing; a duo of players received $75 total for three hours of playing; another student, playing as part of a band, received $80 for four hours of playing; another duo of students received $50 for three hours of playing. In line with these figures, the average pay for such gigs in this area was approximately $10–15 per hour for student players. In one case where the pay was determined by "the door," that is, by how many people attended the performance and paid the cover charge, a duo of students did not receive any pay because there was no audience. In another case, the number of people attending a show was so small that the bandleader lost money because he had to pay his sidemen. Given that any gig requires musicians to prepare the equipment beforehand, dismantle it afterward, and to pay transportation fees, it is clear that gig pay is meager. To be sure, in some cases players also receive food or drink in addition to monetary pay; yet for many students this did not ameliorate what they considered to be a dire situation. Indeed, many students acknowledged that they often did not expect remuneration at all. They played for free in the hope of promoting themselves or gaining valuable performance experience (see also Laing 2003). Such was the case of the students I mentioned earlier who played at Harvard's Winthrop House. Often, however, students' audience simply consisted of their fellow students (compare with Lloyd 2005).[10]

Students reacted in different ways to the dissonance between their hopes of having a performance career and their dim prospects of achieving this goal. Here, too, jokes abounded as a means of both expressing anxiety and commenting on the state of jazz. For example, when I called a student and tried to arrange an interview with him he immediately asked me "How much does this gig pay?" and then burst into laughter. On another occasion, I sat with two Berklee students, John and Alex, in a restaurant near Berklee. When I explained my research to John, Alex said to him, "You see, man, jazz is creating gigs for everyone except for jazz musicians." Throughout my fieldwork, Alex kept joking in front of the other students in my presence that I was the only one he knew who had managed to secure a stable gig out of jazz.

The gradual disappearance of a commercial market for jazz, then, has had significant impact on jazz musicians' job prospects and has provided a strong motivation for them to establish alternative sites of employment—more of which below. It has also compromised the opportunities available to neophyte musicians to learn the craft of jazz improvisation. This, in turn, provided added motivation to establish alternative sites of socialization. To appreciate this factor, it is first necessary to elaborate on how novice jazz musicians learned their craft prior to the full-blown academization of jazz training.

A History of Extracurricular Education

Jazz has many of its roots in traditional West African forms of music making, communality, and religion that survived the Middle Passage from Africa to America. The intertwining of spirit lore, possession rites, communal gathering, singing, dancing, and the playing of instruments was reproduced on the plantations under the politics of white repression (Peretti 1992; Schuller 1986; Wilkinson 1994). After emancipation, however, as blacks were able to travel outside the plantations to cities in search of economic opportunities, the music became more secularized and tied to the spirit of economic enterprise. Rural blacks were drawn to New Orleans in search of jobs. The city had a well-preserved African-Caribbean culture, and European musical influences were well ingrained in the form of a rich band heritage derived from the French military-band tradition. In addition, an array of Confederate band instruments was widely available after the Civil War. Despite the continued racial tensions between blacks, creoles, and whites in New Orleans, the cross-fertilization of these various musical influences, combined with the spirit of economic enterprise, was the infrastructure for the creation of jazz in the first two decades of the twentieth century.

Among the shared conceptual approaches of West African music brought to America was a distinct pedagogical approach—the transmission of musical practices and knowledge from generation to generation via slow absorption through exposure to musical performances and through active participation (Wilkinson 1994; see also Chernoff 1979, 33–36). The emphasis on exposure to music, the active participation in it, and the communal responsibility for the musical education of the young were prevalent in New Orleans in the beginning of the twentieth century, and formative of the ways in which jazz was learned by young musicians in the following decades (Murphy 1994, 35; Peretti 1992; Wilkinson 1994). Music was ubiquitous and thriving in New Orleans at the time. Marching bands sponsored by various African American fraternal organizations paraded the streets to announce the election of new officials, to advertise dance events sponsored by their respective associations, and to escort funerals (Ogren 1992, 24–28). While these bands paraded the streets—a daily phenomenon in the beginning of the twentieth century—the participatory ideal was manifest in the institution of the "second line." Adults and children would march behind the bands to listen to the accomplished musicians and to try to emulate them by singing and playing. At times, bands competed with one another when they happened to meet on the street. In these instances the crowd played an important role in adjudicating between the bands. Aside from parades, music coming from the steamboats or dance halls where bands were playing could be heard in the city. Boundaries between institutionalized performance venues and the street were porous. Although many musicians were musically literate and had formal training, formal train-ing did not so much revolve around jazz; rather, it concerned learning to read music and play instruments (Chevan 2001, 206). Formal training was informed by Western classical music norms, and classically trained music educators often used classical method books for this purpose. The intricacies of jazz playing were learned mainly through informal exchange with fellow musicians. Ear training and direct exposure were the central learning mecha-nisms of jazz in its first decades (Ogren 1992, 30; Wilkinson 1994).

After the Great Migration from 1916 to 1930, during which nearly one million blacks left the South for northern cities, the center of jazz activity shifted first to Chicago and later to New York City. Jazz flowered and grew commercially successful in the northern urban black neighborhoods where it benefited from a growing audience comprised of diverse ethnic groups. In this period, the jazz community continued to provide the educational envi-ronment for young and aspiring musicians. Musicians relied on traditional African American modes of knowledge transmission. This was noticeable in New York City, the center of the jazz world from the 1930s onward (Berliner 1994). Record shops, music stores, musicians' union halls, social clubs for the promotion of jazz, musicians' homes, booking agencies, practice and record-ing studios, and nightclubs all provided sites where musicians interacted with one another, exchanged ideas, and learned the music. Musicians who studied together in high school or who were acquaintances in their hometowns before coming to New York City formed groups and often shared apartments after arriving in the city (McMillan 2001). Stable relationships were often formed between veteran and young musicians, thus allowing for mentoring in issues broader than the production of jazz itself, such as dealing with record companies and coping with life on the road.

Equally important to these forms of knowledge transmission were the myriad possibilities for active participation in music making that the flourishing jazz scenes in New York City and other major cities provided for young jazz musicians. One of the most important of these was the "jam session," an informal get-together of musicians in which they could play and improvise (DeVeaux 1997; Schuller 1991). These informal performances could take place unexpectedly whenever musicians were hanging out together, whether in apartments or in recording studios. Some were more institutionalized than others and took place regularly in after-hours clubs, or were organized by African American associations. A similar but slightly different participatory practice was known as "sitting in." Players could join a group in the middle of its performance for one or two tunes and thus play with veteran musicians, gain performance experience, and establish their reputation (or tarnish it if they failed to attain the expected level of performance). Similarly, when on tour across the country, well-established musicians would sit in with unknown groups to give advice to young musicians.

It is hard to exaggerate the importance of active participation in real-time jazz performance as a learning mode. The reason is not only historical; it is also related to jazz's specific form and the competence it requires. At its core, jazz is improvised music. It is a form of composition on the spur of the moment that weaves together pre-existing and genred building blocks in accordance with given harmonic progressions and the ongoing contribution of other band members. To a large degree, creativity in jazz is group creativity. It relies on the dense back-and-forth communication between players (Sawyer 2003). Hence, training in live performance situations with seasoned musicians has always been a normative ideal of jazz socialization. It has been one of the conditions of possibility for cultivating the ability to contribute to, and benefit from, this kind of collaboration.

To be sure, prior to the rise of academic jazz education, musicians did not learn their craft of improvisation only via real-time apprenticeship. In addition to the traditional pedagogies that emphasized the slow absorption of music, close mentorship, and active participation, records played a key role in how musicians learned to play jazz. In 1917, the first recordings labeled as jazz were produced (Ogren 1992, 93). These were widely disseminated and avidly studied by young musicians who practiced recorded solos with their own instruments. In addition, from the mid-1930s, specialized trade magazines began to appear, such as *DownBeat*, which published transcribed solos from key recordings with commentary (Owens 2003; Murphy 1994, 35). At this time, method books also entered the scene and were used by musicians as learning material.

However, the production and utilization of these magazines and transcribed solos were far removed from the dramatic changes in the cultural reproduction of the music that would take place a few decades later with the full-blown academization of jazz training, which involved the gradual establishment of hundreds of academic jazz programs predicated on rationalized and formalized curricula and pedagogies specific to jazz. Most importantly, as opposed to today's students, jazz musicians of previous generations could test, apply, and perfect knowledge acquired through forms of print pedagogy in the ample live performance opportunities that were available to them all across the United States.

Indeed, consider an image that depicts trumpeter Dizzy Gillespie writing the melody of the tune "Be-Bop" on a blackboard in New York City in 1947.[11] Considered by itself, the image seems to depict a reality that is no different from the current everyday reality in the hundreds of academic jazz programs in the United States. What could be more "contemporary" than someone explaining a bebop tune by writing and perhaps analyzing it on a blackboard? However, if one could have zoomed out from the room in which Gillespie wrote this musical phrase, one would have discovered a bustling jazz scene peppered with numerous venues in which musicians could gain valuable live performance experience that complemented and contextualized whatever print-mediated knowledge they acquired outside of these venues. Today's students face a very different reality.

An Endangered Form of Training

At the time of my fieldwork, many of the Berklee and New School educators I worked with argued that the disappearance of extracurricular performance venues threatened these long-held pedagogical sensibilities that emphasize immersion in live performance situations with experienced musicians. Many young educators revealed that their own musical upbringing had suffered from the same lack. Richard, a Berklee educator in his late thirties who is himself a Berklee graduate, expressed this point in the following manner:

> The times were different. They [the past jazz masters] were playing all the time. You know, from a young age they were sessioning every day, playing day and night. . . . All they were doing was playing music. They got up playing music. They went to bed playing music. Today there's not the chance to play. I mean those guys used to play five nights a week, three to five sets a day, you know. I have never done that as a player, personally. . . . When you're a student you can do sessions and stuff, but you don't have the mentoring that you had back then when like Bird [saxophonist Charlie Parker] would take Miles [trumpeter Miles Davis] under his wing and literally hang with him and teach him, not just necessarily teaching him like I'm teaching students, but just by playing.

Older educators, in turn, often referenced in class the ample and relatively affordable opportunities they had to observe firsthand and learn from the performance of the past masters. Students fully realized the magnitude of these shifts when such stories concerned Boston's past vibrant jazz scene. Carl, a Berklee educator in his midsixties, told his students the following anecdote about his days as a Berklee student:

> I got to catch Monk [Thelonious Monk] in '66. They used to have the Jazz Workshop down Boylston Street. Every Wednesday, Berklee students—you would show your ID and you had to buy Coca-Cola because you couldn't drink, you had to be twenty-one. So seventy-one cents, man. You got to see Monk one week, Miles [trumpeter Miles Davis] one week, Coltrane [saxophonist John Coltrane] the next week, the local cats next week. I got to catch Monk, only the first set, where he played only standards. Solo piano. Wow, you know? He just played standards, only him. Just outrageous. Beautiful playing.

Such tales drew heated commentary about the high prices charged today by top jazz clubs. Students argued that they are unable to attend the performances of the top players in the field. As David, the venerable octogenarian musician teaching at the New School, told me: "The high prices of the clubs kill the music—students have no choice but to learn only from recordings.

Only rich people can go to the clubs nowadays. *And this is why the schools are so important.* Otherwise they [the students] wouldn't get to hear any of it. I myself can't really afford anymore to go to the clubs as often I used to!"[12]

The Academic Jazz Program as a Reconfigured Jazz Scene and Marketplace

David's suggestion that the importance of academic jazz education can only be fully appreciated against the backdrop of these significant changes drives home some of the points I have discussed above. To a great extent, the dramatic expansion of academic jazz education in recent decades occurred against the backdrop of the lack of commercial demand and the absence of commercial venues for jazz. In addition to seeking to democratize knowledge and to acquire cultural legitimacy, then, musicians were driven to establish jazz programs in an effort to create new kinds of jobs and to forge alternative sites of socialization (Ake 2002, 115).[13]

The significance of academic jazz programs in the context of the paucity of performance opportunities and lack of commercial demand for the music is an issue that administrators and educators openly acknowledge. For the financially unstable jazz musician, the academic jazz program provides a haven of financial security. The not-for-profit status of many of these institutions makes them eligible for public funding, tax benefits, and other benefits that jazz has been traditionally denied. When I asked one of the administrators at the New School's jazz program how jazz benefits from being located in a university setting, he said:

> There are practical gains in that it absolutely does provide a financial structure which employs—we are a huge economic factor for a big part of the community of artists. And I'm not saying a very significant factor, but a big factor because we anchor some economic stability for them, for our seventy-three part-time faculty. We have health and benefit plans. To grab a hold of that and have that kind of stability is huge in the life of an artist in terms of survivability and sustainability. So we are an important economic engine and a safety structure that can only come through the economics of the university. [. . .] There's another practical aspect, and that is the encouragement of jazz education to . . . programming in venues. Jazz education and art education in universities are huge arts providers—huge, because a lot of it is underwritten; a lot of it is on this level of presenting some kind of combina-

tion of younger artists but also the faculty. It's a very important vehicle for presenting the work, for performance opportunities. If it were not for higher education, jazz would be completely marginalized in an evermore almost impossible commercial condition.

Academic jazz programs and the institutions in which they reside provide a large share of the venues in which jazz is performed today. Coupled with the teaching jobs they create and the fact that they have become the sites where musicians—both students and educators—are now more likely to interact with one another and where jazz is more likely to be performed, it would be safe to say that jazz programs have become the pillar of the jazz world in the contemporary United States. The *Jazz Improv* conference that took place in NYC in October 2007, organized by the trade magazine of the same name, speaks to this shift. Benny Powell, the legendary trombonist who recently passed away, taught at the New School at the time of the conference. He participated in a panel called "The Eye of the Masters," which featured the New School's educators. During this panel he said: "Now, recently, when a lot of the masters have been dying, to me, when I get there [to the New School] on Wednesday—that's my one day to teach—I give Chico Hamilton an extra hug, I give Jimmy [Owens] an extra hug, because we don't even have meeting places for us.[14] In the days gone by, there was Beefsteak Charlie's or other meeting halls where we could see each other a lot. Now that doesn't happen.[15] So again, that's one of the perks of teaching at the New School."[16]

The expansion of academic jazz education against the backdrop of the lack of extracurricular demand for jazz was made clear in another panel at the *Jazz Improv* conference, sponsored by the jazz program of the Manhattan School of Music. The panel was aptly titled "Can You Make a Living in Jazz?—Yes!" One participant commented that in jazz, as opposed to pop music,

> you have to be a teacher as part of your career, and isn't that a great thing? Because then everyone is staying in the position of sharing what they know and keeping the music growing and sharing it with young people and with anyone who is interested in learning about improvisation and jazz. So it feels somehow divinely inspired, that aspect of it, that you'd need to have teaching to be a part of your career in order to do it, but it's a part that I really enjoy.

Why would this participant say that the life of a jazz artist must have been "divinely inspired" so he or she would have to teach? The answer is that academic teaching, while enjoyable for some, is regarded as a necessity for "getting by" rather than something people choose to pursue.

Furthermore, many of the jazz educators I worked with openly admitted that one of the central contributions of academic jazz education is the production not only of future jazz musicians but, equally important, of future audiences. Although the vast majority of the students will not become performing artists, advocates of jazz education hope that they will maintain an interest in the music. It is safe to say that these students already constitute a large portion of the audience for jazz, as many of them begin attending performances while still in school (Ake 2012). The effort to create audiences for jazz was explicitly highlighted during the formal reception of the January 2007 annual conference of the International Association for Jazz Education held in New York City. The conference was a four-day spree of performances, panels, and merchandise exhibitions attended by thousands of the organization's members. The reception began with a video presentation that featured jazz luminaries explaining how jazz dissemination contributes to democratic and liberal ideals and to the well-being of the world. It continued with a speech by the organization's executive director, who at one point said:

> We are going to grow with the audience for jazz, which is one of my primary concerns, and it's got to be one of your concerns. We're not going to be around, we're not going to have jobs if people aren't gonna get to know this music, unless we find ways of reaching out and touching people with it. One way is providing more resources to you—whatever your job is—to help you do it better whether you're in education, whether you're a musician, whether you're in the industry sector. We want to find ways to help you and this is going to allow us to do it and, finally, to advocate on behalf of this music and its place in our education systems. You know, we have this "no child left behind" system, and we have to make sure that jazz is not left behind either. So advocacy is a central part of what we're going to be doing with this.

The executive director's words make it clear that academic jazz education provides an alternative marketplace for jazz that replaces the rapidly eroding extracurricular one. Indeed, the crucial role played by educational institutions for the survival of the cultural order of jazz was the reason that the unexpected bankruptcy of the International Association for Jazz Education in 2008 was received with such alarm in the jazz community. In an article that discussed this bankruptcy, composer Maria Schneider commented that "the old jazz culture doesn't exist anymore" and that jazz hence depended on "educational institutions, for better or worse" (Ratliff 2008).

Graduation rates from academic jazz education programs also indicate that educational sites have become reconfigured jazz scenes. During Berklee's first decades, prior to the full-blown academization of jazz training, it was the norm for many jazz students to drop out of school after a short time because they were quickly recruited by small and big bands.[17] This prompted Berklee to consider any of its students who studied at least one semester as one of its alumni, thus ensuring that the school was associated with a list of "stars." Today, however, the average jazz student is far more likely to finish his or her four-year course of study, because performing gigs are rare and because attaining a degree is a prerequisite for securing the most common job in the field of jazz today: as a teacher. Indeed, for a number of decades now students have been more likely to play in collegiate big bands than get recruited to play in nonacademic groups (Carey 1986). As an administrator at the New School told me in an interview, the program still faces the problem of student retention. Significantly, however, students leave school today in order to pursue a career in a different musical genre currently at the center of the music industry: hip-hop.

To conclude, although the expansion of academic jazz education was grounded in the ideal of democratization of knowledge fueled by the forces of the market, the nature of these forces has changed over the last few decades from an external demand for experienced jazz musicians to the lack thereof. Thousands of students still enlist in jazz schools annually, but most of them do not necessarily hope to secure a steady performance career. Rather, they seek to become educators or to find some other form of employment within the music world or affiliated industries. This applies to the best of the students, too. Thus in one interview I conducted with Nate, one of the top saxophone students at Berklee at the time of my fieldwork, I asked him about his plans after his graduation, which was about to take place in less than a month. Our exchange epitomized many of the points I have discussed in this chapter: "Well, teaching is not something that I would want to do, but that's obviously something I'll have to do," Nate said. "Why?" I asked. Nate looked at me and responded: "Because 80 percent of the musicians are making their living by teaching. It's hard to get gigs." "But you seem to have gigs," I objected. Nate laughed. "Yeah, but it's like forty-dollar gigs." "An hour?" I asked. "No! Forty dollars a night. It could be less. It could be nothing. It could be just beer!"

In addition to cultural legitimacy, then, academic jazz education has provided the conditions of possibility for the cultural reproduction of jazz that involve new infrastructures of socialization, networking, formation of communities of peers for educators and students, career trajectories, performance venues, markets, and networks of circulation of the music—all this against the backdrop of the disappearance of vibrant extracurricular commercial jazz scenes. Put simply, at the present moment jazz programs *are* the reconfigured jazz scenes of the past. As I show in the next chapter, these transformations did not take place without producing their own ambivalences and contradictions.

3

"THINK-TANK MUSIC"

Public Ambivalences and Contradictions

Visible Markers of Institutionalization

Upon visiting Berklee's campus it is impossible not to be impressed by the visible markers of the institutionalization of jazz in higher education and the many ways in which Berklee's unique identity as a music school with a strong focus on jazz seems to seamlessly blend with the décor and institutional dimensions of a typical university or college campus. Those who are unfamiliar with the very notion of the academic jazz program might benefit from a quick tour of some of these markers. Others might benefit from some statistics that characterized Berklee at the time of my fieldwork there.

Berklee's campus consists of more than ten buildings. Given Boston's highly expensive real-estate market, the school's expansion over the years has been impressive. The school's endowment at the time of my fieldwork there was about $180,000,000. In fiscal year 2012 it reached $248,371,000. The school's endowment was below the average endowment of US and Canadian colleges and universities in FY 2012 ($491,637,000), but higher than the median ($90,051,000). It was ranked 233 out of 843 institutions. For comparison's sake, in FY

2012 Temple University's endowment was $277,479,000, and Barnard College's endowment was $216,447,000.¹ Berklee's relatively comfortable financial state has allowed it to provide its students with top-notch facilities. The school has a number of state-of-the-art performance halls and technology-rich classrooms. As one of the school's treasurers put it, "Berklee set out to be the M.I.T. of music" (Hornfischer 2004), a phrasing that attests not only to Berklee's physical location next to MIT but also to jazz's broader symbolic aspirations to secure a place at the higher echelons of the American cultural hierarchy, in this case through the adoption of sophisticated technologies.

The intersection of Boston's Massachusetts Avenue and Boylston Street, where Berklee's main campus buildings are located, is peppered with the typical décor of an urban American college campus, yet this décor comes with a twist that reveals Berklee's unique identity as a music school with a strong focus on jazz. To begin, the mandatory campus store sells loads of jazz pedagogy material—theory books, video and audio recordings, and DVDs. Indeed, an entire wall is devoted to course material published by Berklee's own press. In the adjacent streets are a number of music instruments stores that cater both to Berklee students and students of the other nearby music schools. Most unusual, perhaps, are probably the only McDonald's, Starbucks, and Dunkin' Donuts stores in the United States that exhibit on their walls black-and-white iconic photographs and portraits of jazz giants such as Charlie Parker, Chet Baker, and Billie Holiday.

Inside, the school also exemplifies the many ways in which Berklee has managed to blend its focus on jazz and contemporary music with the typical décor of a college or university. Most of the classes I observed took place in classrooms and ensemble rooms located in the building at 130–150 Massachusetts Avenue, although many classes take place in other adjacent buildings. On the first floor long corridors lead to classrooms, practice rooms, labs, and studios. Most classes take place in rectangular rooms equipped with a staved whiteboard, a piano, amplifiers for guitars, a drum set, and an audio system. Many rooms are also equipped with an overhead projector and a DVD player. One can observe classes taking place through the tiny windows in the classroom doors: students sitting in their chairs, writing in their notebooks in front of a teacher who explains something about a music score projected on the board with an overhead projector; students sitting quietly while listening to music played with a stereo system; a band playing a jazz standard tune while the instructor is listening. There are also small private rooms in which students can practice by themselves. Although Berklee initially focused mostly on jazz, it has expanded its curriculum to include programs in film scoring, music education, music production and engineering, music synthesis (sound design, digital audio and signal processing, computer programming for music production), and more. These programs incorporate a multitude of rapidly changing and sophisticated technologies.

The library is also located in this building. Berklee takes pride in its extensive collection of music scores, audio and video material, books, and music journals. The library is named after the saxophonist Stan Getz, whose saxophone is proudly displayed in a glass case in the entrance. On higher floors in this building are other classrooms, teacher offices, administration offices, and dorms. Educators' offices are mostly located in their respective departments. Because of scarcity of space, it is not uncommon for a number of educators to share the same office and even the same cubicle, often in rotation. The offices I visited were decorated sparingly with a few posters of famous artists, album covers, or announcements of educators' own past performances hanging on the walls.

The institutionalization of jazz in higher education also finds expression in the very orderly occupational structure of Berklee's educators. There are over five hundred faculty members at Berklee, the majority of whom teach subjects not directly related to jazz. Many of Berklee's jazz educators are themselves graduates of academic jazz programs and many are full-time faculty. Educators are assigned different ranks, as at typical universities and colleges: instructor, assistant professor, associate professor, and professor. Full-time faculty have renewable contracts. However, as one professor told me, once you get to be a professor you need to "really screw up" for your contract not to be renewed. Thus, there is a kind of a tenure system at Berklee.

The composition of Berklee's body of educators and students reflects the demographic transformations that have accompanied jazz's institutionalization in higher education. The overwhelming majority of Berklee's jazz educators are white middle-class men in their thirties to sixties. This reflects the traditional gender composition in jazz (Rustin and Tucker 2008), where women have been typically confined to singing (Pellegrinelli 2008). The predominantly white composition of Berklee's educators is indicative of the broader social changes in the demographics of jazz players that took place in the second half of the twentieth century. Whereas prior to the full-blown academization of jazz training, jazz drew its players mainly from the urban African American lower classes (DeVeaux 1997; Rosenthal 1992), today jazz is practiced by many middle-class white Americans (Lopes 2002).

At the time of my fieldwork, there were approximately four thousand enrolled students at Berklee. Most of these students did not focus solely on jazz performance, but pursued other courses of study. Like their educators, Berklee's students are mostly white men of middle-class background.[2] Latino and African American students are a minority. At the time of my fieldwork, 14 percent of entering domestic American students were Latino, while 15 percent were African American. Given the high percentage of international students among the entire entering class (see below), this translates to a little bit more than 10 percent Latino students and 10 percent African American students out of the entire entering class. The representation of Latino and African American students among the jazz-focused students in the classes I attended was even lower than that. African American jazz-focused students in particular are now a negligible minority at Berklee. As for gender, the entire entering class was 65 percent men and 35 percent women, yet the percentage of women was much lower than 35 percent among students who focused on jazz performance. Most of the classes I attended had few to no women in them.

One crucial difference between Berklee's educators and students is that close to 25 percent of Berklee's students are from non-US countries. In part, this is the result of Berklee's long-time aggressive recruiting strategy outside the United States. The school conducts auditions and clinics all over the world. One very effective recruiting strategy has been to cooperate with jazz schools outside of the United States that were established by Berklee alumni. The school devised this strategy as a response to the dwindling rates of American domestic applicants in the late 1980s. It has been extremely successful in boosting enrollment rates and generating significant revenues. International students often begin their studies in these non-US schools and then complete them at Berklee, where they are often given some financial aid.[3] In 2006, the countries from which most international students came to Berklee were Japan, South Korea, Canada, Mexico, and the UK. The representation of international students among those students who focus on jazz is higher than 25 percent. This situation is not unique to Berklee. The New School's jazz classes were often populated with international students who far outnumbered US students.

These, then, are some of the visible markers of what appears to be the seamless integration of jazz training into the décor and institutional environment of higher music education and the typical college and university. However, upon a closer look the seams begin to show.

Invisible Ambivalences and Contradictions

Jazz's specific trajectory of legitimation through institutionalization in higher education is rife with potential contradictions and ambivalences. To begin, what would cultural legitimacy actually look like after decades of struggle, above and beyond the visible markers of integration? How would jazz educators reconcile their long-held disdain for the markers of exclusionary high culture and academic "pretense" at a time when these markers are now woven into the foundation of their daily pedagogical reality?

Second, many jazz educators have supported their search for a place in higher education by the argument of popular demand. Decades ago, jazz musicians asked how could it be that jazz, as the popular music of its time, was excluded from schools' curricula? However, now when jazz's place in higher education is somewhat secured, the music itself is no longer popular by any means. How would educators reconcile their former rhetoric of curricular representation by popular demand with the fact that jazz is now fast becoming a rarefied art form much like classical music?

Finally, remember that Fred—one of Berklee's high-level administrators, whose words I quoted in the previous chapter—told me in an interview that Berklee's founder vowed not to fall into the "trappings of theory," that is, abstract music theory disconnected from the gritty reality of real-time performance that is truer to jazz's core and conducive to its creativity. How, then, would educators understand the implications of the shift of jazz training into the institutions of higher education that are premised on the inculcation of formalized and abstract bodies of knowledge?

These are not abstract questions. They affect the everyday pedagogical reality in the two jazz programs in which I conducted fieldwork. The remainder of this chapter is organized as an extended tour of three of the contradictions and ambivalences that emerge from these questions as they found expression in two public events at Berklee: a convocation ceremony, and town-hall meetings in which a high-level administrator delivered a "state of the college" address to Berklee's community. As anthropologists have long noted, public rituals, events, and ceremonies are often sites in which society's key values, norms, and contradictions are reproduced and worked out in a crystallized form (Turner 1967). My purpose in discussing these events is to provide the reader with a roadmap of some of the general concerns experienced by the educators, administrators, and students I worked with, with respect to the academization of jazz training.

"Esse Quam Videri": Between Cultural Legitimacy and Academic Role-Playing

It is my first time visiting Berklee's main performance venue, on 136 Massachusetts Avenue, where I am about to attend a convocation. Indeed, this is going to be my very first intimate experience of Berklee's culture, because the school year has not yet begun. I walk through the long pavilion and into the hall. The first thing that strikes me is its size: a two-level concert hall capable of seating 1,220 people, fully equipped with top-notch sound technology. The hall is soon bustling with people—administrators, educators, students and their families, and news media representatives. I hurry and take a seat some ten rows from the stage. The wide stage is well illuminated. A huge bouquet of flowers is placed in the front center and behind it is a row of wooden chairs.

Suddenly, the ear-piercing sound of African drumming explodes into the hall. At first I do not understand where it comes from, since the stage is still empty and the noise clearly does not come from the multitude of speakers that are placed everywhere on the walls. But as faces turn to look behind me, I turn too and see two rows of students entering the hall from the main entrance, one proceeding toward the left aisle, the other toward the right aisle. Drums are strapped to the students' bodies and they beat them with long, wide swings. They are dressed in plain white T-shirts and jeans. A huge cat mascot runs erratically between them, waving its hands, jumping. Each row consists of some ten drummers. The crowd cheers in soaring roars. It whistles, claps hands, and shouts. The noise is unbelievable. Then, following the drummers, people dressed in full academic regalia—long black and gray gowns and hoods—enter the hall, also breaking into two rows. One of the people wears a massive golden medallion around his neck. They walk solemnly, with measured steps, which contrast with the commotion. The crowd becomes louder with cheering. The procession progresses slowly, the drummers beating their drums ferociously while the people behind them walk in their academic garb, some of them smiling. When the leading drummers approach the stage from both of its sides, they turn toward one another until the two rows meet, all the time drumming while the rest of the people in the procession, those dressed in full academic regalia, walk on stage and take their seats. The drummers continue playing for a few more minutes, the crowd cheering and whistling. To the never-ending applause of the crowd, the drummers then disappear through two side doors.

After the drummers disappear and the applause subsides, the dean of students approaches the podium and introduces each of the people on stage—the president, heads of divisions and programs, a student representative, and the recipient of the honorary doctorate, a well-known African American saxophonist. Following additional introductory remarks, the dean speaks to the crowd of students in a deep voice that reverberates through the speakers all over the hall:

> So, what have you gotten yourselves into here? We're now the best contemporary music school in the world, and here we sit in these medieval caps and gowns. Is that what you pictured? Well, just think of your week so far. If moving into Boston, dancing down Mass Ave. intersection traffic, the barbecue today where we had a samba drum line, and traditional jazz that breaks into bebop, and Berklee's check-in, and testing, and auditions—if that didn't do it to ya, tonight will confirm that Berklee is one crazy place. And get used to it. I've been at Berklee as a student, a teacher, and administrator for thirty-nine years. And I still think it's crazy. But it's a great crazy. You need to know that this place is nonstop loud, busy, constantly buzzing and vibrating, but all that buzzing and craziness help make us the best music school on the planet. And don't let the craziness fool you. This place is rigorous. We are here to push you, to draw the very best out of you, as is the purpose of higher education. And after all, this is a college of music. Like all colleges, Berklee has a motto, and in Latin, no less! Esse Quam Videri, which translated means, "to be rather than to appear to be." Now you know that you came here to really be something. So let's get busy. Do what you need to do to be the best at what you want to be. And if I can tell you one thing that I've learned in my thirty-nine years at Berklee, is please don't waste your valuable time here pretending that you are already the best you can be, or you'll not get any better and you'll probably not reach your dreams. And you know, don't try to satisfy somebody else's vision of what they think you should be. We are here to draw the best of you out of you . . .

The dean then narrates the story of his own student days at Berklee some forty years ago, revealing that when he came to the school and noticed that there were numerous great players around him, he first pretended he was better than he really was. However, he soon understood that this was a mistake. The dean then concludes his speech by reiterating the school's motto, saying "So Esse Quam Videri, to be rather than to appear to be."

Following the speech of another administrator, the dean of students introduces the student representative. The dean assures the audience that the representative "is an involved and active student who is also a living and breathing model for our motto—she is doing it rather than just talking about it." The student then begins her long speech. At one point during her speech, she shares with the incoming students her own past fears as a new student at Berklee. After her vocal audition, she says, she soon began to worry about her harmony and ear training placement tests: "I was so worried that I would not test well and that Berklee would point and laugh. But boy was I wrong. The minute I got out of the test, I talked to other students and realized that I was not the only one confused. This is the first lesson I learned at Berklee—you're not alone. It's OK to keep asking, even if you're a senior and you can't remember what a G-sharp Lydian scale is. It's OK."

Following the student representative, the dean of students introduces Berklee's president, Roger Brown, as "your president drummer" to the audience's loud cheers and roars. Brown approaches the podium. He immediately asks: "Do we have any drummers in the house?" The audience roars in approval for a long time. After the applause subsides, Brown begins his speech. At one point, he advises,

> Among you are many gifted musicians, aspiring composers, film scorers, music therapists, business managers, engineers, producers, conductors. There are a lot of different talents here. You're going to hear a few people who are quite formidable players. Try to let that inspire you and not deter you. And here's what I would say. If you were a young Thelonious Monk sitting out in the audience, I would say to you: don't try to sound like Oscar Peterson. Sound like Thelonious Monk. That's what the world needs you to sound like. And if you were a young Bob Dylan, I would say don't try to play like Eric Clapton. You be Bob Dylan. And if you were a young Cassandra Wilson, I'd say don't try to be Sarah Vaughan, you be Cassandra Wilson. And that's going to be hard to do, because you're going to hear people who can really do things you'd like to do some day, and you're going to want to imitate that. But ultimately you got to come back to who you are, what you were put on earth to do, what you were meant to do as a musician, as a human being. So we admitted you to Berklee, not someone else. You're the person we want to have here. You've got something to say that's unique and special, and that's what we want to hear from you.

"Latin scholars being in short supply at Berklee":
Cicero in the Jazz School

As a first step in untangling the cultural logic, tensions, and contradictions that underlie the previous vignette, consider Berklee's motto. The phrase "Esse Quam Videri," "To Be, Rather Than to Seem to Be," as translated during the convocation, is taken from Cicero's essay, *On Friendship*, written in 44 BC. In the passage from which this phrase is taken, Cicero is discussing the contrary natures of flattery, on the one hand, and true friendship, on the other hand: "For not so many [men] desire to be endowed with virtue itself, as to seem to be so. Flattery seems to delight such men: when conversation formed to their wishes is addressed to such persons, they think those deceitful addresses to be the evidence of their merits. This, therefore, is not friendship at all, when one party is unwilling to hear the truth, and the other prepared to speak falsely" (Cicero 1909, 159). The idea underlying Cicero's motto served as a recurring motif throughout the different speeches during the convocation. Yet within the specific context of that event, this idea seems out of place. As I observed the event, I could not avoid feeling the contradiction between, on the one hand, the demand to reject appearance and, on the other hand, the endorsement of this demand in the context of an event that seems to be very much about appearance. How can we explain the fact that Berklee's dean of students advises the students, "Don't try to satisfy somebody else's vision of what they think you should be," in the context of an elaborate production of scholarly ritual that appropriates academic paraphernalia, regalia, and etiquette at a relatively young college for jazz and contemporary music? How can we negotiate the president's admonition to the students that "ultimately you got to come back to who you are, what you were put on earth to do, what you were meant to do as a musician, as a human being," and the fact that Berklee, at least in this public event, basks in the external markers of academia, itself an institution to which, as we shall see, many Berklee educators and administrators are hostile?

To be sure, Cicero's phrase is used by dozens of educational institutions around the world, most of them American, as well as by a few sororities and fraternities, several families, and the State of North Carolina.[4] Yet this ubiquity does not explain the contradictory logic of the use of this phrase on American soil. When New World institutions cling to this marker of the Old World, they seem to betray the very idea encapsulated in it. Such a contra-

diction is all the more acute in the case of Berklee for two reasons. Not only
is it an unlikely academic institution focused on fields of studies very different from those traditionally associated with the Old World university model,
but its preoccupation with the markers of this model, it seems, is even more
incessant than is the case in those American institutions of higher learning
that fall more neatly within the model of the traditional university and that
appropriated Cicero's phrase. Most of the printed material that is handed out
to the audience at Berklee's convocation and commencement, as well as at the
event inaugurating Berklee's president, contains detailed explanations of "Academic Dress." These explanations describe the medieval roots of the gowns,
their shape, the meaning of different colors according to hierarchy and rank
of functionaries and administrators. Perhaps nowhere else is the concern with
the external markers of academe clearer than in the explanation of the presi-
dential medallion—that same medallion that caught my attention during the
convocation—provided to the audience in printed material:

> The Berklee medallion was inaugurated at the 2000 college commencement
> by President Lee Eliot Berk in honor of Berklee College of Music's 55th
> anniversary. In the Middle Ages, medallions wrought in different metals
> such as gold, silver, and bronze became an accepted element of civil and
> academic ceremonial garb. The medallion symbolized a badge of office.
> Adhering to the customs of European educational institutions, American
> universities and colleges adopted the tradition of a medallion made to be
> worn over the academic robe, as part of their presidential ceremonial dress.
> The central circular bronze medallion bears Berklee College of Music's seal,
> upon which is engraved the Berklee motto, *Esse quam videri*, meaning "to be,
> rather than to seem to be." The words "Berklee College of Music" arch over
> the top half of the seal. Treble clefs flank the seal, and the words "Founded
> 1945" run underneath. The entire medallion is edged with a bezel design.
> The decorative links that support the medallion alternate between the letter
> C intertwined by a treble clef and the college's seal. The presidential medal-
> lion has become another important ceremonial symbol of Berklee College
> of Music. It is worn on select academic occasions to reflect the high ideals
> and traditions Berklee has established as the leader in contemporary music
> education. (Berklee 2004, 17).

The elaborate design of the medallion strives to combine the conventional
ceremonial garb with indexes of Berklee's own unique identity as a music

school—for example, the treble clefs. The medallion's detailed design is then mirrored in its detailed verbal description. Both betray an overdetermined preoccupation with this emblem of academe and the idea of a venerable tradition that goes back to "the Middle Ages." This is apparent in the following incident, mentioned in the book that celebrates Berklee's first fifty years: "In 1966 [. . .] President Berk and Administrator Robert Share adopted the college's motto, "Esse Quam Videri." [. . .] Latin scholars being in short supply at Berklee, early versions of the shield and banner [. . .] incorrectly spelled the last word as "videre," but the typographical error was soon corrected" (Hazell 1995, 84). The reason that a mistake such as this could have existed for quite some time was that it was the Latin language itself as a fetishized marker of respectability and cultural legitimacy that was as equally important as, if not more important than, whatever content it conveyed. Note how the dean of students makes sure to emphasize during the convocation that the school's motto is "in Latin, no less!"

In theorizing Berklee's theatrical staging of academic tradition, I turn to historian Eric Hobsbawm's seminal essay, *The Invention of Tradition*, which opens with the observation that "'Traditions' which appear or claim to be old are often quite recent in origin and sometimes invented. Anyone familiar with the colleges of ancient British universities will be able to think of the institution of such 'traditions' on a local scale" (1983, 1). Hobsbawm defines an invented tradition as "a set of practices, normally governed by overtly or tacitly accepted rules and of a ritual or symbolic nature, which seek to inculcate certain values and norms of behavior by repetition, which automatically implies continuity with the past" (1983, 1). More significant is Hobsbawm's suggestion that invented traditions are "responses to novel situations which take the form of reference to old situations" (1983, 2). The recent rise of academic jazz education constitutes such a novel situation, which explains Berklee's elaborately ritualized institutional performance. Berklee's type of invented tradition is indeed one whose purpose is "establishing or legitimizing institutions, status or relations of authority" (1983, 9) in a context in which jazz traditionally lacked culturally legitimized institutions, status, and authority.

My argument that the spectacle of tradition at Berklee's convocation is concerned with legitimizing the jazz program and elevating its status fits well within the larger context of American higher education. Scholars have argued that in the absence of traditional hereditary cast and status systems as in Europe, higher learning in the United States has functioned in the production of status as much as in the production of knowledge (Levine 1986). Beginning in the first half of the twentieth century, higher education has catered to the desire of an emerging white-collar, consumption-oriented middle class for distinctive and prestigious social status. The college became the focus around which the burgeoning middle class's dreams and aspirations for social mobility revolved. It held the key to such social mobility not only by means of professional training but also, and indeed more so, by providing young individuals with the opportunity to acquire important connections and the stamp of social prestige. The concern with social status, connections, and mobility was at the core of the expansion of extracurricular activities such as collegiate athletics, fraternities, debate teams, and student clubs. The college was perceived as an extension, if not the locus, of production of the social structure rather than as an autonomous sphere of learning.

Berklee's case seems to compound these concerns with social status: not only is jazz training organized today within the institutional infrastructure of the college—one of the prime sites of social mobility in the United States—but it also concerns a cultural form that was marginalized and looked down upon in the context of the American cultural hierarchy until quite recently. Hence, if Berklee's concern with the external markers of academe seems somewhat out of proportion, it is precisely because of jazz's historical marginalization and uncertain status.

This overcompensatory emphasis on the external markers of academe is productive of ambivalence because it suggests that while Berklee was founded in an attempt to put an end to jazz's marginalization, this attempt was not entirely free from the same assumptions about what constitutes "legitimate culture," which were responsible for jazz's marginalization to begin with. As sociologist Paul Lopes has argued (2002), efforts by jazz musicians and aficionados to legitimize or "cultivate" jazz in light of its traditionally low status took the form of modeling jazz after highbrow art in terms of its institutional bases. Together with other driving forces, this led to the gradual introduction of jazz into classical music halls, the establishment of jazz societies and collectives, the production of jazz connoisseurship by critics and record collectors, the inception and reproduction of professional magazines, a modernist approach that emphasized formal experimentation, and, indeed, the introduction of jazz into academe, and the structuring of jazz pedagogy by many elements taken from Western classical music pedagogy, including codified "theory" (especially in terms of harmony). The road to jazz's cultural legitimacy, in other words, has entailed the incorporation of the same institutional bases and markers that many individuals in the jazz world associate with the elitism and bigotry that were responsible for jazz's marginalization by gate-keepers for so long.

The educators, administrators, and students I worked with were not oblivious to this contradiction. Although they invested a lot of resources in displaying the external markers of academe, they did not do so wholeheartedly. Rather, their stance remained ambivalent. They both embraced and rejected these markers. The convocation event was replete with attempts to deconstruct and hold on to "academic pretense" at the same time. This duality was evident in the procession of functionaries who were dressed in full academic regalia, which was preceded by students dressed in T-shirts and banging African drums. The frequent cheers, whistles, and hollers that fitted a rock concert clashed with the etiquette of a conventional academic ceremony and the solemnity of the décor. Berklee's administrators did not try to suppress but rather indulged in these contradictions. The dean of students openly admitted the strange aspect of the academic décor in the context of a school such as Berklee, saying, "We're now the best contemporary school in the world, and here we sit in these medieval caps and gowns. Is that what you pictured?" The president was introduced as "Your president drummer," a mode of presentation that constructs him as "one of us" rather than as a businessman-functionary-academic.[5] While bestowing the honorary doctorate—a scene I describe in detail below—the president gave the honoree "his own special stethoscope in honor of his becoming a doctor tonight," thus keeping the entire institution of the honorary doctorate as an emblem of academic honor at an arm's length. The honoree wore the stethoscope around his neck during his long speech. The honoree's speech, as we shall see below, was perhaps the most artful and audacious of such performed distance from the external markers of academe at that event.

"Have you ever heard of Harvard?" The Specter of Differential Value

Perhaps because jazz's ascension into the higher echelons of the American cultural hierarchy is a recent one, and because it was achieved through the emulation of the institutional forms of Western classical music rather than through the cultivation of different institutional forms, the specter of its previous differential and negatively defined value vis-à-vis classical music seems to haunt the educators and administrators I worked with. They frequently compared the jazz program to other music schools, which, significantly, belong to the "Ivy League" of music schools, traditionally known for their classical music programs. However, they also frequently compared Berklee to Ivy League schools properly defined. Thus, Fred, one of Berklee's high-level administrators, proudly told me the following:

> We recently paid a lot of money for a group—they called a thousand households in America, they took them randomly from a phonebook, and they said, "will you participate in this two-minute survey?" They asked them, "Have you ever heard of Harvard? Have you ever heard of Princeton?" The biggest name recognition was Harvard and Yale, and when we asked them about music schools, the most recognized was Juilliard—something like 48 percent knew what Juilliard was. Berklee—much younger, contemporary, and not benefiting from being in New York and having the Juilliard String Quartet and all those things going at the Lincoln Center—our name recognition was 38 percent!, which is very high for a young school.

Note that not only does Fred compare Berklee with Juilliard, he also precedes this comparison with a discussion of the towering institutions of Harvard, Yale, and Princeton, thus indexing the frame of reference within which Berklee should be and wants to be understood.[6]

The anxiety over cultural legitimacy and its expression in the form of the recurring comparison of the jazz program to "elite" schools—both music schools and research universities—at times takes the form of messages whose implications are ambiguous, which are nevertheless endorsed because they serve the purpose of reasserting Berklee's status, which always seems to be in jeopardy because of the past history of jazz as an excluded subject of academic study. They further reveal the articulation of prestige discourses, which are always tenuous. They never seem to reassure, and hence they need to be repeatedly asserted. Consider the following example taken from another public event held at Berklee, a town-hall address delivered by a high-level administrator to Berklee's entire community. At one point this administrator said:

> There's another interesting measure, which is what colleges call yield rates, which is how many students you have to admit to put a class together. So let me explain what these numbers mean. At the NEC [New England Conservatory] they have a yield rate of 29 percent. That means that when a hundred students apply and are accepted, 29 of those actually come to the institution.

At Berklee, our yield rate was 65 percent, which is extraordinary because it's equivalent to, you know, Yale and Harvard. What that tells us is that when a student is accepted to Berklee, it's more often their first choice and they come here.

The implications of these figures are somewhat ambiguous. To begin, the NEC is a conservatory dedicated mainly to classical music, although it has a very good jazz program. While Berklee has a classical music program, it is negligible in its overall curriculum. Hence what this comparison actually implies is unclear because it involves students in different fields (e.g., classical music and jazz, among others), each field entailing a completely different structure of competition with other programs. Moreover, to a certain degree, Berklee's success has been based in the fact that it has frequently been the first school to offer programs and courses pertaining to musical genres and technologies that have not yet entered other contemporary music programs. Lastly, for years the school has promoted an admission system in which most applicants were admitted if they had the money to pay tuition—a policy that contributed to the extreme expansion of the school to the point where in 2007 the school finally had to put a cap on the number of the students it admitted and establish a more rigorous audition system. Thus some of the students applying to Berklee may have had fewer viable options for attending other schools than students applying to the NEC and other institutions.

At a different town-hall meeting on the state of the college, the administrator compared the school's tuition to that charged by Juilliard, Eastman, Oberlin, and the NEC. This comparison not only revealed yet again the preoccupation with Berklee's position vis-à-vis the more established schools for music that connote high art, but also how it impacts institutional decisions on the administrative level:

Our tuition is still low relative to other four-year colleges. It's not so low that it's affordable, right? But it's low. So you're like the least expensive of the unaffordable four-year private music colleges [laughter]. In my opinion it doesn't do us much good. If you're a very talented musician focused on high quality educational experience, you would think: "Hmmm, do I really want to go to the cheapest one?" And if you have the means, if you're from a family of enormous wealth, you don't care; you don't pay any attention to how much the college costs. You just want to go to the best place you can go. And

if you're not wealthy, you need scholarship support, and by having such low
tuition we're unable to offer as much scholarships as we need to. So the challenge for us will be to raise tuition, to try to get at least to the medium level
of these other colleges as we dramatically increase the scholarship support
that we offer.

While the goal of providing more scholarships is commendable, the primacy
of differential value underlies the problematic assumption about the prefer-
ences of prospective affluent students.[7] The contours of the differential value
discussed in the previous chapter apropos Pierre Bourdieu's notion of the
field of cultural production continue to haunt some of the jazz educators and
administrators I worked with even as jazz appears to be securely positioned
in the American cultural hierarchy and institutionalized in higher music
education.

"Nothing conservatory about it": Between Aesthetic
Modernism and Popular Market Demand

In her ethnographic study of IRCAM, an institute for music research founded
by composer Pierre Boulez in Paris in 1977, anthropologist Georgina Born
discusses at length some of the key contradictions and ambivalences that
structure this example of the institutionalization of the European musical
avant-garde. On the one hand, the ideology of the modernist avant-garde is
based, among many factors, on the denigration of the present state of things,
the promise of the production of better art, and a disregard for outside market
demand as a criterion of evaluation of its own production. On the other hand,
its institutionalization at IRCAM has meant that the avant-garde ceased being
"marginal and critical of the dominant order as in the earlier period of modernism [; . . .] itself established, it has not only undermined its initial raison d'être
but it must also continuously legitimize its present position of official subsidy
in the absence of a large audience" (Born 1998, 4). Born argues that even as
IRCAM continues to hold on to avant-garde discursive strategies of maximizing cultural capital, orienting itself to the future, and disregarding market demand, it must also adopt a discourse of legitimation in which the "assessment
and manipulation of demand are pivotal" (29). Born discusses in detail the
ways in which IRCAM members attempt to negotiate markers of high modernism such as the scientification of art, the reliance on theory, the adoption

of high technology, experimentalization, and the rejection of popular culture, within an institutional environment that often prescribes and symbolizes norms, procedures, and meanings that are inconsistent with high modernism.

The contradictions that structure Berklee in particular and many other academic jazz programs in general are similar in many respects to the contradictions that structure IRCAM, yet they are also crucially different. To begin with the similarities, Berklee, too, is suffused with the tension between, on the one hand, the discourse of modernist high art and its institutional markers—including theory, the use of sophisticated technology, and an insulated institutional environment where knowledge is produced for its own sake, and, on the other hand, popular culture and market demand. Furthermore, as in the European avant-garde, many commentators in the jazz world argue time and again that jazz's institutionalization in the academy has neutralized its previous anti-institutional status, which presumably was also responsible for its creativity.

However, unlike the modernist avant-garde, jazz lacked cultural capital prior to its academization. Its presumed oppositional status was not primarily the result of its adoption of the discourse of the modernist avant-garde. This does not mean that musicians were not influenced by the rhetoric of high modernism prior to jazz's academization. Indeed, some of them adopted it from the very outset (Monson 2007). Rather, this rhetoric was never as dominant as the rhetoric of legitimation through market demand prior to the music's full-blown academization, certainly not in the public imagination. At that point, jazz's oppositional stance emerged mostly due to its systematic marginalization on racial and class grounds by gatekeepers at the higher echelons of the American cultural hierarchy. Only later, in tandem with the decline in the commercial demand for jazz, did the music begin to be more fully suffused with the high-modernist rhetoric of autonomy from the market. Thus, if the institutionalization of art at both IRCAM and Berklee embodies a key tension between high modernism and popular culture, the European musical avant-garde and jazz arrived at such institutionalization from entirely opposite directions and for entirely different reasons. They represent two very different trajectories of legitimation. In broad brushstrokes, IRCAM's case represents a shift from dominant legitimation through the rhetoric of the avant-garde to increased legitimation through the assessment of popular demand, while Berklee's case represents a shift from dominant legitimation through popular demand to increased legitimation through the rhetoric of high modernism. This means that although the contradictions at both places have often involved the same terms, their meanings and the ways in which they are negotiated have been different.

Commodifying Academia

At Berklee, the negotiation of the tension between high modernism and popular demand often finds expression in the commodification of the markers of high art and academe and the creation of an institutional form that often appeared to the educators I worked with, not to mention to external observers, as a very strange hybrid of these two modes of legitimation. This commodification has been exacerbated by the strong competition between a growing number of jazz schools and programs that try to differentiate themselves from one another by different claims to excellence, truth, and cutting-edge pedagogical methods. This competition, much like the quest for cultural legitimacy within the broader field of American music, often affects decisions, from the institution's self-presentation—the focus of this chapter, to decisions about pedagogy—the focus of the following chapters.

The convocation provided examples for the commodification of the external markers of academe I am concerned with. The entire event resembled a rock concert. At one point, the president called out the names of the "star" guest clinicians who were going to visit the school during the coming academic year. The audience responded with ear-piercing cheers. The conferral of honorary doctorates at Berklee often resembles Emmy-like events in which the degree is granted to music "stars" chosen not so much for the value of their musical output as for their popularity.[8] This practice has not gone undisputed at Berklee. During one of the town-hall meetings, the high-level administrator addressed the commodification of the honorary doctorate and thus pointed up the tension between the two forms of legitimation:

> I just want to pause for a second. I know there's a little bit of controversy within the college. Sometimes there's a pushback about why we would invite a celebrity like Paul Simon or Melissa Etheridge to get an honorary doctorate. Well, I think there are a lot of compelling reasons for that, and I think that we need to keep doing that because part of what makes people excited about Berklee is that element: talent on the highest level or entertainers who have achieved some great stature. The Paul Simon piece of the sixtieth [anniversary] was what made the Wang Theatre sell out. As much as I love

the other musicians who were there, honestly, it was the star power of a Paul Simon which made the place sell out and got us the kind of visibility and publicity that we got, and I want to remind people that unlike USC [University of South Carolina] or Notre Dame, we don't have a homecoming football game that we can use as a great fundraising tool, but we have things like this. So it's essential for us to engage with the larger world, with famous entertainers, celebrities, and get them excited about Berklee as well.

These words point at the tension between the two forms of legitimation, a tension that emanates from jazz's specific history. Berklee has continued to grant honorary doctorates to a number of musicians who, as a number of educators bitterly told me, deserved it less for their musical talent than for the public visibility they brought to Berklee. Berklee's attempt to negotiate these two strategies of legitimation found expression at a commencement ceremony that took place in May 2007 in which honorary doctorates were granted to "Grammy-winning superstars Gloria and Emilio Estefan, U2's groundbreaking guitarist the Edge, and to late jazz pianist and composer Andrew Hill," as Berklee's website put it. This choice represents the full spectrum of legitimation, from art that is defined by its market demand (the Estefans) to high-modernist jazz (Andrew Hill), with a musical representative that seems to occupy the middle slot between these two poles (the Edge). Significantly, during the event, in the midst of shaking hands with the graduating students who were coming on stage one after another, it was announced that the Estefans must leave the ceremony because they have "a gig in the Bahamas." Such an announcement was received with applause rather than disappointment. The increased commodification of the honorary doctorate at Berklee finds expression in the list of its recipients. Whereas by 1996—i.e., during the school's first fifty years—Berklee awarded approximately eighty honorary doctorates, during the seventeen years that have passed since 1996 it has awarded approximately one hundred and twenty more.[9]

Perhaps by far the clearest example of the ways in which the markers of academe are commodified and the tension between the two forms of legitimation finds expression at Berklee was a standardized letter sent from the Office of Public Information to students on the dean's list. I learned about this letter while interviewing Craig, a Berklee student, in his apartment. At one point when we discussed his grades, Craig said, "You certainly know by now that Berklee has the highest number of students on the dean's list [laughter]. Almost everyone I know is on that list." When I asked him what advantages there are to being on the dean's list, Craig responded: "Nothing. You just get this letter. I get it every semester!" Craig opened a drawer, took out a piece of paper and handed it out to me. I took it and read:

> Please accept my congratulations on your Dean's List status at Berklee for fall semester 2006. I am writing to ask a favor, though by no means an unpleasant one. Enclosed, you'll find a press release about your excellent work at the college. I am asking you to send this press release to your local newspaper, so that everyone in your area can know this happy news. Weekly newspapers that focus on neighborhood and family events—rather than large-circulation, daily newspapers—are the best places to approach with a notice like this. The Editor, or Managing Editor are good people to whom you can address this notice. Your effort will make all the difference. We appreciate the help very much.

I then read the press release. The first five-line paragraph announced that the student was on the dean's list, which required such and such GPA. The next two paragraphs—the bulk of the press release—were devoted to celebratory descriptions of Berklee, its curriculum, its different programs focusing on "practical career preparation for today's music industry," and its illustrious alumni, ending with "Berklee is the world's premier learning lab for the music of today—and tomorrow." Thus the dean's list, a marker of academic excellence, was appropriated and commodified in a very straightforward way.

"But I don't know if Hip Hop is music": The Return of Aesthetic Modernism

The contradiction between the two discourses of legitimation—the one focusing on aesthetic modernism and the other on market demand—came into relief during my interview with Fred when we discussed Berklee's long-held philosophy of reflecting market demand and being attuned to what the students want to study rather than imposing preconceived notions of "high" art. Fred emphasized that the pragmatic ideal of reflecting contemporary market demand still plays a key role in the school's philosophy. In response to my question about the significance of the small number of Berklee students who pursue jazz studies, he commented:

The fact that today there are many more guitar players [interested in rock music] than horn players [interested in jazz] and that many of them are not interested in jazz—we do not treat it as imbalance. There is no imbalance. There are indeed more people who want to be guitar players and we must go with that because our thing is to reflect reality. Or the fact that the biggest major, the major that students choose at the end of the first year, is music business: you have to understand that popular music sells. Students want to be Kenny G.,[10] not necessarily in terms of the music, but in terms of the sales. So our purpose is to turn a craft into a living. The music industry is the fourth-biggest industry in the economy. Take for example the Beatles. The sheer numbers may mandate that we have a special category for people who reach millions of people. The communication factor changed a lot. Dante or Beethoven cannot compete with Spielberg. So we simply emulate that. We take the position that it is not up to us to define what art is but rather to get the kids where they want to go. . . . The motto is not to create ideologues because I don't know what noble [art] is.

Thus, the school's central concern with democratizing knowledge in response to market demand presumes its refusal to determine in advance what is and what is not art and to make curricular decisions on this basis.

However, this sensitivity has resulted in the fact that while the number of students and educators who focus on jazz has remained consistent with historical numbers, their proportion within the school's student body has declined. Jazz is taught today at Berklee in a totally different atmosphere than the one that existed at the time the school was founded, that is, when jazz was widely listened to and played over the airwaves. These shifting conditions have produced a number of challenges. Berklee's seemingly self-assured and proudly pragmatic philosophy of "reflecting market demand" is not so easily adhered to anymore. It was one thing to celebrate this philosophy when the market demanded jazz; it is another thing altogether to do so when the market demands rock and roll and hip-hop. Exclusionist definitions of art and creativity, as well as the tension between the marketplace and artistic value, enter Berklee through the back door. Thus, immediately after endorsing this pragmatic ideal, Fred continued:

But I don't know if hip-hop is music, or rock and roll. Successful jazz is usually defined as art. It is evaluated by fellow musicians and some critics, in contrast to rock and roll, where the public decides and defines. Rock doesn't play the role of art. Popularity doesn't define art. Students today come with a platinum consumer-based motivation, but platinum is not art. It is almost a contradiction to say that it is. And I am troubled by the institutionalized concerts [i.e., concerts organized at Berklee] because they are conservative. The students don't come with artistic requirements, but with what will advance them economically. I am upset about this. I mean, they don't have to sell tickets at this stage, so why are they not making art? This is failure: the school doesn't attract these kinds of students. The students are not experimental. The emphasis on pragmatism excluded experimentation and it bothers me. There is the money and the infrastructure [to experiment]. So it is a loss. Students are so interested in making a buck. And we are dealing here [in the school] with the balance between the two trends—between art and rock and roll.

Berklee's modus operandi has continued to be to respond to market demand. But as the market has diversified and forced contemporary music programs to come to terms with the demand for different musical genres whose artistic value many educators and administrators openly question, these educators and administrators have begun to express a sense of malaise about the effects of this philosophy. Ironically, against this backdrop, many educators have suggested the conservatory model for music education as a possible solution to the continuous pressure to introduce forms of music of presumably dubious artistic value into Berklee's curriculum. They do so despite the fact that they remain highly ambivalent about this model because it connotes the past systematic marginalization of jazz by institutions dominated by the Western classical music tradition. Thus, just prior to my fieldwork, Berklee hired an external advising firm and asked it to develop new branding strategies. Among the suggestions this firm came up with was the tagline "Berklee—Nothing Conservatory about It." At face value, this tagline nicely captures what Berklee has been all about: the emphasis on reflecting market demand, being open and innovative, and not being trapped in ideologies and dogmas. However, many educators hotly rejected the tagline because they felt, as one of the school's public relations administrators told me, that "the pros, the good thing in being alike and understood as a conservatory, far outweighed anything you could [gain] by being perceived to be putting [it] down." The malaise that resulted from Berklee's efforts to reflect market demand has led many of them to conclude that modeling the jazz program after the conservatory, with its notion of conserving knowledge that is valuable independently of market demand, is perhaps not such a bad idea. As we concluded our meeting, Fred said, "I argued [in a board meeting] that we need to create an institute within Berklee to protect jazz, because I think everybody at Berklee, even nonjazz people and nonmusicians in the administration, believe that it's the American art form and we must honor that." Thus, while the strategy of legitimation through responsiveness to external market demand has not entirely disappeared, a growing number of educators and administrators have mobilized something akin to the "great books" approach in order to justify the importance of conserving jazz irrespective of its market value.

In adopting the external markers and norms of the very institutional structure from which it was excluded decades ago, jazz has acquired a conflicted identity and clashing strategies of legitimation. What's more, many of the educators and administrators I worked with firmly believe that jazz music itself has suffered as a result of its introduction into academe and its cultivation within a conservatory institutional model, a point they often articulate by comparing jazz's present state to its creative heydays prior to its full-blown academization. These anxieties received a palpable form during Berklee's convocation.

"It doesn't have the same ring": Between Signs of Present Standardization and Tropes of Past Creativity

After Berklee's president finishes his speech at the convocation, he introduces the recipient of the honorary doctorate, a successful and highly regarded African American saxophone player. The president describes the honoree's long list of musical achievements, as well as the congratulations that his fellow musicians sent in honor of the occasion from all over the world. To the continuous cheers of the crowd, the president invites the honoree to approach him, whereupon one of the administrators sitting on stage puts a pink scarf around his neck. After the president gives the honoree his stethoscope—an attempt to defuse the marker of academe that is the honorary doctorate—the honoree begins his speech, from which I quote in detail:

I remember when I left New Orleans in 1979, before most of you were zygotes or even thought of, to come to Boston. And this particular area of Boston's Back Bay was what modern city planners would call an area in transition. And I called my father about two days after getting here, and he's never been to Boston, so he asked, "What's it like?" I said, "Man, the cars drive really close to one another and they run the red lights a lot." And he said, "Really? They don't get tickets?" I said, "No. The cops just ignore them. And when you say hi to people they look at you really strange." And he's like, "Really?" "Yeah . . . ," I said, "and there's a bar across the street, like a bar, and it seems like it's for us." [And he said:] "There's a school full of musicians, why not open a bar?" [. . .] Now, growing up in a city with a twenty-four-hours liquor license, it wasn't nirvana for me, but there were a lot of guys from Pennsylvania going: "Yeah!!!" And I said, "There's a lot of hookers hanging around, Dad. I've seen them on Bourbon Street [in New Orleans], but I've never seen them that close." And he said, "Well, go talk to them, ask them how they're doing"—which is actually what he said. He said, "That's part of humanity, man; it might help your music." So a couple of us would go across the street and just talk to them, say, "Hey, how are you doing?" . . . And it was a nice little thing in addition to the university—we'd be like, "Hey, man, let's go talk to the hookers" . . .

And my roommates were great because I had—my first roommates—two guys, on one side the cleanest guy I've ever been near in my life. And the other guy was the absolute dirtiest guy I've ever been around in my life. [. . .] And he would order pizza and leave the boxes under the bed. Of course it was only a matter of time before a mouse came into the room, and then the first guy said: "That's it, I'm gonna kill him, there's a mouse in the room." And I was like the peace maker because we don't have a lot of mice in New Orleans, but we have big old rats, and I said, "Come on, man, it's just a mouse."

So I go outside now, and there's a Starbucks, a Store 24 where the pizza shop used to be, where the homeless guy used to come and stick his finger in your pizza and say, "Do you want that?" And people would gladly—I never understood—they would gladly, they'd just give him the pizza after that. And I was from New Orleans, I said, "Man, you can't let the man win like that." So one time he did it to me and I said, "Yeah," and I ate it right in front of him. And I vomited later, but the point was he left me alone after that. He would see me and say—"No, that ain't gonna work on him; he's crazy," you know.

So there are a lot of memories. These memories are random, yes, but the thing about being a musician that is often not talked about is that one of the things that make music great is the sum total of your personal experiences. And these are all fun things that I remember in addition to the scholarship,

the academic things, that I've incorporated, willingly or not. I've incorporated all this experience and friendships in the music because the ultimate
experience in playing music is to find a way to reach out and touch humanity. And too many times we hear about, you know, Mixolydian scales, and,
what did you call that—the G-Sharp Lydian? [Looks at the student representative who spoke before him], which I still don't know what that is. I was
never good with my scales. But it's one of those [things], being in Boston,
with the homeless guy, and the hookers—

Oh, I forgot the best part. The pope was coming to town, and it was
amazing. In thirty-six hours everything was gone. The bar was gone, the
hookers were gone, and much to our chagrin, it never came back. It was just
gone. And now there's a Starbucks and a Store 24, which is cool in its own
way, but you don't have the same kind of memories: "What are you doing?"
"Oh, I'm hanging out at the Store 24"—it doesn't have the same: "Man, I'm
with hookers in front of a bar, and I'm nineteen." It just doesn't have the
same ring, I don't care what you say. So we win, you guys lose.

Throughout the honoree's speech the audience burst into laughter. He continued to advise the students to benefit from the exposure to the various cultures
that different students bring with them to Berklee, and also to seek out exposure to as many musical genres as possible. After he told them to respect but
also to question their educators, he informed them about an all-girls college
nearby where the male students can find girls. When one of the administrators on stage told him that this all-girls college does not exist anymore,[11] the
honoree said: "Oh no, it's gone? This is a terrible place! First the hookers, now
this? What's next?"

"We win, you guys lose": A Long-Held Structure of Oppositions

The honoree's speech is an artful and poetic articulation of mounting concerns among the educators I worked with that jazz, via its introduction into
the university, is fast becoming or has already become a standardized cultural
form that is only a pale shadow of its glorious past. At the bottom of such
concerns is a contradiction between the search for cultural legitimacy and
notions about the bedrock of true creative jazz. Efforts to cultivate jazz and
to grant it cultural legitimacy have borne fruit: jazz's status in the American
cultural hierarchy has become firmly secured. At the same time, many of the
people I worked with shared the suspicion that the music's creative energies

are grounded in, and can only be sustained by, interactional norms, behaviors, and epistemologies that are radically at odds with the practices and ideologies that characterize the institutional bases of high-art. Thus, the past anxiety over jazz's cultural marginalization, though never entirely gone, has been replaced by a different kind of anxiety: that jazz's present cultural legitimacy and institutionalization might ultimately lead to its death by cultural standardization, abstraction, and theory.

What distinguishes the honoree's convocation speech from numerous other expressions of concern over jazz's cultural standardization is the crystallized way in which it reveals notions associated in the popular imagination with this polarity of creative agency and institutionalized rationality as it pertains to jazz. In his speech, the honoree superimposes a number of binary oppositions on one another that collectively strengthen the opposition between "institutionalized" and "creative" jazz. At stake are the fantasies and imageries that animate many people's ideas about the interactional norms, behaviors, and values that presumably structured the creativity of the past jazz masters and the opposite norms, behaviors, and values that presumably obstruct the cultivation of creativity in today's academic jazz programs.

First, the honoree artfully constructs an opposition between the past and the present and between players of his generation and today's students. He repeatedly contrasts himself and his cohort of fellow students with his student listeners during his speech, as when he begins with "When I left New Orleans in 1979, before most of you were zygotes." Second, there is a strong gendered aspect to this generational opposition. The honoree and his cohort of mostly male players were more masculine: they interacted with "hookers" and they found "girls" in the all-girls college nearby. Today's students, so it is implied, have neither hookers nor an all-girls college at their disposal, i.e., they cannot perform masculinity and hence are more effeminate than their predecessors. Third, the honoree contrasts New Orleans as a gritty urban setting and today's sanitized urban centers. Before contemporary urban centers became sanitized, so he suggests, they resembled New Orleans in that they had rats and mice running around in the streets and "homeless" people trying to take advantage of you. Fourth, the honoree stages a moral opposition between a lenient past social environment that was tolerant toward prostitution, traffic violations, and hard drinking, and today's more conservative institutional settings that are as sanitized and as flavorless as the chain stores that populate them such as Starbucks and Store 24.

Fifth, the honoree constructs an opposition between "humanness" as the raw material of true creativity and abstract theory as the source of sterile art. Note that in the middle of his speech he turns to the student representative who spoke before him and says, "And too many times we hear about, you know, Mixolydian scales, and—what did you call that—the G-Sharp Lydian?, which I still don't know what that is. I was never good with my scales." In contrast to the student representative who is worried about knowing her scales, he quotes his father apropos the grittiness, the rats, the hookers, the liquor, the homeless guy—saying that all this is "part of humanity, it might help your music." As I will suggest in the following chapters, this contrast between theory and humanness implicitly invokes a long-held contrast in jazz aesthetics between literacy and aurality as unequal modes of knowledge transmission and production, where the latter mode is presumed to be more in line with the masterpieces of the past jazz masters, whereas the former mode is associated with the dangers of excessive conceptual mediation.[12]

A sixth opposition that plays a role in the honoree's speech is that between marginalization and cultural legitimacy. He conjures this opposition by invoking the pope's visit to Boston in 1979, which marked the disappearance of the gritty bar across the street from Berklee and an end to the hookers' presence. This anecdote is about much more than the simple fact that the city council took actions to prepare the ground for the pope's visit. Rather, it is a description symbolic of the cultural dynamic behind the introduction of jazz into the university and its transformation into a legitimate form of high art. For the emergence of the institutional infrastructure of high art in the United States in the nineteenth century has been understood by its upper-class architects to be a form of sacralization, the creation of sacred texts purged of all the superficialities and profanities of popular culture, as well as the creation of sacred spaces such as the museum and the concert and theater halls, which would be symbolically and physically disconnected from the cacophony of the lower classes (Levine 1988). Tropes of pollution and purification played a key role in such processes of sacralization. Thus a nineteenth-century cultural entrepreneur wrote that "Light music, 'popular' so called, is the sensual side of the art and has more or less devil in it" (Levine 1988, 136). The honoree's narrative about the pope's visit is thus an artful allegory of the cultural dynamics of jazz's ascent into its present cultural legitimacy, respectability, and, indeed, sacrality as indexed by its academization, which presumably depended on a form of purification of jazz from the humanness, grittiness, sensuality, and moral leniency of the past learning environment of the honoree's student days. The price of such purification, according to this narrative, has been jazz's creative vigor.

Note, finally, that the honoree's narrative implicitly invokes another opposition: that between African American and white musicians. This opposition is implied in some of the previous, explicitly stated oppositions. First, past jazz, as opposed to present, was performed by a majority of African American players. Second, New Orleans, the mythical birthplace of jazz, indexes African American culture as opposed to the present gentrified urban centers that the honoree refers to, which are increasingly populated by white middle- and upper-class Americans. Indeed, note that the honoree, an African American, is addressing a crowd of mostly white students both as a member of an older generation of musicians and as a native of New Orleans.

The honoree's speech builds on all these oppositions to support the basic and most important opposition between better and lesser jazz performed by past players and today's students, respectively, as a result of the shift in the mode of jazz training represented by the academization of jazz. It all comes down to his almost festive summary: "We win, you guys lose." The oppositions that structure his speech can be rendered as in figure 1. If this structure of oppositions seems to conjure some of the very essentializing notions and ideologies that were used to marginalize jazz in the first half of the twentieth century, it is because this is precisely what it does. Jazz was excluded from institutions of higher music education in part because it was associated with Af-

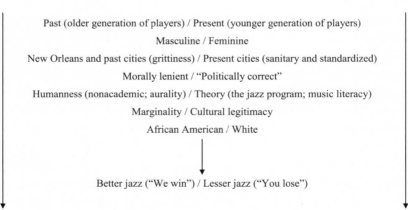

Figure 1. Structure of oppositions superimposed on one another in the doctoral honoree's speech

rican American musicians who were stereotyped as morally lenient, sexually uninhibited, and lacking in theoretical sophistication.[13] That this structure of oppositions is inadvertently reproduced by the honoree—a socially mindful, highly educated person who is well versed in the convoluted history of jazz and who is aware of the essentializing discourses that suffuse it, is indicative of just how deep the anxieties provoked by the rise of academic jazz education are, and how much the opposition between institutionalized rationality and creative agency is entrenched and made salient when people are asked to comment on jazz's present institutional form of training. This is one of the most ironic consequences of the rise of academic jazz education in the contexts I have worked in, namely, that in many respects it has subtly reproduced the essentializing divides that it was supposed to make obsolete—an irony that will recur time and again in the following chapters.

Abstract Ideas Have Concrete Effects

It is crucial to note that the implications of this specific orientation to jazz's mythical past and feared present are not restricted to the sphere of abstract ideas and notions. As anthropologists have shown, societies that orient themselves to a mythical past often shape their present in accordance with their perceptions of this past even if they understand this past to be a "golden age" that can never be fully recuperated (Berdahl 1999). Similarly, in their attempts to mitigate the threat of cultural standardization presumably produced as a result of jazz's academization, many of the educators, administrators, and students I worked with tap into the tropes that occupy the left side of the structure of oppositions in figure 1, which they associate with jazz's past mythical creativity. These tropes organize their efforts to rescue jazz from its presumed cultural standardization due to its academization. They attempt to introduce the notions, ideologies, behavioral norms, and epistemologies associated with this mythical past into the classroom in order to infuse the jazz program with the charismatic creativity of the past jazz masters, those musicians who learned their craft in ways that educators, administrators, and students believe were mostly different from the modes of training that pervade the academic program. These pedagogical strategies, their challenge to long-held notions about the opposition between creative agency and institutionalized schooling, and their unintended consequences are the focus of the remaining chapters.

4

CHARISMA INFUSION

Bringing the "Street" Back into the Classroom

A "Scandal" in the Classroom

It is the middle of the semester at the New School in late October 2007. I am sitting in a classroom with six students—all men in their twenties—waiting for the teacher of the ensemble class to arrive. The teacher, Thomas—a man in his early seventies with an impressive performance history with some of the most well-known past jazz masters—is already fifteen minutes late. Two of the students are discussing some jazz concerts they plan to attend the following week, while others play their instruments. Suddenly the door opens and Thomas enters the classroom. He closes the door behind him, remains standing by the door, and immediately says to the students:

> [Thomas:] Sorry I'm late. I was jerking off in the bathroom and my
> old lady caught me so I had to fuck her.
> [Student 1:] Wow!
> [Thomas:] What's the lesson in that?
> [Silence.]
> [Student 2:] You should always lock the door.

[Thomas:] No!

[Student 3:] Start jerking off earlier?

[Thomas:] No! [Silence.] When you're late for a gig don't apologize. Why?
    And make it good! Because if you crack up the bandleader he's going
    to give you an easier time than if you say, [simulating a childish voice]
    "Oh, I'm sorry, man, I was late because of traffic," you know. So you
    better have your "late" lines together. [Thomas laughs; students join in
    laughter.]

Even though by the time I started my fieldwork at the New School I had already recorded similar interactions between educators and students at Berklee, I was still puzzled by this interaction. My puzzlement did not originate so
much from the content of Thomas's words per se as from the discrepancy between his words and the institutional norms of the New School as a research
university. As I focused my attention on these kinds of interactions, I noticed
that they frequently involved a very specific group of educators. They were
mostly older musicians, all men, who, in contrast to most of the professional
educators I met in the two jazz programs, had ample performance experience
with the great jazz masters of the past. The persona they adopted in these interactions was iconoclastic, gritty, rough, and male-centric.

I suggest that rather than an institutional anomaly, the behavior displayed
by some of these educators (of which Thomas's performance, to be sure, is
an extreme example) is the unintended consequence of a strategy devised
by program administrators to negotiate the increasingly predominant suspicion that such programs have become sites of cold technicism and cultural
standardization, which result in a lesser form of jazz—"think-tank music," in
Branford Marsalis's artful phrasing (Young 2006). This strategy is based in the
hope that these musicians who played with the great past masters will be able
infuse the program with the masters' charisma. At its core, it embodies a key
contradiction.

"They have no idea what it's like out there": Out of the Academic Bubble

On the one side of this contradiction, these educators do, indeed, bring with
them valuable knowledge into the classroom. This knowledge surpasses the
specifics of theory and instrumental technique that are the focus of much of
academic jazz training. First and foremost, their presence in the classroom

allows students to benefit from the invaluable skills these musicians possess, which are the product of years of contributing to the creation of some of the masterpieces of the genre. To play with these musicians in class is an incredible opportunity, as I myself experienced firsthand when Pierre, my Berklee guitar student friend, asked me to play in his group in a master class led by a well-known saxophonist. After we played Thelonious Monk's tune "Reflections," this master joined in, and the three of us—the master, Pierre, and I traded fours on the tune. I will always remember this player's incredible energy and rhythmic complexity, which stood in such a contrast to Pierre's and my staid and stiff playing. It was like suddenly being caught in the middle of a hurricane.

However, the knowledge these masters bring with them to the classroom is wider than pure musical skills. It encompasses information about the nitty-gritty of a musician's working life; the history of the music rendered through stories and anecdotes; valuable contacts with other well-known musicians that students might benefit from; and interactional practices between mentors and protégés grounded in traditional modes of training that contribute directly to students' improvisational skills, and which are highly different from the interactions one finds at a typical university classroom. Indeed, in a number of the classes I attended, some of these educators recruited their top students to their own bands. In that respect, these jazz programs have indeed managed, in part, to reproduce long-held modes of training that have become endangered with the decline of extracurricular jazz scenes.

This added pedagogical value is apparent in the vignette that opens this chapter, in which Thomas demonstrates the highly volatile context of the jazz musician's work life in the "real world," where one can get instantly fired for being late to a gig—a context rarely addressed in the well-protected and insulated confines of the classroom. Many students arrive with a consumer-based approach that is highly incompatible with what would be required from them if they are fortunate enough to be hired as sidemen by the leading musicians of the jazz world. Musicians like Thomas, who are recruited by programs' administrators because of their association with the past masters, are better equipped than regular educators to clarify to students that this consumer-based approach will not do, because their special status grants them partial immunity from the program's supervision and expectations about how "typical" educators ought to treat their students—immunity that is grounded in their charisma.

In classes I attended, these musicians would often explain to their students that they model their authority after that of the masters in whose bands they had played. They would tell students who are late to class that they should treat the class as a gig. Frank, a New School educator in his late sixties, shouted at a drummer student who failed to enter the class on time: "Remember, you are always one phone call away from getting fired. One phone call! There is no second chance!"

In another class at the New School, Paul, an educator in his early seventies, scolded the students in the band in short bursts of terse commands for over thirty minutes. During the break he told me: "I try to teach them like they used to teach you on the gig, in real life. There are no apologies—it's serious. . . . If they behave and play like that outside of school they won't get any calls. They have no idea what it's like out there, absolutely no idea. I try to show them how it is." "Showing them how it is" means simulating a bandleader who has complete authority over his sidemen. Greg, another New School educator in his early seventies, explained: "There are times when democracy doesn't work. There's a time when the only thing that works is a dictatorship. . . . In my band I'm the manager; I'm a dictator, but I'm a caring dictator. I'm a listening dictator. I like to get feedback, I like that, just don't be a pain in the ass about it. But I like the feedback and I'll think about it and then once I'll make my decision, that's it—that's the way it's gonna be." Perhaps the starkest example I recorded of an assertion of authority by an educator who belongs to this group of musicians took place in a class at the New School visited by a prospective student. While the class was discussing a composition of one of the students, the prospective student suddenly intervened and suggested that the voice and the horns should enter at different points than prescribed in the current arrangement. Dave, the educator, a tall and imposing man in his mid-seventies who appears in some of the most iconic recordings in jazz history, interrupted him abruptly and said, "Listen, I appreciate the suggestion but in this situation you should just sit and shut the fuck up." When the student answered with "No, I just wanted to—" Dave interrupted him again and said, "No, just shut the fuck up." Everyone pretended as if nothing had happened. After a few minutes the prospective student left the room.

Indeed, at times such assertions of authority implicated me as well. As an observer sitting in class, I, too, was, at least in principle, a subject in these educators' kingdoms. Often, the "dictator" would assert his authority over me as a message directed both to me and to the students, as if saying: "Look at this—here, in my class, even this guy is under my authority." Thus in one class Frank addressed the band and then suddenly me:

[Frank:] OK, should we make another attempt at it? Let's have the man
    from Israel kick us off. The Israeli, kick us off, man. Give us a tempo.
[I remain in my seat and count:] 1, 2, a-1, 2, 3, 4—
[Frank:] No, no. We want to go upstairs [i.e., at a faster tempo]. Would you
    mind coming over here? It's hard sitting over there. It's your band, your
    orchestra.
[Eitan:] My band?
[Frank:] Yeah, come up and play. Nobody gets away. I'm the only one sitting
    in this class. Kick us off, man.[1]

And Back into New Forms of Charismatic, Stereotypical Indigeneity

Often, at the same time that these musicians imparted valuable knowledge,
only a tiny share of which I covered above, they also reproduced some of the
marginalizing ideologies that had previously been responsible for the exclusion of jazz from institutions of higher music education. Note that Thomas—
the educator featured in the vignette that opens this chapter—does not convey
knowledge about the tough reality of the working musician with the typical
register of the university professor. He uses a register that, as I will suggest
below, has been associated with the mythical creativity of the past jazz masters and that connotes iconoclasm, anti-institutionalism, lowbrow behavior,
and male-centric interactional norms. These are precisely some of the tropes
that the doctoral honoree whose speech I analyzed in the previous chapter
implicitly associated with the great jazz of the past. Not only does Thomas's
use of this register reproduce the status of "authentic" creativity in jazz as the
antithesis of the academic environment, it also reproduces the stereotypes
that many gatekeepers projected onto jazz musicians to keep jazz away from
the institutions of higher music education.

In unpacking the contradiction between these musicians' pedagogical
value that prompts administrators to recruit them as educators, and their
anti-institutional persona that reproduces a host of stereotypes and marginalizing ideologies, I use two theoretical frameworks. The first pertains to what
the sociologist Max Weber called "routinization of charisma" (Weber 1978c).
Weber highlighted the processes that often follow periods of charismatic fervor, when such fervor is institutionalized in permanent and routine social
structures. The establishment of the Catholic Church following the charismatic movement initiated by Jesus is an example of such routinization. The
recruitment of musicians who played with the charismatic past jazz masters to

serve as educators in academic jazz programs is another case of an attempt to routinize charisma in a permanent organizational structure. Such routinized charisma might occasionally threaten to backfire and undermine the institutional structure itself, as in the incident that opens this chapter.

An added theoretical framework I use is the anthropological study of the politics of indigeneity, which traditionally defines *indigeneity* via territoriality, or "first-order connections (usually at small scale) between group and locality" that connote "belonging and originariness and deeply felt processes of attachment and identification" that distinguish "natives" from "others" (Merlan 2009, 304). However, recent moves in this literature have detached indigeneity from territory and emphasized the multiple dimensions of relationality between indigenous and nonindigenous groups (Muehlebach 2003, 250–251). These studies have suggested that indigeneity is a relational category that is based in an opposition between one group perceived to have some primordial connection to specific aspects of culture that do not necessarily involve territory, and another group perceived to lack this connection.

I suggest that the recruitment of some "golden-age" musicians into the New School and Berklee is productive of unexpected indigeneity. In this context, "primordiality" has nothing to do with territoriality, blood ties, or the periphery of modern life. Rather, these musicians' performance experience with past masters motivates people to see them as "indigenous" to the cultural order of jazz (compare with Povinelli 2002), and this forms a powerful opposition between these musicians and the majority of educators in academic jazz programs who lack such performance experience with the past masters and who received their education mostly in academic jazz programs.

The academic jazz context displays a number of additional classic features of the politics of indigeneity. First, administrators assume that these sought-after musicians possess "traditional" knowledge of jazz that has the potential to mitigate the standardization processes presumably unleashed by the professionalization and modernization of jazz and thus to revitalize contemporary jazz education and infuse the classroom with jazz's past charismatic vitality (compare with Davidson 2010).

Second, anthropologists have argued that projections of indigeneity often result in the expectation that indigenous people "enact a legible form of primordialism" (Comaroff and Comaroff 2009, 94), radical difference, and cultural authenticity as indices of their possession of indigenous knowledge (Povinelli 2002). Similarly, in everyday pedagogical interactions with students, a number of these musicians enact this difference as a legible sign that they possess "traditional" knowledge that has the potential to mitigate the eroding forces of institutionalized rationality, of which the jazz program is an example. Frequently, such enactment reproduces long-held stereotypes about jazz musicians in American culture. Thomas's "scandalous" mode of teaching is an example.

My argument, then, is that the musicians I discuss respond to a very specific set of *expectations* about the primordial essence of the creative jazz musician (compare with Cattelino 2008; Deloria 2004). The "scandalous," then, is a product of the American public imagination and its set of expectations about such an essence. My purpose in discussing this aspect of the attempt to reconcile creative agency and institutionalized rationality in the two academic jazz programs through the recruitment of these musicians is thus not to perpetuate these essentializing discourses but rather to suggest that they survive and are reproduced in the least expected place, namely, the academic jazz program, albeit not predominantly so, since the majority of educators in such programs are not musicians with significant performance history, nor do all musicians with significant performance history exhibit the patterns I describe in this chapter. These are important qualifications.

To unravel the contradictions that result from the recruitment of some of these musicians into the academic jazz program, we must begin from the criticism that academic jazz education is a site of cultural standardization—the very criticism that has led the administrators I worked with to search for "golden-age" musicians to begin with. This criticism has a basis in the everyday pedagogical reality at Berklee and the New School. Two particularly significant components of standardization are, first, overspecialization and abstraction of theory; and second, the rise of a professional class of educators who gained most of their performance experience and training in academic jazz education rather than through prolonged apprenticeship with the past masters.

"It's the same thing!" Compartmentalization and Abstraction of Knowledge

Although fifty minutes had passed since the start of class, fifty more minutes remained in a session of a course at Berklee. The topic of the day was "chromatic approach to chord tones." The course followed one among a series of successful commercial jazz pedagogy books. The chromatic approach involves different ways of arriving at chord tones while improvising on a harmonic progression that consists of a series of chords. Chord tones typically fall on the first, third, fifth, seventh, ninth, eleventh, and thirteenth degree of each chord. A chromatic approach to a chord tone might simply be a half step below that tone. However, there are more complicated chromatic approaches, such as starting from a half step above the chord tone and then going to a half step below the tone before reaching the chord tone itself.

I closely observed the educator's strategy that day. Once he explained a particular chromatic approach, he asked the students to apply that approach to a single chord tone over a play-along recording of a blues harmonic progression.[2] First they applied the chromatic approach to the first degree of each chord in the harmonic progression. In the second chorus, they applied it to the third degree, then to the fifth degree in the third chorus, and so forth. Each chord tone represented a unique challenge because of its derivation from a relative place in the scale and because most harmonic progressions contain chords of different qualities (some are major seventh, some dominant seventh, some minor seventh, etc.).

The thirteen students had a difficult time handling these intricacies. Most students find it easier to hear the lower chord tones (such as the first, third, and fifth). Because the exercise involved higher-degree chord tones, and because the chromatic approach was of a more complex type, an increasing number of the students could not execute the exercises. Their attempts resulted in a growing cacophony. I sat among the students and observed as they tried to correctly approach the chord tones that always seemed to pass too quickly. They struggled with the play-along that marched on regardless of their difficulties. Some students just gave up and waited until the educator replayed the track, which he did over and over again.

Suddenly, in a moment of silence, music from an adjacent room filtered into the classroom. An ensemble class led by one of the "star" educators of the school—a well-known saxophone player with impressive performance experience—had been rehearsing in the next room throughout the semester at the same day and time as this class. Today, as the students had excitedly mentioned, the ensemble was rehearsing with a substitute musician who had been invited by the regular saxophonist because he had to go on tour. The substitute educator was an even more well-established saxophonist than the regular one. The well-respected ensemble consisted of advanced students. Frequently I saw students gathering outside the door of the rehearsal room to listen and observe through the small window in the door. At that particular moment, the music from the adjacent room could be heard clearly. A student exclaimed: "It's the same thing!" The educator then listened for a second to the music that infiltrated from the adjacent room and then said, "Yes, I know! You see?" Everyone listened attentively and then burst into laughter. One student hummed the phrase that we all heard emanating from the adjacent room. It definitely resembled the chromatic approach that the class had been practicing at that moment. Then the voice of Jamey Aebersold, the producer of the play-along device, boomed from the speakers, counting off the beginning of the play-along track, and the students entered with a chromatic approach on the third beat.

The students' and educator's reaction to the infiltration of the music from the other room was a significant moment of self-reflection on the course and the pedagogy it represents. This class belongs to a group of five courses that follow a series of commercially successful method books that are well known in the field of jazz education. Week after week, the students labored to master material that was only tangential to skillful improvisation. The method of presentation and practice made this material even more difficult to remember and learn. The formal and laborious nature of this approach is evident in a teaching moment I recorded in my field notes from one of the first classes in this course. The educator entered the classroom and without saying a word wrote the twenty-four permutations of the pattern 1 2 3 5 that represents the degrees of a scale based on a given chord. The educator continued to explain seventy-two further permutations for three other chord types (minor, half-diminished, and diminished chords). After the students practiced this basic pattern, he instructed them to treat the first degree as an eighth degree;[3] this produced a panoply of permutations at each degree. Soon the whiteboard was covered in scrawled numbers. Had a stranger entered the classroom, she might have mistaken it for a higher-level math class. In the particular moment of silence that I described above, music filled the classroom; it filtered in from an adjacent room where "the real thing" was taking place. To the surprise of the students, the musicians next door produced music that bore some resemblance to the abstract body of knowledge they had been studying for weeks. Laughter erupted as one student exclaimed: "It's the same thing!" Another student hummed the musical phrase, as if attempting to corroborate the similarity between abstract class material and real-world music produced by the ensemble playing in a neighboring room. This expression of disbelief indexes the gulf, or degree of distance, between music theory and "real music" experienced by some of my interlocutors at Berklee.

This disconnect is grounded in the fact that most academic jazz programs exist within the institutional environment of the college and the university. More specifically, many programs are housed at four-year colleges that grant a bachelor of music degree and which therefore combine music studies with the liberal arts education required for accreditation purposes. These institutions put a premium on compartmentalization of knowledge into discrete subjects. Many jazz programs align themselves with these institutional norms by dividing jazz into different areas of expertise and formulating general rules of action, guidelines, and modus operandi meant to structure learning to the point where the different aspects of knowledge students acquire often become ever more abstract and disconnected from one another (Ake 2002). This compartmentalization is highly visible at Berklee. At the time of my fieldwork, the school offered concentrates such as composition, music business, music education, film scoring, music synthesis, and more, in addition to the performance concentrate where most jazz courses are located. The curriculum consisted of both material shared by all concentrates and material that is specific to each concentrate. Students in all concentrates had to take credits of "Core Music" (Arranging, Harmony, Ear Training, Introduction to Music Technology), "Traditional Studies" (Traditional Harmony/Composition, Traditional Counterpoint, History of Music, Conducting), "Private Instruction," "Ensembles/Instrumental Labs," and "General Education" (College Writing, Art History, Western/World Civilization, Physical Science Selection, Social Science Selection, and General Education Electives). The courses specific to the Performance concentrate included Additional Private Instruction, Harmonic Considerations in Improvisation, Styles Survey, Recital Preparation and Workshop, and Ensembles/Labs/Approved Electives (such as Performance Ear Training).

Further compartmentalization takes place within each topic. Thus, in one semester, Berklee offered eleven different courses under Arranging, sixteen under Ear Training, twelve under Harmony, seven under Music Technology, dozens of improvisational classes, and more than one hundred different sections of ensembles and instrumental labs. The wealth of subject matter offered in any one concentrate is significant. The improvisational courses in one semester consisted of Improvisation Techniques 1 to 6; Harmonic Considerations in Improvisation; Standard Jazz Repertoire 1 and 2; The Music of Wayne Shorter; The Jazz Language; Jazz Interpretation; The Jazz Line; Melodic Structures in Improvisation; Pentatonics in Improvisation; Thematic Development in Improvisation; Performance and Analysis of Bebop; and more. The same variety of topics exists in smaller programs, but they offer fewer courses under each topic. Some academic jazz programs are thus highly departmentalized and formalized in the sense that they define distinct areas of expertise and competence. As the vignette above about the class on chromatic approach to chord tones demonstrates, within some areas of expertise the pressure to specialize finds expression in courses that focus on very specific and arguably minor aspects of jazz improvisation. As Chris, the teacher of this class, told me in an interview, his course "is sort of the spice—I don't see it as the general cooking, which is not together at all." In other words, because of institutional forces of specialization and compartmentalization, students are often expected to master higher-level and frequently esoteric improvisational skills before they master the basics of the music.

In addition to topical compartmentalization, courses are structured by syllabuses that address topics by date, similar to courses at research universities and liberal arts colleges. Berklee uses the same template for the syllabuses of almost all the courses it offers. Syllabuses are divided into course description, course objective, required text, coursework and out-of-class preparation, grading criteria, final grade determination, attendance policy, and deadline for course withdrawal. Furthermore, students are evaluated and assigned grades. Most courses administer some form of examination that tests students' mastery of the material. This drive toward examination has played a significant role in the jazz program's parceling of jazz competence into increasingly finer categories of evaluation. At Berklee, for example, students are evaluated according to a five-digit (each digit in the range of 1 to 8) rating system in their auditions to the school and throughout their studies. The first four digits stand for "reading, instrumental skill, improvisation, and groove and rhythmic interpretation." The fifth digit is an overall number representative of all the other digits. In their audition, students are required to play a prepared piece, to improvise on a tune that is selected by the committee, and finally to sight-read musical examples.

The vast number of courses and topics now covered in many jazz programs can give the impression that today's jazz students have infinitely richer material on which to draw in their improvisations as compared to musicians of previous generations. To some degree, this is true. However, a closer look reveals that although this specialization has increased the scope of material accessible to students, not all of them necessarily benefit from this increase. The compartmentalization and specialization of jazz often produces a fundamental disconnect between the material learned in multiple classes any one student enrolls in and his or her ability to implement it in actual playing. As Jerry, an educator in his midfifties who has been teaching at Berklee since his graduation from the school, told me:

> I think that both harmony and ear training should be more performance-based. They teach harmony over here [points to his head], they teach ear training over here [points to his ears], and the playing is here [points to his fingers], and so many students don't connect them. Like you need to have the harmony and understand how you can *play* the harmony . . . you must to be able to connect that. I know so many students that pass ear training and they [have] so much work to do with their ears because they didn't even conceive of using their ears and their horn together.

The bifurcation between theory and practice and the effects of compartmentalization of knowledge became clear to me one day during an upper-level theory class at Berklee in which the educator encouraged his students to apply course material to their playing. Although this playing necessitated the use of a play-along device's recorded rhythm section and thus did not involve live interactivity with other musicians, this educator sought nevertheless to close somewhat the gap between theory and practice. However, only after two and a half minutes of playing did one student realize that the educator had accidentally played the wrong play-along track. Thus, there was no connection whatsoever between the students' playing and the background track in terms of the harmonic structure. All who were present in the classroom laughed upon this realization, but the laughter was of awkward embarrassment.

This short vignette brings to mind the cultural critic Georg Lukács's argument that hyper-rational social systems often produce objects that end up being disconnected from the larger context within which these objects are supposed to operate (1999). Such systems undergo further subdivision and specialization and eventually become incoherent, losing touch with the purposes for which they were originally devised. The reification and compartmentalization of some areas of expertise at Berklee have similar consequences to those discussed by Lukács.

Even in small jazz programs that pride themselves on being less formalized, the pressures toward formalization, departmentalization, and specialization are powerful. Thus around the time of my fieldwork, administrators at the New School's jazz program distributed a form entitled "Common Values for All Ensembles," which states twenty-eight different "values" under "Individual and Collective Responsibility," "Listening and Communication Skills," "Musical Values," and "Professionalism and Performance." Mark, a musician who teaches at the New School and who had performed with some of the founding figures of jazz, expressed dismay: "Did you see that? Even this program is beginning to be incorporated!"

"Teachers Teaching Teachers": The Rise of a Professional Class of Educators

Another focus of concern for critics of academic jazz programs has been the qualifications of the majority of educators in such programs. Over the last few decades, as part of the general decline in the popular demand for the music, the number of extracurricular performance venues has decreased while the number of jazz programs has increased. Consequently, many (though certainly not all) of the younger educators in today's jazz programs did not benefit from prolonged apprenticeship with experienced masters prior to taking their academic positions. Rather, most of their training took place in academic jazz programs. In addition, the present performance activity of many of the younger educators is fairly limited. This is a state of affairs they openly acknowledge. For example, Chris, a Berklee educator in his midforties, told me: "The scene can only support so much musicians, so somebody—and god bless them—[saxophonist] Joe Lovano gets all the work, [guitar player John] Scofield gets all the work. . . . So there's room for only a few. Then there's the second tier. So the second tier—like I'm with X [a musician he frequently performs with]—we get to play maybe thirteen, ten weeks a year in Europe and that's where we are. Then there's the third tier, which doesn't get that much but does a lot of local playing." The majority of the jazz educators I met at Berklee belong to the last group—people who play locally and irregularly. These transformations have forced many jazz programs to recruit musicians who are professional educators more than professional performers.[4]

The bifurcation between performance and teaching has been compounded by the rise of a so-called "in-breeding ideology" at some schools that recruit musicians from within a pool of their own graduates to serve as educators. This has been particularly prevalent at Berklee. As Tim, a Berklee faculty member in his fifties who is also an alumnus of the school, told me: "It's much easier—they [Berklee's graduates] know already the different methods of teaching, the building, and the atmosphere. They don't need to be trained to know what to do, where's this hall, where's that copy machine. But especially it's because there is a certain system of teaching to Berklee—you know, its own language, the chord-scale theory. They've been through that, so it makes things easy." In their reliance on musicians who have been trained in the same knowledge they produce and inculcate, some academic jazz programs have become highly self-referential systems, sites of professional teaching.

Within the jazz world, this trend is derogatively and somewhat simplistically referred to as "Teachers Teaching Teachers" (Nicholson 2005). It denotes the growing reliance of jazz programs on musicians who have not had extensive extracurricular performing experience with experienced musicians. As a number of the more experienced musicians told me, the problem is not only with how knowledge is imparted but also with its quality. Frank, a musician in his seventies who teaches at the New School and who had played with a number of past jazz masters noted: "Most of the teachers in these programs are teachers teaching teachers. Where do they get their experience from? Try being on the road for fifty weeks a year with Cannonball [alto-saxophonist Cannonball Adderley]—that's experience! After three months you already played all your shit out, you exhausted it all. Then you really start learning!" These criticisms are voiced not only by the more experienced educators who have a vested interest in such descriptions. They are also subscribed to by the professional educators who are typically their target. Albert, a Berklee educator in his late thirties, told me,

> My time was much easier than Miles's [the legendary trumpeter Miles Davis], who had to go to the clubs—he was in it! You know, he was living it, so it was much deeper for him to learn the stuff and get the influence than it was for me, which was much easier. I had a record, I could transcribe, I could get transcription books and cheating—I didn't really learn the stuff. I mean I learned the aspects of certain things in music, but I don't have the depth in my learning that the older cats have in some ways.

Albert conceptualizes the divide between today's jazz educators and the past jazz performers by means of metaphors of depth and immersion: while Miles Davis was "in it," "living it," and thus "it was much deeper for him," for Albert everything was "much easier," like "cheating," with the result that he did not really "learn the stuff" and does not have "the depth." To be sure, Albert knows very well that the past jazz masters also transcribed the solos of the musicians they admired. Rather, he suggests that these musicians supplemented this mode of acquiring knowledge with prolonged performance experience and mentoring by experienced musicians. Many of the jazz educators I worked with, being the products of academic jazz education rather than of extensive apprenticeship with the great masters, feel they lack knowledge grounded in extensive, concrete performing experience. It is significant that Albert's commentary points up printed pedagogical aids as mediating this "fall from grace," for these aids have come to index and be identified with academic jazz education at large.

The Charisma of Past Jazz Masters

In an effort to deflect the criticism that they are sites of increased abstraction, compartmentalization, and professionalism divorced from significant real-time performance experience, administrators in the two jazz programs have actively sought to recruit musicians who played with the past masters at some point in their careers and who thus index the knowledge, myths, lore, and charisma associated with them. The past masters are considered to be exemplary practitioners of the music, the mythical loci of the creative practice of jazz. During class, educators frequently refer to them with accolades such as "perfect," "amazing," and "the real cats." Educators and administrators direct most of this veneration to a number of performers who were musically active in the years between the 1940s and the late 1960s. This period in the history of jazz, which encompasses several stylistic shifts—from bebop, hard bop, postbop, to the beginning of free jazz—is considered to be the golden age of jazz within the jazz program, epitomized by legendary recordings (e.g., *Sonny Side Up*), recording labels (e.g., Blue Note Records), and groups (e.g., the Second Miles Davis Quintet). Educators often invoke musicians like saxophonists John Coltrane, Charlie Parker, and Sonny Rollins, trumpeters Miles Davis, Dizzy Gillespie, Clifford Brown, and Lee Morgan, pianists Bill Evans and Bud Powell. These musicians form such a habitual point of reference that educators and students refer to them by nicknames like "Dizzy," "Bird, "Trane," "Clifford." Within the cultural order of jazz, the past jazz master is revered in terms of his musical knowledge to such a degree that he becomes a charismatic force that orients the field around him. The past masters' charisma is important to note because it is the source of value of those musicians recruited to programs because they played with these masters at some point in the past.

In his foundational study of charisma, Max Weber highlighted two dimensions that are important in the context of the jazz program. First, charisma is associated with exceptional abilities and skills. Weber defined charismatic people as "bearers of specific gifts of body and mind that were considered 'supernatural' (in the sense that not everybody could have access to them)" (Weber 1978b, 1112). Second, the charismatic quality is inherently relational and dialogical. It is a performative practice that depends on the audience as a "co-author" of the meaning and function of charismatic domination. Weber argued that the charismatic leader's authority is established only when adherents recognize it: "The mere fact of recognizing the personal mission of a charismatic master establishes his power. . . . this recognition derives from the surrender of the faithful to the extraordinary and unheard-of, to what is alien to all regulation and tradition and therefore is viewed as divine—surrender which arises from distress or enthusiasm" (1115).

These two features played a prominent role in the panels I attended at the *Jazz Improv* conference that took place in New York City in October 2007, organized by the trade magazine of the same name. The conference included dozens of panels in which musicians, many of whom are now educators in jazz programs, convened to share their memories of the masters with whom they had worked. Indeed, the New School's jazz program was one of the conference's sponsors, and many of the New School's educators participated in such panels. Two panels entitled "Eyes of the Masters" and "Thad Jones Retrospective" were devoted exclusively to the New School's educators. As I moved from panel to panel during the three days of the conference, I could not resist the impression that they served as assemblies in which believers convened and shared stories, testimonials, and personal witnessing of the miracles that the charismatic masters had performed. In many ways, these assemblies functioned as sites where the charismatic superiority of the masters was certified and re-enacted. Frequently, this attitude took the form of participants providing descriptions of the past masters' unnatural musical capabilities.

The various panels confirmed Weber's emphasis on the charismatic leader's exceptional abilities and on acts of recognition by believers as the basis of the leader's authority. For example, in a panel on the Thad Jones/ Mel Lewis Orchestra, one saxophonist who teaches at the New School commented: "It was known among the Shaolin Monks that Thad Jones could go through walls [laughter]. No, but he did some magic. It was known that—this is the truth—it was known that Thad Jones could look at a score and hear the music as he's reading it, hear all those parts as he's reading it. So that's like walking through walls for me." Characteristically, this statement provoked other participants in the panel and some audience members to offer their own accounts and testimonials of Thad Jones's ability to hear the music just by looking at a score of a big band. A trumpeter, also a New School educator, said, "We did a recording date [. . .] and there was a section there, the brass was just roaring [scats for seven seconds a convoluted line to convey the nonlinearity of the piece]. Thad stopped and said, 'Wait a minute, wait a minute: third trombone, that's an E-flat, not an E natural.' [Laughter. The trumpeter feigns amazement.] What? How could you do that? What? How do you know that? How did you hear that?" The trumpeter offered a few additional testimonials of similar "miracles," concluding with the same enactment of amazement: "You can't do that! No one can do that!" He thus time and again pointed to the nonhuman and extraordinary nature of Thad Jones's capabilities. He added the following words, apropos another participant's testimonial about seeing a past master writing a big band arrangement from scratch within an hour and a half: "I wasn't there, but I've seen him do it. You know, the term *genius* gets thrown a lot. But these people were geniuses. They did stuff that normal people can't do. And . . . once in a while Thad would pick up his horn and play some of the most incredible stuff that you can ever imagine." Even though he was not there to witness this specific "miracle," the trumpeter saw similar "miracles" on other occasions, "stuff that normal people can't do." In accordance with Weber's assertion that "the mere fact of recognizing the personal mission of a charismatic master establishes his power" (Weber 1978b, 1115), here, too, participants are encouraged and feel compelled to offer accounts of the masters' magical acts as a practice of "testifying," which constitutes and reaffirms the masters' charismatic powers.

Participants in the various panels related to the masters as charismatic leaders not only by providing descriptions of their exceptional musical capacities but also by giving accounts of the ways in which these masters were able to influence the players around them. Consider the following testimonial given by trumpeter Valery Ponomarev during a panel on the drummer Art Blakey: "Once Art Blakey heard the arrangement and he starts playing—from that point on, whatever you wrote moves immediately to another level. It becomes either a great tune or a masterpiece just by him touching it. That was incredible. That was his special touch and gift. . . . It was a metamorphosis." Blakey, by his mere presence, can transform the musical situation into something else. He is able to take it to "another level," to transform it by virtue of his "special touch and gift." These descriptions reverberate with charismatic notions through and through. Indeed, Ponomarev titled a series of tribute concerts he organized with the participation of Blakey's former band members, "Our Father Who Art Blakey." This title is a paraphrase on the Pater Noster, or the

Lord's Prayer, which starts with the words "Our Father who art in Heaven"—probably the best-known prayer in Christianity. In this clever title the trope of the jazz master as a charismatic figure finds its clearest expression.[5]

Charismatic "Natives" and Professional "Settlers"

Musicians who are recruited by administrators because they played with the past masters for an extensive time at one point in their career partake to a certain degree in the masters' charisma in a process that is akin to one of the three modes of routinization of charisma described by Weber (1978b, 1139): transference of charisma by contact or association with the charismatic leader. The notion of association or contact finds ample expression particularly at the New School, which emphasizes this mythical connection in order to present itself as a site of traditional pedagogy rooted in jazz's rich history. In this way the New School program attempts to differentiate itself from other jazz programs. A yearly publication distributed to students contained the following message: "Our curriculum is based on the respected tradition of artist-as-mentor, and is taught by accomplished, active artists with significant *links* to the history and evolution of jazz. . . . Students at the New School work with the *creators*, not just the *interpreters*, of jazz and its offshoots" (emphasis added). I suggest that the opposition between musicians who are "creators" with "significant links" to the roots of the music, and musicians who are mere "interpreters," is meant to index the distinction between musicians who at some point in their career played with the past masters for an extensive time, and musicians who are "merely" professional educators in that they received most of their education in academic jazz programs. One of the administrators at the New School's jazz program explained to me the value of the musicians who are recruited into the program because they played with the past masters in these words:

> These are the giants who have walked with the giants—standing on the shoulders of the giants, the people who are connected to the very origins of this wonderful tradition. And touching that is huge for those who understand that—the students who can or do begin to appreciate that. So it certainly begins with that because spiritually—in terms of the truth that they carry from those kinds of [. . .] connections—how they carry themselves—it's the sum total—I mean that sort of leads them to the experience factor because they all carry a lifetime of experience in this music, its community, its creation, its practice—they embody that.

The administrator's reference to "origins" and his use of the phrase "walked with the giants" paints a portrait of a mythological and almost primordial world populated by "giants" with whom these musicians had a first-order connection (Merlan 2009, 304). Furthermore, he uses the words "truth," "experience factor," "spiritually," and "embody" to characterize the knowledge these musicians possess because they played with the past masters. His choice of words here resonates with mythologized indigeneity across various social contexts, which frequently relies on a conception of truth that is embodied rather than codified, abstract, and rationalized (Kuper 2003; Merlan 2009; Pelican 2009). The tropes of "contact," "touch," and "link" express the desire for a reconnection with a mythical and charismatic era that holds the promise of quasi musical salvation in the present. As one New School student told me in an interview apropos pianist and New School educator Junior Mance, who had played with Charlie Parker: "There is Junior Mance telling a story about Charlie Parker and I am like—'Wow, I am one link from Charlie Parker!'"[6]

To be sure, some of the professional educators I worked with also attempted to establish proximity to the past masters. Yet their strategies of doing so reveal their limitations. Consider a class taught by Frank, a Berklee educator in his early sixties. Frank belongs to the group of "professional educators" in that he has not had ample performance experience with the past jazz masters (although he has probably had more experience than most professional educators). At one point, after discussing the 1949 *Birth of the Cool* recording by the Miles Davis band, Frank told the students: "I once heard Miles in Detroit. I sat so close to him that he almost emptied his trumpet into my beer. And if he did, I would thank him!" While saying this, Frank raised his hands in an imaginary gesture of thanking. Shortly thereafter, in another class at Berklee, James, another educator in his midsixties, told a story that was starkly similar to Frank's. In the middle of playing a recording of the Thad Jones/Mel Lewis Orchestra, James commented: "I had the chance to hear this band at the Village Vanguard right in the beginning in the sixties. I used to sit that close next to the sax section [demonstrates with his hands a distance of approximately two feet]. Wow, what a sound! And Sir Roland Hanna [the band's piano player]—he was a spitter—he spat all over the parts and on me [mimics the movement of cleaning his shirt]. And Thad was another one—he would empty his trumpet into your whisky if you didn't watch it." These stories represent an attempt on the part of some of the professional educators I worked with to partake in the past masters' charisma through evidence of association with these masters. These educators claim proximity to the masters by means of stories about their literally being "anointed" by the charismatic masters through the trope of "contact with the master via the latter's saliva," as it were. Indeed, anointment is another of the strategies of routinization of charisma highlighted by Weber (1978c, 248). However, this is only pseudo anointment, because the past masters only accidentally "anointed" the educators who narrate these stories—they did not mean to do so. Short of playing with these past innovators, then, some of the professional educators I worked with have to rely on their experiences of having seen them perform, of attending their performances as audience. Such strategies can only go so far in imbuing these professional educators with charisma. It is one thing to have seen the past masters perform; it is quite another thing to have played with them for an extended period of time.

The opposition between musicians who played with the past masters and are now teaching in jazz programs and professional educators is reminiscent of the opposition between "natives" and "settlers," to extend the indigeneity framework a bit further. Anthropologists have argued that within the politics of indigeneity, the former are often portrayed as possessing primordial, embodied, and experiential knowledge, whereas the latter are portrayed as having knowledge mediated by modernization, rationalization, and abstraction (Povinelli 2002). This opposition found expression when Charlie, a New School educator in his eighties who has an impressive performance history, said in class:

> I just had an argument with somebody whose name I won't mention about blues scales. He wrote a book about blues scale. As far as I'm concerned there's no such thing. [...] I told him, I said—"there's no such thing as a blues scale!" He put up the book anyway. He wanted me to do an endorsement. I showed him endorsement! I don't have a PhD, but I know what I've heard! [...] Listen, how are all those people who played the blues first—they didn't know anything about the scale—the field people and all that. I mean, why try to confuse it and make it all technical by saying what scale it is? If you can't get it from listening to it, leave it alone.

This story opposes two figures: Charlie, the educator who played with numerous past jazz masters, and the professional educator who wanted to publish a blues-scale method book. The phrase "I don't have a PhD, but I know what I've heard!" as well as the invocation of the "field people" situate Charlie as having a first-order connection to the roots of the music while ascribing to the professional educator a highly mediated and temporally late connection to the music. Charlie contrasts the PhD with "hearing," and the book on blues scales with the "field people." These oppositions correspond to the opposition between modern forms of mediation, rationality, and abstraction as opposed to "indigenous" immediation. Charlie *heard* the masters—he was "there." He did not learn the music in a jazz program that grants degrees—a late development in the jazz world that for many people is the source of jazz's current problems. Correspondingly, he does not need a book on blues scales—a textual artifact that iconizes the mediating logic of academic jazz education itself—in order to play the music. He is in touch with the roots of the music, as he metaphorically argues by the trope of the "field people" that connotes a presumably more authentic and early point in the history of jazz, a time purified of the mediating conceptual machinery of the academic jazz program.

Another New School educator, a musician with an impressive performance history with the past jazz masters, performed a similar polarization during the panel titled "The Eyes of the Masters" that took place in the *Jazz Improv* conference, which featured the New School's educators. At the very beginning of the panel, this educator said:

> The state of jazz, in my opinion, is rather poor because we've had jazz education for the last forty years and we had jazz educators who are not skilled at performing this music, and they have turned out players who lack the essence of this music: originality, emotional projection, and innovation. And I want to say that the people that we have on the faculty of the New School are the epitome of what jazz music should be about, and I would say a large percentage of those people on the faculty are the epitome because of their past histories, no matter how young or old they are, and I think it's time that we look at the elements that the master musician has that he or she can bestow on a young student who wants to learn and work hard at this music.

Addressing the perceived crisis of cultural standardization, this educator assigns a certain recuperative hope to the "histories" of some of the New School jazz program's educators; their primordial connection to the music may have the capacity to mitigate this crisis. As opposed to "jazz educators who are not skilled at performing this music," by which he means professional educators, he situates musicians who played with the past masters and who are recruited to teach as "the epitome of what jazz music should be about." This epitome does not encompass knowledge learned in abstraction, but rather experiential elements acquired through extensive and significant performance history. The optimism pinned onto these musicians enlists tropes that have long embodied the potentialities and promises associated with jazz in American culture. These tropes, when enacted in class by some of these recruited musicians, reproduce essentializing discourses about the sources and meaning of the creativity of the past jazz musician.

Bringing the "Street" back into the Classroom

I want to suggest that some of these recruited musicians who are charismatic by virtue of their performance experience with and connection to the past masters inadvertently cater to the expectation that they "enact a legible form of primordialism," radical difference, and cultural authenticity as evidence that they possess knowledge that can salvage the jazz program from its presumed deadening rationality (Comaroff and Comaroff 2009, 94). They do so in the form of bringing back "the street" into the classroom. The trope of "the street" denotes the various poles that the doctoral honoree whose speech I analyzed in the previous chapter associated with past mythical jazz: male-centric behavior, gritty urban sceneries, lowbrow interactional norms, and, more subtly, "blackness." These tropes are supposed to be the opposites of the presumed sanitized, "politically correct," and subtly white institutional environment of academic jazz education.[7]

This contrast and the trope of the "street" that often plays a prominent role in it find expression in the following interaction that took place in a class at the New School between a student and Tim, a musician in his seventies who played with some of the most venerable past jazz masters:

> [Student:] I think I am trying to play too soft, like I'm thinking too much
>   about playing soft.
> [Tim:] Well that's possibly instead of hearing soft. . . . That's the thing, isn't
>   it? That's the crux. That's the game of having a classroom about jazz.
>   Let's think and talk about jazz. Ha! The true classroom would be on the
>   bandstand and you all would be in my band and I'd be beating you up
>   night after night until you couldn't take it—you'd either leave the gig in
>   tears or you just stuck through it and you got better. That's what I went
>   through. Embarrassments, threats, guns pointed at me.
> [Student:] Guns?
> [Tim:] Yeah!

Tim proceeded to tell the students a story that took place in the early 1970s in a supposedly Mafia-owned club in Cincinnati in which he was threatened with a gun by the manager when the band wanted to quit. He then continued:

> [Tim:] All the clubs in the United States were Mafia-owned. . . . You guys have no idea. . . . You have no idea. You guys got it made, man. You got it made.
>
> [Student:] But do you think the music has kind of been hurt because of it, because the scene has changed?
>
> [Tim:] Yes, because there's no *street* in it. And there are no *characters*! Everybody is so leveled down! Man, when I came [to the scene]—man, there were always characters who had a walk, you know. You know, this guy had his walk, and that guy had his walk, and the hats, and the clothes, everybody had—you could always tell who the guy was by the hat or the uniform or the suit. . . . Now everyone is afraid to be a character. Everybody's like—it's all white-breaded out. It's like—everything is politically correct. There was nothing politically correct on the scene when I came up on it—Jesus Christ. . . . *In those days* your first goal was to get your own *sound* no matter what instrument you played to establish your individuality so people would know who you are. I have a hard time telling anybody from anybody else these days because there are very few distinctive, really distinctive sounds, because that's not part of the thing anymore.

In this interaction, Tim draws on his past experience in a jazz scene characterized by a colorful "street" scene as a foil to the presumed monotonous playing of today's students and to a bland urban landscape. He associates the musical diversity and "health" of the past, when more musicians had a distinctive sound—one of the core values in the jazz aesthetic—with a past cultural diversity expressed in terms that connote urban grittiness, organized crime, sartorial individuality, lenient morality, and abundantly available real-time performance opportunities. He refers to all these dimensions as "the street." He suggests that the "street" is opposed to the present "sterility" of the jazz program and the urban landscape in which it is situated. Ultimately, as in the doctoral honoree's narrative, Tim argues that the shift from "the street" to the school has resulted in the demise of jazz itself.

Some of the musicians I observed in class who had ample performance experience with the past masters enacted three key tropes that invoke the charismatic street as a locus of jazz's past creativity. These tropes consist of stereo-typical enactments of sexually uninhibited masculinity, lowbrow behavioral norms, and blackness. This enactment is not merely the figment of these musicians' imagination, nor did they wholeheartedly subscribe to the discourses and ideologies of creativity that they performed in class in front of their students. Rather, during such enactments, these musicians aligned themselves with a specific, identifiable register: they reverted to a quasi occupational jargon (Agha 2007; Bakhtin 1996) that, in the American public imagination, is associated with the "real, mythical, and creative" jazz musician.

"When you have your chick beside you in bed"

The vignette that opens this chapter, in which Thomas "explains" to his students why he was late to class, is a radical example of a performance of charisma that mobilizes the trope of sexually uninhibited masculinity associated with the past creative jazz musician. To be sure, the jazz community has traditionally been embedded in a heterosexual "malecentric context" (Vargas 2008, 329) and male musicians have often voluntarily asserted their masculinity through various forms of conduct. Yet the genred personhood of the mythical jazz musician prior to the full-blown academization of jazz training in higher education was also overdetermined by the belief projected onto it in the American public imagination, according to which jazz musicians possess uninhibited sexuality responsible for their creative genius. This mythical dimension, which was often motivated by the racial identification of the jazz musician as a black person, found expression in commentary written by white male authors in the middle of the twentieth century. These authors were fascinated by what they perceived to be the liberating aspects of jazz musicians' being-in-the-world that offered an alternative to the presumed confining mainstream white culture as portrayed in a number of key sociological essays in the 1950s. These essays focused on the malaise of suburbanization and the growing corporate world (for the most well-known example, see Whyte 2002). Norman Mailer's 1957 essay, "The White Negro," is one example of the widespread public fascination with the jazz musician's presumed uninhibited sexuality and being:

> Knowing in the cells of his existence that life was war, nothing but war, the
> Negro (all exceptions admitted) could rarely afford the sophisticated inhibi-
> tions of civilization, and so he kept for his survival the art of the primitive,
> he lived in the enormous present, he subsisted for his Saturday night kicks,

relinquishing the pleasures of the mind for the more obligatory pleasures of the body, and in his music he gave voice to the character and quality of his existence, to his rage and the infinite variations of joy, lust, languor, growl, cramp, pinch, scream and despair of his orgasm. For jazz is orgasm. (Quoted in Monson 1995, 403–404)

Far from being a nonreflexive use of sexually explicit register that reproduces and reifies one of the most persistent gender-based stereotypes in the history of jazz, I suggest that the vignette that opens this chapter emanates from a performance of a legible sign of charisma or "the street" whose value is grounded in its transgression of the university's norms and in its being an index of the imagined past creative apex of jazz music. This is supported by the following exchange, in which Alfred, a Berklee educator in his midfifties, responds to a student who complained about the challenge of making it on time to early classes: "Excuse me for the un-PC phrasing, but getting up in the morning and playing is almost the best way to get up except for when you have your chick beside you in bed. When you have your chick—that's the best! [Students laugh.]" By prefacing his words with "Excuse me for the un-PC phrasing," Alfred explicitly positions himself against the institutional norms of the school and behaves in what he takes to be the manner of a golden-age musician.

Similarly, when I ask Chris, a Berklee educator in his midsixties who possesses a significant performance history with some of the great past masters, what he would add to the school's curriculum, he answers, laughing: "Cheerleaders! Culturally diverse cheerleaders!" and other male educators present in the room laugh. First, by responding with "cheerleaders" Chris cues male-centric norms and performs the primordial personhood of the sexually uninhibited jazz musician. Second, by qualifying his words with the phrase "culturally diverse," he, like Alfred and Tim, mocks the "politically correct" ideals and norms associated with the school, thus occupying an adversarial position. Remember again Tim's complaint that now "it's all politically correct" and "everyone is afraid to be a character. Everybody's like—it's all white-breaded out" as opposed to "the street," the jazz scene of his youth.

That these and the other educators I discuss below have managed to enact in class such performances of uninhibited male sexuality indeed points to their charismatic status, which protects them to a certain degree from the program's supervision. This supervision is limited mostly to gender and diversity seminars and online tutorials that they are required to pass. At the New School, online tutorials were instituted after the program "had some problems in the past" with educators' conduct, as one of the program's administrators told me in an interview. At the same time, administrators must be careful not to alienate these musicians by supervising them too tightly. This is a risk whose full meaning is embedded in the history of the music. As this administrator put it:

> Bringing the culture into the institution is possible, but it requires a lot of effort and trust. [...] There's a huge baggage that every jazz artist carries: ... the value of this art form not [being] recognized in contemporary culture. And because of that there's this coming together as a community of "we get it" against the world, a bond of agreement. It's important that we as an institution have a way that we can link into that. [...] So it's ever more important that as administration you have the faculty believing that I get it, and that I value them, we value them, and that we are all working together to the best of our ability under tough conditions. I intersect with "the Man," the institution; so I need to give them the feeling that I am with them against all this world.

The administrator expresses here succinctly the tremendous administrative challenges of balancing the institutional norms of the university with the very different set of expectations that many musicians, especially the older ones, bring with them to the school and, ironically, are also expected to enact.

"Very cheap, very kind of trashy . . . not very sophisticated for the most fucking part"

A second trope of the charismatic "street" as a locus of jazz's past creativity enacted by some of these educators concerns stereotypical notions of "lowbrow" norms of conduct. Consider the following vignette, which concerns Chris, the Berklee educator whose words I quoted above. In one class, Chris argued that the fact that his jazz classes are attended by a majority of foreign students actually enables him to get away with behavior that for him evokes the great creative apex of jazz prior to its full-blown academization, behavior that today clashes with the institutional norms of the university. This is what he told his students in class:

> You know, it's interesting. Most of my classes, I think, are—you are the only American, right? [Chris is pointing at an American student.] Yeah, most

of my classes are like this—my ensembles, I have maybe a few more of the American crowd in the ensembles, but all the classes that I have ever taught have had way more foreign students than American students. And when I swear—you know, fuck this, this fucking chord, this fucking tune, mother-fucker, you know, the way people do in music, and in jazz anyway—it's kind of like a very verbally, very cheap, very kind of trashy, you know, not very sophisticated for the most fucking part [laughing]. But when I swear, most of the foreign people, they don't know what the fuck it means! They don't know what fuck—they don't know what fuck means. It's like me swearing in Italian—I don't have the same feeling of like—"I just swore." When I swear in Italian or Spanish I don't have the same feeling, but when I swear in English I have the feeling "I am swearing." That's why I like to swear in English, because it feels like I'm swearing. It feels like I'm accomplishing something [laughter]. But when I swear in a foreign fucking language, man, it doesn't mean fucking shit to me. And the hip thing about having a lot of foreign students is that a lot of them aren't offended by the word *fuck* because [. . .] they won't recoil and say—"You just swore! My teacher swears in class!"

Chris feels that he can use profanities in class because his students are foreigners and are thus not imbued with what he and many other educators consider to be the school's and contemporary American culture's castrating "political correctness." His words suggest that he intentionally enacts the stereotypes associated with the past creative jazz musician and his speech register as lower-class, coarse, and unrefined, and that he is fully aware of the reified status of such stereotypes: "In jazz anyway—it's kind of like a very verbally, very cheap, very kind of trashy, you know, not very sophisticated for the most fucking part."

Similar stereotypes of jazz as a lowbrow musical form have been dominant throughout most of the twentieth century, as legendary jazz trumpeter Dizzy Gillespie noted in a 1957 *Esquire* article: "Jazz . . . has never really been accepted as an art form by the people of my own country. . . . I believe that the great mass of the American people still consider jazz as lowbrow music. . . . To them, jazz is music for kids and dope addicts. Music to get high to. Music to take a fling to. Music to rub bodies to. Not 'serious' music. Not concert hall material. Not music to listen to. Not music to study. Not music to enjoy purely for its listening kicks" (quoted in Lopes 2002, 1). I suggest that this trope still plays a key role in the American popular imagination despite jazz's ascent into the higher echelons of the American cultural hierarchy. By reverting to an explicitly lowbrow sociolinguistic register, then, Chris enacts a legible sign of charismatic creativity that invokes the era that predates the professionalization of jazz and its cultivation in the model of high art.

"I spent three years in a totally black environment"

A third dimension of the charismatic creativity of "the street" that some of the musicians I worked with tap into is the most important but least explicitly acknowledged: blackness. Most of the past jazz masters who are revered within academic jazz education left their mark between the 1940s and the late 1960s—an era that predates the full-blown academization of jazz. In this period, jazz was still an expressive cultural form predominantly grounded in African American communities. Consequently, most of the educators who can establish significant "lineage" to the jazz masters are African American, too, while most of the professional educators who cannot trace this descent are white. Because of this correlation, blackness is a primary yet rarely fully acknowledged marker of charismatic primordialism in academic jazz education (and the jazz world at large).

Blackness plays a much more important role than meets the eye because it underlies the previous two dimensions of charisma in accordance with well-established racial ideologies in American culture. These ideologies frequently associate the black person with a more "authentic" and unmediated path to existential truth and with uninhibited sexuality, which stand in contrast to the presumed inauthenticity of abstract, rational modernity. In this framework, rational modernity can be salvaged by infusing it with the "primitivity" of blackness (Gioia 1988a; Monson 1995; Torgovnick 1990). Views of jazz musicians who played with the past jazz masters as superior to professional educators who received most of their education in jazz programs are thus informed to a certain degree by a taken-for-granted correlation between blackness and musical excellence.[8] Though this correlation is rarely explicitly asserted in post–civil rights era jazz programs, it often surfaces in subtle ways.

For example, one of the New School's administrators told me that one of the program's biggest problems is "finding black teachers who can teach the theory stuff, the theory courses. All of our black teachers are doing the ensemble courses." Even as they express a desire to increase the representation of African American musicians across all pedagogical areas, these words reveal the prevalent institutionalized division in this program between educators who have performance authority and are allowed to direct ensembles, and those educators who do "the theory stuff." The lopsided composition of these groups reproduces a deep-seated racial coding of immediation (performance) and mediation (theory) as black and white, respectively (Monson 2007). This division manifested earlier, as well, in the case of the octogenarian African American New School educator—a person with the most impressive performance history among my interlocutors—who refused to endorse the book written by a younger New School educator—a white man with little performance experience. The history of jazz is a repository for stereotypical correlations between black jazz musicians and Dionysian primitivism, intuition, immediacy, and conceptual ignorance. An early, ostentatious example is a white jazz critic's commentary from 1938: "Those who create [jazz] most successfully are the ones who know the least about its abstract structure. The Negro, like all folk musicians, expresses himself intuitively" (quoted in Gioia 1988a, 33).[9]

The function of blackness as a legible sign of primordial charisma in these pedagogical settings becomes most explicit in the case of the few white musicians considered to be "indigenous" to the music because they played with the past masters at one point in their career. Perhaps because they are marked as "not black," some of them consider it necessary to explicitly highlight their past participation in black culture as a formative stage in their musical apprenticeship. For example, Rick, a white educator in his early seventies who had significant performance experience with a number of past jazz masters, recounted to his students his experience of playing with a legendary jazz master (whose name I omitted):

[Rick:] Believe me, I spent three years with [X]—I didn't hear English spoken for three years. I didn't see white people for three years. I spent three years in a totally black environment. And that's so different from this [i.e., the school]! You have no idea. You just don't know. We would play all the black clubs. Even the people in the clubs thought I was black! They thought I was passing! You know? [laughs].

[Student:] I thought Greg [another educator who has significant performance experience] is black the first time. "You dig?" [supposedly imitating Greg].

Rick proceeded to share a story about a concert he played with this master in Chicago that was organized by "a drug dealer." He described how during the intermission the DJ shouted sexual profanities into the microphone and how, after the concert, the musicians feared they would get robbed by the concert's organizer because there was barely any audience attending the show. Rick then concluded: "It's another scene, you know. I think I told you about this: when we played in James Brown's club, the sign on the door said 'Please check your guns and knives at the coatroom.' It's a different scene." Importantly, these words followed an exchange in which two students questioned Rick's authority with respect to two musical topics, prompting him to frame the jazz program as a "sterile" environment that does not resemble the real performance situations of the past, and thus to reclaim his authority. Rick establishes his authority via evidence of his participation in black culture and proximity to a black jazz master. The ultimate evidence of Rick's musical authority, charismatic primordialism, and participation in "the street" is that he was considered black by "black audience." Building on this, one student mentioned that he mistook Greg, another educator, for a black person. He then imitated Greg—"You dig?"—a phrase that presumably connotes "black speech." Greg, who apprenticed with the jazz master Art Blakey, passed as black in the mind of this student not only because of his dark complexion and the fact that his ethnic identity was hard for him to identify. More importantly, he passed as black because of his lineage and his designation by the program as a "living link" to the tradition of the music, a title that smuggles in blackness as an identity marker and that solved for the student his uncertainty about Greg's ethnic identity. Most crucially, though, note that Rick associates creativity with "blackness" that is expressed in terms of danger and transgression. Tropes such as the use of nonstandard English (which Rick suggests is not English at all—"I didn't hear English spoken for three years"), drugs, violence, and sex—stereotypes that have frequently mediated images of African American people in the white American public imagination (Entman and Rojecki 2001; Jones 2005)—abound in Rick's story. At a more general level, they exemplify the fantasies and fears beneath Western modernism's notions of primitivism—often articulated in terms of "blackness"—as a locus of true creativity (Gioia 1988a; Torgovnick 1990).

Jazz and the Continued Lure of the Primordially Unmediated

In their attempt to counter the criticism that academic jazz programs have become sites of professionalism that is cut off from "real" jazz, and in which the music is compartmentalized and abstracted until it loses its meaning, administrators in the jazz programs I worked in recruit charismatic musicians with links to the past mythical era of the music with the hope that they can unify this disjointed knowledge into a coherent whole and inform the jazz program with charismatic authenticity. They thus attempt to negotiate between creative practice and institutionalization, and to some extent they manage to reconcile the two, a fact that bears witness to these educators' tremendous pedagogical value. Yet many times this strategy of negotiation also inadvertently reproduces some of the discourses that represent creativity and institutionalized schooling as oppositional to one another. Furthermore, they reproduce discourses that had originally motivated the exclusion of jazz from institutions of higher education to begin with. Such strategies of "routinization of charisma" thus seem to undermine the very institutional structure they seek to maintain.

The story I have told in this chapter is not limited to a few academic jazz programs. A similar dynamic finds expression in contemporary discourses about the potential of jazz to revitalize and authenticate American culture at large and especially American youth. These discourses reproduce stereotypical dimensions of the "jazz tradition" much like some jazz programs do. For example, concerns about the decline in public funding for art education in the United States have prompted institutions and interest groups to attempt to reverse this trend. Against the backdrop of Congress's 2007 decision about whether or not to reauthorize the No Child Left Behind Act for another five years, the nonprofit organization Americans for the Arts sponsored a series of advertisements that advocated an increase in public funding for the arts in general and art education in particular. Two advertisements were specifically concerned with jazz music. Presenting its message in a witty style, one of these advertisements was titled, "No wonder people think Duke Ellington is a member of the royal family." Following a short description of the life of the legendary jazz pianist and bandleader, the advertisement added:

> Kids don't get enough art these days. Not in their schools. Not in their communities. They don't have enough access to theater, poetry or jazz. So you can see why some kids might confuse a jazz legend named Duke with royalty named duke. But it's time to set the record straight. It's time to get hip to a new kind of groove. (American for the Arts 2007)

The advertisement ended:

Jazz is Art. Art is Jazz. Dig? The arts transform lives. In fact, the more a kid
gets, the more knowledgeable that kid can become in subjects like math and
science. Everything is affected. Everything is related. So make sure your kids
get their daily dose of art. Take them to a museum, a dance performance,
a jazz concert. They'll be less likely to confuse a duke with *the* Duke. And
they'll be more well-rounded, finger-snapping members of society, daddy-o.
(American for the Arts 2007)

This advertisement uses a "hip" jargon that connotes "jazz dialect" as a marked
"black speech," which it posits as a crucial ingredient in the education of
young Americans. In doing so, the advertisement suggests that jazz has a role
to play in the shaping of future generations of Americans. Indeed, public fascination with the idiosyncratic speech idioms and behavior of jazz musicians
considered to be indicators of "hipness" and "cool" has been a recurrent feature in the history of jazz (Ake 2012; Monson 1995). Together with unique
modes of dress and comportment, these speech idioms mapped onto imagery
of hypersexualized black male subculture that represented for many alienated
young American white males the existence of an alternative, much more "authentic" lifestyle. The advertisement inadvertently draws on these connota-
tions of unmediated creativity, sexuality, and charismatic authenticity—if not
primitivity—that can mitigate excessive alienation and rationalization when
it also reminds the readers that "Royal dukes [as opposed to the jazz legend,
Duke Ellington] are squaresville, man. They have no rhythm. And they wear
crowns." Thus, stereotypical imaginings of jazz's charismatic primordialism
continue to play a role in fantasies of salvation from modernity's presumed
alienation, sterility, soullessness, and vampiric rationalization in American
culture.

5

RITUALS OF CREATIVITY

Inhabiting the Echoes of the Past

Their Mystical Experience, My Modern Discomfort

One morning, I found myself sitting in a high-level improvisation class at Berklee. This week, the students had to transcribe any of pianist McCoy Tyner's solos and play it in synchrony with the original recording. Tyner's style is characterized by the ample use of pentatonic and tetratonic scales and out-of-scale playing, often in neck-breaking tempos. These features render his solos difficult to transcribe and play in real time, especially if one plays them with an instrument other than the piano. One after the other, the students stood up and approached the educator, gave him an iPod or a CD with the recording they had chosen, and, after preparing themselves for playing and indicating that they were ready, waited for Tyner's solos to begin. Once the solo began, they joined in, playing in synchrony with their respective instruments. Such synchrony depended on their levels of proficiency. At times, one could barely hear Tyner's playing because students managed to perfectly laminate their own playing on top of his. However, during particularly difficult passages, one could hear Tyner's playing re-emerge. The rest of the students remained in their seats. They listened carefully. Frequently, when a student gave a particularly accurate performance of one of Tyner's solos, as was the case when a violin player gave an impressive rendition of Tyner's complicated solo on the tune "Passion Dance" from his 1967 album, *The Real McCoy*, the students would burst into loud applause, clapping their hands and exclaiming "Yeah!," "All right," "Wow," and "Note-for-note!"

Sitting among the students, I was struck both by this performance, which seemed to me to display a talent for formulaic imitation, and by the students' and educator's enthusiastic responses. As I proceeded with my fieldwork, my puzzlement only deepened. Of the twenty-four classes that I observed at Berklee, twelve involved some form of this practice, in which students had to learn a jazz master's recorded solo and play it in class in synchrony with the original recording. I perfectly understood when educators explained to students that this exercise would help them incorporate into their playing prototypical stylistic features of jazz improvisation that the masters epitomize in their solos and that cannot be learned in class in an abstract fashion. But I had difficulty with their descriptions of the emotional experience this practice generates. For example, Steve, a Berklee educator in his midforties, described to his class the desired experience:

> It should sound like you're double-tracking the player. As a matter of fact, the experience that the class should have when they hear you performing should be you performing with the [recorded] rhythm section because you're so tight with the soloist that he just melts away and it's just you. That's how it should be. And that happens, too. It's kind of actually mystical when you're doing it. You're like performing, and it's like you're doing exactly what he was doing, and then you're like, "Gee, what was that person thinking when he was doing this thing?" You're like becoming him.

Note that Steve does not describe a state in which the player in the present "loses" himself, as it were, in the past recording. It is the master who "melts away" and then "it's just you." In other words, Steve seems to argue that playing in synchrony with and on top of the master's recording can enhance the student's sense of individual creativity in the present. The student inhabits the master's creativity in order to experience and reenact it *as his or her own*. In this process, the master's presence is felt the most in its perceived acoustic absence, that is, when the student perfectly laminates his or her playing on top of that of the master's. Such fusion of student and master is a "mystical" experience. Karl, another educator, described this experience of inhabiting and re-enacting the master's creativity by saying that in such moments of fusion with the master "you can kind of imagine what that performer experienced at the time he was playing . . . the feeling that they might have had at that moment."

I suggest that my initial discomfort vis-à-vis these sensations generated from meticulous imitation is the result of modern sensibilities that abhor imitation and see it as antithetical to creativity. In this chapter, I would like to clarify the cultural logic of this pedagogical practice and its challenge to the long-held opposition between creative practice and rule-governed or institutionalized social behavior. In addition, I will highlight the pedagogical value that professional educators bring to the classroom. From the previous chapter it might seem as if these educators must limit themselves to the gray mechanics of everyday pedagogical routine while musicians who played with the past masters get to occupy the charismatic centers. Yet to assume this would be a mistake. Professional educators, too, manage to open up creative spaces in the classroom by tapping into a charismatic era with which many of them had no direct connection and experience.

A specific dimension of academic jazz training has motivated the educators I worked with to engage their students in the formulaic and meticulous imitation of the masters' past recorded improvisations despite their awareness of the widespread belief about the opposition between creative agency and imitative social behavior. This dimension is concerned with the repercussions of the key role played by print pedagogy in the jazz program.

Written in Stave: The Ubiquity of Print Pedagogy and Its Discontent

One of the first things that stuck me during my fieldwork at Berklee was the ubiquity of printed pedagogical material of all kinds. These artifacts included not only staved notebooks, in which students wrote down their notes, but also specially produced method books for teaching and learning jazz improvisation. The first time I visited Berklee's campus bookstore I could not but marvel at the hundreds of different pedagogical method books adorning every shelf in the store and catering to every possible topic and subtopic of jazz improvisation. Indeed, from the mid-twentieth century, the publishing industry has begun to play a growing role in the institutionalization of jazz training, producing ever more specialized pedagogical material (Lopes 2002, 261) and actively participating in school cultures by sponsoring summer camps taught by famous clinicians who employ their method books, and establishing fellowships for students (Murphy 1994). In some cases, jazz programs were named after producers of jazz pedagogy material.[1] Some jazz schools have by now established their own publishing presses, such as Berklee's own Berklee Press.

There are several reasons for this expansion of print pedagogy in the context of academic jazz education. First, degrees in jazz studies have often been offered in colleges and universities whose main field of expertise was, and frequently still is, Western classical music training. As scholars have noted, the typographic holds a privileged place in the culture of classical music. The written score is the basis of musical pieces, and method books are the primary tool for instrumental training. In the context of classical music, as ethnomusicologist Bruno Nettl puts it, "music" means "notated music" (Nettl 1995, 36). The institutional environment thus no doubt encouraged jazz programs to increasingly adopt this element in what is perhaps a case of "institutional isomorphism," that is, the incorporation by an organization or actor of the institutional norms and rules of the external environment within which it operates (Powell and DiMaggio 1991). In addition, it is highly likely that this proliferation of textual artifacts geared directly toward jazz pedagogy has been informed by conscious efforts to confer prestige upon jazz or to assign it cultural legitimacy in the model of classical music. Lastly, the typographic medium allows the transmission of knowledge to more students simultaneously and in "a short amount of time," as one educator told me, thus pointing at cost-efficiency considerations (Porter 1989, 138).

Even so, the seamless adoption of the system of notation that emerged in the context of the Western classical music tradition is surprising, given the different sensibilities and orientations and the competing ideologies and meanings of classical music and jazz. Some of jazz's distinct aesthetic features, such as its approach to phrasing, timbre, and articulation, cannot be represented by the notation system used in Western classical music. For example, this system of notation represents fixed pitch levels that are separated from one another by half a tone. Yet experienced jazz musicians often create meaningful improvisations by bending notes and producing distinct timbres. In this regard, one scholar has devoted an entire chapter to documenting the futility of trying to capture these recalcitrant musical elements in traditional notation or in other forms of graphic representation (Winkler 1997).

To some extent, the nature of these elements of jazz provides another explanation for jazz programs' heavy reliance on the notation system used in the Western classical music tradition. The migration of jazz training into the college and the university entailed the adoption of the professional ethos that prevails in these contexts. This ethos mandates standardized and rationalized knowledge testable against clear-cut criteria (Abbott 1988, 8; Larson 1977, 40). Hosted within colleges and universities, jazz programs devised clear definitions of the hurdles that students must pass through and implemented evaluative criteria of their progress on the way to obtaining a degree. They delineated the knowledge that a neophyte jazz musician should master, how that knowledge should be conveyed to the student, and how mastery of this knowledge should be tested (Ake 2002). The typographic medium is a convenient means for achieving these requirements. Writing allows for the formulation and codification of fixed rules whose mastery can then be easily tested. Adopting the notation system that emerged in the context of the classical Western music tradition makes institutional sense precisely because it abstracts jazz from many of its pragmatic elements that are difficult to evaluate or operationalize in line with clear-cut, codified criteria.[2]

Jazz musicians, however, have traditionally placed a premium on elements such as the creation of personal sound and style through development of distinct timbres and modes of articulation. This emphasis, like many other of jazz's aesthetic elements, can be traced back to West African aesthetics. The musicologist Olly Wilson has called the emphasis on personal sound in the West African context "the heterogeneous sound ideal." He described this ideal as "a common approach to music making in which a kaleidoscopic range of dramatically contrasting qualities of sound (timbre) is sought after in both vocal and instrumental music. The desirable musical sound texture is one that contains a combination of diverse timbres . . . [a] fundamental bias for contrast of color—heterogeneity of sound rather than similarity of color or homogeneity of sound" (Wilson 1999, 160). In the context of jazz, the heterogeneous sound ideal found one of its clearest expressions in the big bands of the 1920s and 1930s (Wilson 1999, 168), in which musicians employed devices and techniques of sound production such as plunger mutes and growls to create distinctive sonorities. This ideal has continued to inform jazz aesthetics (Berliner 1994, 67–68).

The expansion of print pedagogy in academic jazz training would not have constituted a problem if the number of opportunities to implement in live performance the knowledge mediated by such a pedagogy had not decreased as a result of the decline in jazz's popularity. After all, most of the admired past jazz masters were fluent in this notation system, and some of them avidly learned scores of classical music compositions. However, in contrast to today's students, players of past generations had ample performance opportunities in which they could cultivate crucial elements in the jazz aesthetics that are not encompassed by this system of notation.

According to some of the educators I spoke with, the overwhelming incorporation of the notation system used in the Western classical music tradition into the academic infrastructure of teaching and learning jazz, coupled with the lack of opportunities students have to implement the knowledge thus acquired in live performance with experienced practitioners, has impacted students' mastery of a number of stylistic features that are crucial to jazz's modes of signification. For example, many students fail to develop a unique personal sound, which is one of the core aesthetic norms in jazz. Hal, a Berklee educator in his sixties, pointed up this fact after I had asked him to talk about the proficiency of students who graduate from jazz programs:

> You know, I saw some time ago a show on TV. There were a few young trumpet players and Jack Sheldon [a veteran trumpet player]. They played "Confirmation" [a Charlie Parker tune], I think. All those young players were like a cookie cutter. They all sounded the same, playing really fast and high, using small mouthpieces to boost their range, and having that electric sound. All of them were the same. The first played high and fast, and then the other higher and faster, and the third and that. But then Jack Sheldon played, and after four notes you could tell that it was him. That's sound.

Hal argues that Jack Sheldon, who had ample opportunities to apprentice with the past masters, managed to develop a distinct sound and improvisation style that most of today's young musicians—because of their increasingly abstract training—lack.

Some educators also voiced their concern that the increased reliance on printed pedagogical material and the absence of real-time performance opportunities have impacted students' ability to master subtle rhythmic processes that cannot be acquired from notated music. In a conversation I had with Frank, a venerable drummer in his eighties who had apprenticed with a number of past masters and who currently teaches at the New School, he argued that his students have difficulty learning to swing:

> I think that we are not concentrating on a way of teaching students how to swing. . . . Whenever we go to the listening sessions [i.e., student performances at the New School] and we're listening to students, we hear a lot of

notes, but it ain't no swinging. They will be playing a lot of notes and they will be playing basically the right changes and everything but it ain't got that thing. And when you talk about that you'll hear a lot of old musicians saying "Well, you gotta be born with it." But that's a cop-out—I don't buy that. I think that we as teachers should find a way to teach—maybe not teach, but help students to learn—how to swing. . . . That's my biggest ax to grind because I haven't heard any teacher come up with any combo or a process to teach or to help a student [learn] how to swing. Listening helps. But I think you gotta pick certain people that really swing hard and make the student really listen to them.

The elusive notion of swinging is frequently understood as a player's ability to produce a kinesthetic response in a listener by placing notes in a specific relation to a beat. Swing encompasses subtle rhythmic nuances that are very hard to represent via traditional notation systems. In contrast to discourses that blame students for their own compromised ability to swing, Frank suggests that the jazz program has not yet been able to create the proper training. He suggests aural learning: "You gotta pick certain people that really swing hard and make the student really listen to them." However, the opportunities to benefit from such a mode of training have become rare.

I should emphasize that, for the most part, the educators I worked with did not subscribe to an imagined dichotomy between the presumably pure notions of aurality and literacy (although some certainly did, as chapter 7 makes clear).[3] Rather, they had a subtle understanding of the shifting conditions that have tilted the balance toward print pedagogy in jazz education. They argued that although they use many intricate hearing practices in their teaching, these practices have become increasingly oriented to, and organized around, reading and printed materials. The meaning and function of aurality as a key modality of knowledge production and transmission in jazz training has shifted. This is what my interlocutors reacted to.

Performing Distance from Print, Gravitating to Sound

A few of the Berklee educators whose classes I attended attempted to distance themselves from print pedagogy through the defacement of the objects associated with it.[4] For example, upon entering the class with a pile of sheet music under his arm, one educator, Sam, stopped, looked at the class, and said: "Music, who needs it? I don't, at least not written music!" and then threw the pile into the air to the students' laughter. At the beginning of one ensemble class, a student from a different class entered and asked if he could take some music stands. Mark, the educator, immediately responded: "Take them. Go Ahead. We don't need no freaking stands here!" A different educator announced in the first class of his course, when he arranged the room after the previous class: "Here you don't need writing—we don't need those music stands."

Whiteboard markers were similarly manipulated and abused. One educator, whenever a marker would become weak while he was writing, would throw it behind his back or at the board, shaking his head in disgust. Paul, another educator, had a different ritual: at the beginning of class he would take his markers out of his briefcase and try to build standing structures with them on the piano, to the laughter of the students. This would continue for a few minutes. At a certain point the structure would collapse and the markers would fall on the floor and be left there for the remainder of the class.

Educators would often warn their students about the limits of printed pedagogical material, especially when it is not recontextualized in real-time performance. Peter often did this. Once, for example, he had just finished explaining some basic formal compositional categories. He was writing on the board the students' assignment for the following week: to transcribe one of saxophonist Sonny Stitt's blues solos and perform it in class. In the middle of writing the theoretical considerations that students should pay attention to when transcribing the solo, Peter turned to face the students and said (referring to the rating system that indicates students' proficiency levels):

Cats, about the transcriptions. I have some level 7 in here, I have some level 2. I don't grade on the transcription. You do the best you can, you get an A for it. That's it. But you got to hear it. It's one thing writing all that stuff on the board, but if you don't hear how that stuff's articulated—you know, the way that cat swings, the way you swing on a bebop scale or diminished [scale] and all that. I mean, I can write all those licks on the board and it wouldn't mean a damn thing. Who cares? You got to hear the articulation. The only way to get to the heart of Stitt, the feeling, you know—make a loop out of it, and if you can't, slow speed it, make a loop and sing it for about a week. Don't even play it. Just sing it at a slowed speed. Then after about a week when you get it into your ear, then start to play it. Then write it down. So writing it down should be the last thing. You see what's happening? But you really want to get into the articulation. So when you come into my improv classes you don't tatatatata [mimics bad swinging]. I don't want to hear that shit! I want to hear authentic articulation! You know what I'm saying? I can't teach you that. You're gonna hear that. You know, like anything else: you want the accent? You're gonna have to hang around with the accent.

Peter emphasizes to his students that there are some key things he cannot teach them, such as specific modes of articulation, which can only be acquired when one bypasses printed pedagogical material and focuses on aural learning.

Against the backdrop of these considerations, the pedagogical strategy I explore in the next section is supposed to mitigate the increasingly significant role played by print pedagogy at Berklee. If students lack a nuanced understanding of the pragmatics of jazz, then "hanging around with the accent," as Peter put it, or listening to the past masters' recordings time and again, is one way of gaining it. At the same time, I suggest that this practice is also motivated by the powerful emotional and experiential effect it produces, which is grounded in the unique possibility this practice provides for students to fuse with the charismatic creativity of past jazz masters and to inhabit it and the stylistic features it consists of. Here enter the "mystical" feelings that puzzled me when I first witnessed students enacting this pedagogical practice.

In the previous chapter I discussed the ways in which the past masters' charismatic power is asserted and acknowledged time and again in various contexts outside of the jazz program. Such charisma is the subject of commentary in the classroom as well. For example, during a class at Berklee, John, an educator in his midfifties, expressed to his students his desire to fuse with saxophonist John Coltrane after playing the recording of the latter's solo on the tune "Impressions" from the record *Live in Stockholm, 1961*:

Imagine being on stage with someone like Coltrane, screaming like that. These guys, the band, were playing every other night, two-week tours, ten cities, ten big concerts, and at night you're standing on the stage and this cat is right there playing in that just unbelievable way that no one would play like that at that time, and there still hasn't been anyone playing like that that really got there [like Coltrane]. . . . Can you imagine being in the presence of that? I'm not talking about the audience here. I'm talking about the band, being on the stage, being Miles Davis, that kind of presence, being next to that, and experiencing that. That can change your life, it really can. Even being in the audience and hearing it live can change your life.

John describes Coltrane's musical superiority and charisma and his desire to commune with him—"being on the stage" with him. He also references the existence of a past jazz scene in which musicians could play almost every night with experienced jazz musicians. Thus educators and students at Berklee look up to jazz masters not only because they presumably epitomize the laws of improvisation in their very playing, but also because they index a charismatic era that no longer exists, the creative apex of the music, the "passing of an age," as one of the administrators at the New School's jazz program told me, with the awareness that "it's never quite going to be the same—those conditions of, particularly the shaping of this community and its social interaction, are not going to be replicated."

Short of providing their students with an opportunity to actually play with the masters and thereby assimilate key stylistic features, the jazz educators I worked with use advanced media technologies to enable students to transcend the limitations of print pedagogy and immerse themselves in the legendary masters' recorded sounds. By means of rule-governed and formulaic appropriation of such technologies, students manage not only to "be on the stage" with a past jazz master such as John Coltrane, as it were, but also to fuse with him, if only for brief moments, and thus to partake in his and other past masters' charismatic authority and individual creativity. This practice blurs the distinction between rule-governed social behavior and creative practice, as well as between institutionalized rationality and creative agency, and in doing so it represents an attempt—an often successful one—to infuse the classroom with the charisma of the past jazz masters. The conditions of possibility for such blurring lie in the medium of sound and the availability of these new technologies of sound mediation.

"Did you hear that?" Entering the "Acoustic Unconscious"

I was sitting among eight students in a course at Berklee in which students learn how to transcribe jazz masters' recorded solos. They also have to memorize these solos and play them in class. Larry, an educator in his early forties, explained that the students were going to choose a past jazz master's recorded improvisation to work on during the semester. He approached his laptop, which was connected to speakers, in order to play one master's recorded solo, then said: "I am very into technology. I am very technology-comfortable. One program that I use, which you probably already have on your computer, is the Amazing Slow Downer. Did you hear about it?" Some students nodded in approval. "The Amazing Slow Downer," he said slowly. "It's amazing! Really, it is. We are going to play—first we will play [the recording] and then I will tell you why it's amazing, OK?"

Larry then played the recording of Miles Davis's solo on the tune "Walkin'" from the 1954 album of the same name. He immediately began to sing the solo together with the recording. After a few measures, he stopped the recording and began to sing the solo again, this time without the recording. He said, "Every note! Not like"—and then sang a phrase from Davis's solo inaccurately, rhythmically speaking. The students laughed. "Right? Exactly what's there. So that's where I want you to spend your time. That's the point, all right? To really nail every nuance of what's going on. And the Amazing Slow Downer is so amazing! It's certainly an option for that—look at this!" He played Davis's recorded solo again with his laptop. The moment the solo began he slowed it down from about 60 to 20 beats per minute. When Davis played what would be an almost unnoticeable embellishment in normal speed, Larry stopped the slowed-down recording, sang the embellishment, and said "Did you hear that? It's really—the Amazing Slow Downer is amazing! It's one thing you can do. The other thing you can do is—let's say you're practicing—" He took the same embellishment and looped it. In the process, he altered its tempo, first speeding it up to 120 beats per minute and then slowing it down again to 20 beats per minute. The students laughed. One student exclaimed, "Nice!" and Larry concluded, "I have no problem with using the technology to slow it down. Why? Because it's more important that you'll hear it right!"

To make sense of this vignette, it would be productive to draw from one of the many lines of inquiry given impetus by the vast work of Walter Benjamin, namely his exploration of the impact of modern media technologies on perception. Within this line of interrogation, the notion of the "optical unconscious" has been especially significant. In his celebrated essay "The Work of Art in the Age of Mechanical Reproduction" (Benjamin 1969b), Benjamin argued that modern media technologies have empowered the subject by providing her with the critical distance needed in order to recognize the forces that impact her life, much in the same way that psychoanalysis has increased our awareness of how the unconscious structures everyday behavior. Benjamin focused on the technologies of film and photography. He took note of a number of film technology's features that he believed contribute to its revolutionary potential, such as slow motion and the close-up. By enhancing the subject's perceptual capacities—allowing, for example, a novice athlete to examine a slowed-down video recording of his performance—these features extend "our comprehension of the necessities which rule our lives" (Benjamin 1969b, 236).[5] Although Benjamin acknowledged film's revolutionary potential also in the realm of "acoustical" perception (235), he explored this potential exclusively in the visual realm. I suggest that to account for students' and educators' use of the Amazing Slow Downer, we need to develop the notion of the "acoustic unconscious," that is, the dynamic of acoustic perceptual enhancement by means of advanced technology.

The Amazing Slow Downer's features parallel in significant ways those features of film that Benjamin emphasized in his discussion. It is a software program that enables one to slow down or speed up digitized music with little distortion of pitch and timbre.[6] To be sure, jazz musicians have always incorporated jazz masters' recorded solos into their playing by meticulously manipulating them ever since the first commercial jazz recordings were made publicly available. Yet a description of musicians' use of previous technologies reveals their limitations in comparison to the Amazing Slow Downer:

> Early record players had controls enabling listeners to slow a record's speed by gradations until they could catch a particularly fast passage, albeit at a lower pitch, transposing the retarded phrase into its original pitch immediately thereafter. Those lacking such equipment slowed the turntable by applying slight finger pressure to the record. Tape recorders with half-speed controls, which drop the pitch a complete octave, are an additional help, as are recent compact disc players, which allow for the repeated play of isolated passages. (Berliner 1994, 96)

Note that players already had to possess well-developed skills of transposition and pitch-recognition, as well as a deep familiarity with the idiom of jazz, to benefit from such technologies. In contrast, the Amazing Slow Downer and similar digital technologies allow players with lower skills to penetrate even deeper into the mechanics of the masters' solos. In the past, musicians had to perform the masters' solos numerous times in order to arrive, through increased familiarity with them, at "an illusory transformation [in which] . . . the solo seems to ensue more slowly, presenting, paradoxically, ever finer yet enlarged details. . . . Each pitch reveals its individual character, its own articulation, inflection, timbre, dynamics, and rhythmic feeling" (Berliner 1994, 97). By contrast, today's students begin from such a perceptual transformation with the help of the Amazing Slow Downer and proceed from there into familiarity with even finer details of the solo's acoustic features. Thus, Larry's question to his students, "Did you hear that? It's really—," whose topic was a specific embellishment, was about an acoustic reality that was suddenly revealed by means of slowing down Miles Davis's solo. Such an embellishment, which would go unnoticed when the solo is played in normal tempo, is a slip of the "improvising" tongue, to draw on Benjamin's appropriation of Freudian theory. Thanks to the Amazing Slow Downer, it can be the focus of analysis in the classroom.

A software program like the Amazing Slow Downer, then, increases exponentially the spectrum of nuances that are available for educators and students to analyze. But in addition to these gains, it allows them to imitate more accurately the masters' recorded solos, so they can then play those solos in synchrony with the original recordings in the classroom. Through this practice, students fuse with the masters. This rule-governed practice blurs spatiotemporal boundaries and ritually bridges between students' playing and the masters' recorded playing, as well as between the present of the classroom and the values, social reality, and charismatic authority indexed by the recordings. It consists of rule-governed orientation to a past textual authority that is also productive of individual creativity in the present. I call this practice a "ritual of creativity" in order to capture this duality, which I suggest challenges the long-held institutionalized dichotomy between rule-governed social behavior and creative agency, as well as the notion that the academic jazz program is overwhelmingly a site of cold technicism and rationality that are antithetical to creative agency. Recall that one educator described the sensation of performing the masters' recorded improvisations in synchrony with the recordings in the following manner: "It's kind of actually mystical when you're doing it. You're like performing, and it's like you're doing exactly what he was doing, and then you're like, 'Gee, what was that person thinking when he was doing this thing?' You're like becoming him."

"You're like becoming him": Ritually Inhabiting the Masters' Creativity

The powerful sensation of inhabiting the masters' creativity experienced during such "rituals of creativity" emerges for a number of reasons. First, the source texts that students replicate are emblematic texts of individual creativity. They are improvisations created by legendary musicians. These improvisations have entered jazz's canon. Any improvisation on the tune "Passion Dance," for example, is indexically connected to Tyner's famous 1967 original improvisation on this tune for those who are knowledgeable members of the jazz community. Hence, students do not produce replications of just any text. In their case, the source texts are imbued with charismatic energy and carry the meaning of individual creativity that expresses itself on the spur of the moment.

Furthermore, when students and educators engage in "rituals of creativity," they do not make their own playing and past masters' playing commensurate by abstracting two qualitatively different entities into a quantitative common denominator (Espeland and Stevens 1998), as when two different colors are expressed in terms of the numerical values of their wavelengths; nor do they translate from one arbitrarily and nonmotivated cultural code into another as in the translation from English to French (Benjamin 1969a); nor, for that matter, do they engage in dubbing, a practice in which "the moment of fusion is always deferred" (Boellstorff 2003, 238). Rather, they engage in the synchronous iconization of a quality (Eisenlohr 2010; Peirce 1998, 272), that is, sound. The source text of individual creativity that students replicate—the past jazz masters' improvisations—is available in the form of recorded sound. This allows students to produce texts that iconize the source text—to produce texts that consist of the same quality as the source text—in synchrony with it and thus to experience a kind of fusion with the master in those moments when the two texts are perfectly laminated on top of one another. These moments are indexed by the "disappearance" of the master's recorded solo "in" the student's playing. It is a ritual practice that is based on the production of a very precise "diagrammatic" or "figurational equivalence" (Silverstein 2004, 626) between the two spatiotemporal planes of the classroom and the original mythical event in which the improvisation was created and recorded. This practice has profound experiential results for students who feel that in those moments they become the masters, as it were, inhabiting the very moment in time in which their solos were created.[7] It is for this reason that the educator quoted above says that "you can kind of imagine what that performer experienced at the time he was playing . . . the feeling that they might have had at that moment," for in those moments students and educators feel they inhabit the creative decisions made by the master. To be sure, in such a practice "the seams show" too (Boellstorff 2003, 236)—students do not always manage to iconize the masters' solos in perfect synchrony with their recordings. Yet from time to time they do manage to do so, and this has profound experiential effects.

As a practice that involves the attempted matching between a source text (the recorded solo) and a target text (the student's playing of the solo), playing the masters' recorded solos in synchrony with their recordings is an exercise in intertextuality (Briggs and Bauman 1992). Yet note the peculiarity of music: the source text (the past masters' recorded improvisations) consists of sound that unfolds in time. This accounts for the fact that the recorded solo of a Charlie Parker allows its synchronous iconization in a way that a Picasso painting does not. One can replicate a *Guernica* and one can even laminate the replication on top of the original, but one would not have the experience of painting the *Guernica* in synchrony with Picasso's act of painting it because one does not have as detailed a representation of the unfolding of the decisions made by Picasso that one can inhabit.[8] Thus, the peculiarity of the practice I am focusing on here derives from the fact that it concerns not only the replication of the products of creativity but also the ritual inhabitance of the very *act* of creativity as it unfolds in time.

Note another point. The educator I quoted above describes nicely what scholars of intertextuality have noticed in many contexts, namely music's "capacity for closely regulating pitch, timbre, tempo, volume, and other features," and thus its ability to "provide a powerful resource in attempting to suppress intertextual gaps" (Briggs and Bauman 1992, 158; Eisenlohr 2010). The notion of intertextual gaps pertains to the fact that "the fit between a particular text and its generic model—as well as other tokens of the same genre—is never perfect" (Briggs and Bauman 1992, 149): there are always interfering factors of some sort that prevent the production of a perfect fit between the source and the target texts. Inasmuch as the practice I have just described involves the synchronous replication of sound, it allows students to greatly minimize the intertextual gap between the recorded improvisations of the solos and their own replication of these solos. However, whereas scholars of intertextuality have documented a correlation between the suppression of intertextual gaps and "highly conservative, traditionalizing modes of creating textual authority," and between maximizing intertextual gaps and "building authority through claims of individual creativity and innovation (such as are common in 20th-century Western literature)" (Briggs and Bauman 1992, 149; Handman 2010), in the practice I discuss here a radical, rule-governed form of minimizing intertextual gaps (i.e., imitation) enhances and complements the experience of individual creativity. When a student inhabits a master's improvisation, she inhabits the latter's creative faculty as it unfolds in the moment, thus ritually replicating the creative act itself. It is precisely the duality of such a ritual of creativity—as a form of rule-governed inhabitance of individual creativity that is experienced as such by the person perform-

ing this practice—which accounts for the fact that some of the educators I
worked with do not consider it plagiarism when they require their students to
incorporate the masters' solos into their own solos during their final recitals
without disclosing the former's provenance to the audience.

Alienable Creativity

I was standing next to Henry, a man in his fifties, the instructor of an ensemble class I attended throughout the semester at Berklee. The students in this
class were of medium-level proficiency. Today was the ensemble's final recital,
which took place at one of Berklee's concert halls. Following Henry's instructions, each of the students had prepared a solo of a different well-known jazz
master. Today they were to play these solos on stage with the ensemble's
rhythm section without informing the audience about the solos' provenance.
After each student finished playing a master's solo, he or she seamlessly continued with his or her own improvisation. The audience did not notice the
transition. When the piano player played the late pianist Michel Petrucciani's
solo on the tune "Autumn Leaves," Henry turned to me and said with excitement, "They [the audience] don't know it's a Petrucciani solo!" Moreover,
when the student played an impressive passage in Petrucciani's solo, Henry
joined members of the audience in applauding the pianist.

   At the time, I was deeply puzzled. After all, if Henry's purpose was merely
to have the students learn the stylistic features of good improvisation, he did
not have to require them to play the solos in public without disclosing the
improvisations' authors. What was the rationale for this requirement, which,
on the surface, undermines individual creativity and connotes the specter of
plagiarism and the charge that jazz is a site of false individuality?[9] In a conversation, Henry explained the reason for his decision in the following manner:

> For them to be able to do that in a kind of a concert situation, performance
> situation, not a classroom test situation, makes it that much more chal-
> lenging. If they do it, they're going to feel, internalize it more strongly. . . .
> If one of them has never played a really good solo before on their own and
> if they've never played before, maybe even before an audience, then all of a
> sudden to play a solo that got good phrasing, good lines, good time-feel, all
> that stuff, and they play kind of true to the way it was recorded—they have
> accomplished something. *They internalized good lines and good feeling in the*
> *moment when it is supposed to happen, you know, with a rhythm section.*

Henry's goal was to make his students experience as faithfully as possible the act of improvising a great solo. Not disclosing the original authors of these improvisations was a means to this end, a way of precipitating this specific ritual transformation in which the student inhabits the master's individual creativity so he can become an improviser in his own right. Furthermore, as Henry makes clear, performing the masters' solo with a live rhythm section whose members react in real time to the student's reenactment of this solo further contributes to the student's sensation of inhabiting the original moment of the solo's creation. When Henry exclaimed to me that "they [the audience] don't know it's a Petrucciani solo," his excitement was not about the success of an act of "deception." Rather, he admired the degree to which the student inhabited the master's solo.

I take my initial discomfort provoked by Henry's pedagogical strategy as further opportunity to examine some key modern assumptions about the relationship between creative agency and rule-governed social behavior such as imitation. Anthropological accounts of the reenactment of myths by "traditional" people are a good way to begin this inquiry. Consider the following description of a myth recitation by a Brazilian Indian:

> Nil of the *macuco* . . . tells the origin myth. While doing so, he appears to grow distant, perhaps slipping into trance, yet not fully. He is here, but also elsewhere. Where? Inside the myth? Transposed back—in search of lost time—to some earlier world? Has he reinhabited that world, grasped its generative core, produced the words as if they were his own creation? . . . Is it possible for him to produce—not copy—those old words, inhabiting them so thoroughly that the abstract culture (the spirit of the time) carried along with them passes through him and recreates them? He is not simply copying the words in a rote way, but rather extracting from them some secret they contain, their life and vitality, which he, in turn, employs to produce them, in an act of creation. (Urban 2001, 91)

Anthropologists have recognized that performers of past "traditional" texts can inhabit these texts and experience them as the products of their own creation. What is it that makes it difficult for us to acknowledge that something similar can take place in the case of the recitation of emblematic texts of modern creativity such as the improvisations of past jazz masters? Why does it seem to us improbable that people can inhabit emblematic texts of modern individual creativity so thoroughly as to produce—not copy—them "in an act of creation"? Should we not be even more pressed to acknowledge this possibility in light of the fact that jazz students have at their disposal technologies of sound mediation that precipitate the production of figurational equivalence between the original moment of the master's improvisation and their own replication?

The answer, to a large extent, lies in the fact that we perceive individual creativity as a prototypical form of an inalienable possession (Weiner 1992). This meaning of creativity has its origins in the rise of possessive individualism as a modern normative ideal and the centrality of property rights as a defining feature of the modern autonomous individual (Leach 2007). This genealogy found expression, for example, in efforts made by bourgeois writers at the end of the eighteenth century to secure the economic benefits that can be accrued from defining individual creativity as inalienable (Woodmansee 1996). Similarly, tropes of possessive individualism pervaded early Romantic notions of organic creativity. Thus, in an essay that had a tremendous impact on Romanticism, *Conjectures on Original Composition*, Edward Young expressed his disdain for learning by arguing that "learning is *borrowed* knowledge; genius is knowledge innate, and quite *our own*" (Young 1759, 36; emphasis added). For Young, creativity cannot be based in any form of debt or behavior governed by existing rules. The intricate connection between creativity and notions of inalienability that have structured modern capitalism continue to find expression in new forms of virtual sociality (Boellstorff 2008, 205–236). The presumed inalienability of the creative faculty, then, which situates it in opposition to rule-governed social behavior, has a historically specific genealogy. Acknowledging this genealogy would require us to rethink Henry's pedagogical strategy as something other than an intended act of deception. Whereas anthropologists have already established that the inalienability of the artwork depends on the artwork's "intermittent forays into the commodity sphere, quickly followed by reentries into the closed sphere of singular 'art'" (Kopytoff 1986, 83), as in art auctions that boost the singularity of an artwork by attaching to it an exorbitant price tag (Appadurai 1986, 14; Myers 2002), my concern is to show the possibility of the alienability of the creative faculty itself, not only its products, through its replication and rule-governed inhabitance, and thus to collapse the opposition between rule-governed social behavior and creative agency.

Furthermore, in assessing students' acts of replication, we need to take into account recent anthropological studies that have emphasized the creativity that imitation necessitates in order to be successful. For example, Hussein

Ali Agrama (Agrama 2010) has called into question a number of assumptions about tradition, temporality, and creativity that underlie liberal philosophy's critique of the fatwa and similar forms of authority rooted in tradition and rule-governed behavior. He asks, "Might it not take great creativity just to do good imitation, as in the case of the comedian who mimics a president or famous political figure, or an actor, for whom it may take creative skill just to follow a script well, to surrender himself to it?" (Agrama 2010, 8). Anthropologists who have studied the phenomenology of imitation have answered in the affirmative: "Copying or imitation, we argue, is not the simple, mechanical process of replication that it is often taken to be, of running off duplicates from a template, but entails a complex and ongoing alignment of observation of the model with action in the world. In this alignment lies the work of improvisation. The formal resemblance between the copy and the model is an outcome of this process, not given in advance. It is a horizon of attainment" (Ingold and Hallam 2007, 5). Similarly, I suggest that the task of producing a synchronous iconization of a master's solo while its recording plays in the background is a creative act. Students need to realign their playing with the recording time and again, making instantaneous decisions about when to decelerate or accelerate their playing or, at times, stop playing altogether so as to "catch up" with the recording. In addition to matching pitch and rhythm, such synchronous iconization requires students to inhabit the timbre, volume, and indeed "feel" of the masters' playing.

Once we overcome our initial modern discomfort, it also becomes easier to note the continuity with many creative practices, jazz included, that structures Henry's pedagogical instructions. Replication, repetition, and quotation have been part of the cultural logic of jazz from its very beginning. The aesthetic sensibilities expressed in repetitive and imitative musical structures such as riffs and call and response (Monson 1994; Snead 1981), as well as in the ironic replication of and thus commentary upon previous musical structures and other players' solos (Gates 1988; Monson 1999), have always informed notions of creativity in jazz. Although jazz musicians have tended to be ambivalent toward the replication of someone else's entire solo in a live performance (though at times they have engaged precisely in this practice [Berliner 1994, 99]), they have never objected to "musicians borrowing discrete patterns or phrase fragments from other improvisers . . . ; indeed, it is expected" (Berliner 1994, 101) as a pedagogical strategy. Musicians have gone to great lengths to achieve this borrowing. Such discrete patterns, which improvisers weave together to form their solos, can be a few measures long.

Thus improvisation involves imitation insofar as it is a recombination of pre-viously available building blocks created by other improvisers (Nettl 1995; Solis and Nettl 2009). When students replicate in public parts of a past mas-ter's solo and weave them with their own improvisations, they engage in a practice that is not that different from what jazz players have always practiced, albeit on a slightly different scale. All these are added reasons that Henry and his students did not consider their performance as plagiarism. Beyond jazz, dialogism and various forms of borrowing have been the mode of operation of numerous domains of modern creativity (Boon 2010).

Jazz educators also adhere to modern normative ideals of individual cre-ativity that emphasize uniqueness. Indeed, they often warn their students against the peril of both permanently sounding like someone else and display-ing little internal stylistic variety in their solos. However, they also acknowl-edge and practice the possibility of inhabiting, experiencing, and reenacting another person's individual creativity. They do so not only as an homage to a revered ideal (compare with Vann 2006) but also as a pedagogy that has become increasingly important against the backdrop of the changing condi-tions of existence of jazz, and that has become increasingly possible due to the availability of new technologies of sound reproduction.

However, these practices of replication encapsulate a key paradox: the very same conditions of possibility that frequently allow students to overcome the gap between the interactional plane of the classroom and the representational plane of jazz's mythical past, often also keep the two planes apart.

"Damn!" The Specter of Asymptotic Approximation

One October morning as I was waiting for the elevator to arrive in one of Berklee's campus buildings, I heard the sound of a tenor saxophone coming from one of the adjacent rooms. I recognized John Coltrane's solo on the tune "Giant Steps," recorded in 1960, a stepping stone for every serious improviser. However, it was not only John Coltrane I was listening to. Rather, someone else was playing the solo on her saxophone on top of and in synchrony with Coltrane. I could hear the rhythm section that accompanied Coltrane on that famous recording, but I could barely hear Coltrane himself, because the player in the room perfectly laminated her own playing on top of Coltrane's. I approached the closed door and listened attentively. After a few seconds, the saxophonist stopped playing and emitted a loud "Damn!" while Coltrane's re-cording continued for a few seconds. The player then stopped the recording, replayed the track and joined in again. After a few dozen seconds she stopped again, this time emitting an even more impatient "Damn!" She stopped the recording, replayed it from the beginning and joined in again. This pattern repeated itself five times until I had to go to a meeting. To my ears, her rendition was perfect—whenever she played I could barely hear Coltrane's playing—so tightly was her playing laminated over Coltrane's. What motivated this player to repeatedly stop her playing? Why was she displeased with her synchronic iconization of Coltrane's solo?

As I amassed more data on educators' and students' use of the Amazing Slow Downer, it became clear to me that one repercussion of using this and similar technologies of sound mediation is that they increase students' perceptual capacities and standards for precision. I have often observed students laminating their renditions of the masters' solos on top of the original recordings. To my ears, their renditions were perfect. And yet, more than once, students would stop their playing because they were displeased with their replications. One student who was working on Cannonball Adderley's solo on the tune "Work Song" looked at me with surprise after I asked him why he stopped his playing time and again. He responded: "Don't you hear I don't get it right in the seventh bar of the A section?" When I asked him to explain in greater detail, he said:

> When you listen to the recording, you slow it down and you listen to it again and again, you know? You become so familiar with it. I mean, I listened to this Cannonball solo probably like a hundred times, really slowing it down, every note, and the feel. . . .. So when you play it with the recording, you are so familiar with it—I want to play it like it was, to really get to the feel of it. And after you've used the Downer [i.e., the Amazing Slow Downer] long enough you can immediately tell when something is not right, when you or someone else still haven't gotten there, because your ears can hear now at that level, you know?

The student described the effects of the prolonged use of the Amazing Slow Downer in terms of heightened sensitivity to the tiniest asynchronicities between a recorded solo and its real-time replication.

To some extent, at issue is the development of new skills around new technologies. As Tim Ingold, drawing on François Sigaut, argues, "As fast as machines have been contrived to do what had previously been done by skilled hands, different skills have sprung up for handling the machines themselves.

[Sigaut] calls this 'the law of the irreducibility of skills,' in the light of which 'the entire history of technics . . . might be interpreted as a constantly renewed attempt to build skills into machines by means of algorithms, an attempt constantly foiled because other skills always tend to develop around the new machines'" (Ingold 2000, 332). Enhanced by the prosthetic ear of the Amazing Slow Downer, students are now able to decipher more nuances in the masters' solos, which they can master to good effect, experiencing a ritual transformation in which they feel they fuse with the masters. However, now they are also better able to perceive the tiniest asynchronicities and mismatches between their own playing and the masters' recorded playing. In these moments of frustration produced by the perception of such asynchronicities, the interactive plane of the classroom and the representational plane indexed by the recordings of the jazz masters become disjointed again; the recording returns to its pastness; and the student is no longer fused with the master (compare with Parmentier 2007). The frustration displayed by the saxophonist who attempted to produce a synchronized iconization of Coltrane's solo on the tune "Giant Steps" is the result of this dynamics.

Moreover, the use of the Amazing Slow Downer is productive of frustration even prior to actually playing the replication—that is, at the preliminary stage in which the student must become familiar with the intricacies of the master's solo. On the one hand, educators often emphasize that the purpose of slowing down the masters' solos with the help of software such as the Amazing Slow Downer is to enable students to cope with the solos' complexity. As Henry put it in a class that revolved around the music of trumpeter Miles Davis, the software allows you to "slow it down to a tempo where you can deal with it." Slowing down the recorded solos is supposed to make it easier for students to decipher the notes played by the legendary musicians and the intricacies that make their solos masterpieces. Note that many of these solos, especially those that were created in the bebop era, are characterized by neck-breaking tempos. Slowing them down enables students to identify more quickly the solos' building blocks and thus to prepare better replications, which would then result in a fusion with the masters when these replications are played on top of their recordings.

On the other hand, as I attended more classes it became clear that although using the Amazing Slow Downer indeed helps students deal with the solos, it does so only relative to a specific level of complexity of the solos' features—the level students encounter *prior* to the use of this technology. Beyond that level, the Amazing Slow Downer reveals new complexity *within the slowed-down reality itself.* Consequently, in order to deal with this newly revealed complexity, students have to spend more time with the recording and, in addition, slow it down even further, a step that reveals further complexity and so forth. This stepwise increase in their perception of the solo's complexity ultimately defers "closure" for them in the sense that they do not feel satisfied with their replications.

To fully appreciate this dynamic, it is necessary to understand the experience of having to account for the nuances of a significantly slowed-down recording. When greatly slowed down, a short embellishment can become as complex as an entire measure prior to its manipulation by the Amazing Slow Downer. To begin, every note stretches. What were infinitely short spaces between the drum kicks, the bass notes, the piano accompaniment, and the soloist, suddenly become palpable. Accounting for the soloist's notes in relation to this thickening context becomes a daunting task. Furthermore, as one continues to slow down the recording in an attempt to deal with this newly revealed complexity, one discovers more nuances that need to be accounted for. Like a fractal shape whose complexity is repeated at different scales, the slowed-down recording reveals the same complexity at a higher acoustic resolution. This is further complicated by two facts. First, when the recording is sufficiently slowed down, even the onset of notes becomes difficult to pin down. Second, at such reduced speed the different notes cease to index one another in a meaningful configuration as they do when the jazz improvisation is at its normal tempo and exhibits the ongoing musical interaction and call-and-response between band members (Monson 1996; Sawyer 1996).

This is why moments of epiphany in class—when a hitherto unnoticed element in a master's solo is suddenly revealed via the Amazing Slow Downer—are frequently not the end but rather the beginning of a long process of further clarification of the specific element. The class seldom proceeds to unearth "other nuances" in a master's solo with the help of the Amazing Slow Downer. Rather, after educators identify a specific embellishment, it typically becomes the focus of heightened group attention in an attempt "to really nail it," as one educator put it. I have observed many classes in which, after certain musical segments of only a few seconds in length were pinned down via the Amazing Slow Downer, they were further slowed down and looped dozens of times in a successive fashion for what could easily amount to twenty minutes.

Thus, paradoxically, these technologies represent for students and educators the possibility of inhabiting the masters' creativity by making it more accessible, but they often frustrate this promise both by gradually revealing the solos' endless complexity and by training students to perceive this complexity.

It is a form of "asymptotic approximation" in which the potential to embody the ideal never fully materializes, although it often materializes enough to generate powerful sensations of fusion with the masters. In other words, this pedagogical strategy enables the reconciliation of rule-governed social behavior and creative practice on one level while frustrating it on another level, a feature shared by many of the pedagogical strategies explored in this book.

Entering One's Own Acoustic Unconscious?

Against the backdrop of their concerns about the ubiquity of printed artifacts in the jazz program and the disappearance of live performance situations in which neophyte musicians can apprentice with seasoned musicians, the educators I worked with instruct students to ritually orient themselves to the past masters' individual creativity available in the form of their recorded improvisations, and thereby inhabit this creativity. This "ritual of creativity" demonstrates the alienability of the creative faculty and the co-constitution of rule-governed social behavior and creative practice. At the same time, it keeps rule-governed social behavior and creative practice polarized.

I do not want to argue that such practices always work in the same way and for all individuals. Thus, in one class at the New School, Paul, a venerable pianist in his seventies, played with the sound system one of his own recordings made some forty-five years ago, in which he plays with a number of well-known jazz masters. While the recording was playing, Paul suddenly approached the piano and hesitatingly attempted to replicate his recorded solo in synchrony. Perhaps for Paul, inhabiting and replicating his own past individual creativity in synchrony with his recording created a bifurcation between creativity and imitation. Perhaps, rather than ritually bridging the past and the present, his act of replication in class only accentuated for him the schism between the present of the classroom and the vibrant performance jazz scenes in which he had participated and indeed helped form as a young man. Perhaps it only invoked for him the disappearance of these scenes as loci of creativity, a disappearance that has motivated jazz educators to search for advanced sound technologies that would allow students to experience immersive interaction with these scenes' echoes. It was uncanny to witness this incident, for at that moment Paul entered his very own acoustic unconscious, as it were. It was a moment—one out of many—that highlighted the multiple potentialities and contradictions that underlie the institutionalization of creativity in the academic jazz program.

TRANSCRIBING CREATIVITY
AS CREATIVE TRANSCRIBING

Legitimizing Theory and Expertise

Performing Exegesis in the Classroom

Imagine you enter a room full of people. The people are sitting. Each of them is leaning over the same written manuscript. The manuscript is also projected on a screen and a person is talking while pointing at the projected manuscript with a pointer. When you ask the people what this manuscript represents, they tell you it represents the words of wise people who lived in the past. The people in the room are collectively trying to decipher the rationale for the words the wise people said, for there is no doubt, so they tell you, that every word of the ancient wise people has profound meaning and that this meaning can be harnessed to great effect in the present by anyone who is able to understand it. If you managed to engage in this little thought experiment, I would guess it made you think of a religious congregation practicing something like religious exegesis.

The image of religious exegesis frequently came to my mind when I attended a dozen of classes at Berklee and observed a pedagogical practice that entailed the production and analysis of transcriptions of the past jazz masters' recorded improvisations. Indeed, it is impossible not to notice the prominent role played by the jazz transcription in Berklee's culture. Some educators utilize transcriptions as a means of teaching "improvisational concepts." There are courses in which students learn to transcribe jazz solos. In yet other courses, such as ensemble classes where the focus is on performance, educators make frequent reference to the importance of jazz transcribing, and they often use transcriptions during class as reference points for exemplary solo construction. In the program's library one can find hundreds of booklets of published jazz transcriptions of every important past jazz musician.

Although musicians used transcriptions as learning devices prior to the full-blown academization of jazz training in one form or another, they did so mainly by producing their own transcriptions from records (Owens 2003).[1] The commercial production and dissemination of jazz transcriptions received added impetus after that point because knowledge codified in print allows for its standardization, can be more efficiently imparted in class to many students at the same time, and is central to these programs' claim to be sites of expert knowledge.

A jazz transcription is the textual artifact that is the result of notating music from jazz recordings (Berliner 1994, 95–105). The notated parts are usually the solo parts played by musicians who have been canonized within the jazz tradition. Educators harness their transcribing skills mostly to the musical output of the charismatic performers who were musically active or who made their greatest impact in the years between the 1940s and the late 1960s. Frequently, educators' rationale for doing so resembles the explanation given by Fred, a Berklee educator, during a course focusing on the music of trumpeter Miles Davis. At the beginning of this class Fred played an excerpt from Davis's solo on the tune "But Not for Me" from Davis's 1957 album *Bags' Groove* using the stereo system.[2] The sounds filled the room while everyone listened attentively. Fred then replayed the recording measure after measure, each time stopping and rewinding it. He instructed the students to transcribe what they heard. He then replayed the recording again, this time asking the students to say out loud the notes, which he then wrote on the staved whiteboard. When he finished, he looked at the transcribed solo in front of him and said:

> And if you're interested in improvisation, you want to become an improviser, you write down the solo, you're writing down the chord changes above and you analyze it—that's fantastic to learn it. You're reading somebody's mind! How they are thinking in terms of their improvisational thoughts,

you know: are they thinking harmony, are they thinking scales, why pick this note, why pick that note? You can't ask Miles Davis; you can't ask Charlie Parker why he played those notes, because he's not around, but you can check him out and it's almost as good. You can read their mind. It's like reading the mind of a genius!

Fred presents the act of transcribing and then analyzing Davis's solo as a simple and transparent process of reading the theoretical considerations that have informed Davis's playing when he recorded his solo—considerations that students can implement when constructing their own improvisations.

However, I suggest that the pedagogical practice of producing and analyzing jazz transcriptions at Berklee is far removed from the unproblematic deciphering of pre-existing improvisational considerations, as Fred presents it. It has to do with what anthropologists and other scholars interested in modern institutions have long emphasized: the role played by inscription in the production and reproduction of institutional authority. Specifically, scholars have highlighted the ways in which institutions buttress their authority by detaching a given stretch of discourse from the situation of its occurrence and then strategically recontextualizing and interpreting it in ritualized institutional events that revolve around the production and analysis of printed material. Such strategies have become "a key to understanding the way institutional power works through discourse" (Park and Bucholtz 2009, 486; Silverstein and Urban 1996).

For example, Jaffe (2009) examined two media productions about sociolinguistic variety in the UK and the United States. He focused on the strategic manipulation of the representation of the speech of the individuals who were the subject of these productions. Specifically, he analyzed the transcriptions of this speech posted on the companion websites of these productions. In these websites, the speech of people identified as dialect speakers was likely to be represented with nonstandard spellings, a choice that contributes to their image as authentic speakers but also stigmatizes them as deviating from the standard norm. In contrast, the talk of the sociolinguists whose role is to provide expert commentary on the former is likely to be represented with standard spellings. This choice reproduces the "contrast between lay and expert knowledge about sociolinguistic diversity" (Jaffe 2009, 574; see also Bucholtz 2009; Park 2009). Similarly, Goodman (2002) shows how the codification of North African native lore in printed artifacts by French colonizing and nationalist institutions during the nineteenth and twentieth centuries erased these local cultures' heterogeneity and situated pragmatic character and thus allowed institutional agents to strategically position these cultures within various ideological frameworks of social and hierarchical difference (see also Bauman and Briggs 2004). These and similar accounts have shown that institutions, through the strategic transcribing and subsequent recontextualizing of discursive events, naturalize their authority and their claim to be sites of exclusive, rational knowledge.

Similarly, I suggest that some of the classes I attended at Berklee are sites in which institutional authority is legitimized and creative agency and institutionalized rationality are reconciled through strategies of capturing on paper and recontextualizing ephemeral discourse—in this case the past jazz masters' recorded improvisations.[3] The success of these strategies is defined in terms of their ability to symmetrically align the academic jazz program's expert knowledge with the past jazz masters' intentionality as it is presumably revealed in the masters' improvisations. This alignment takes place despite the fact that past jazz masters, for the most part, created their masterpieces irrespective of contemporary academic jazz education's expert knowledge. I argue that in addition to any pedagogical value, the purpose of these institutional practices is to legitimize a body of expert knowledge commonly known as chord-scale theory, which has been the target of mounting criticism in the past few years as part of the general critique of academic jazz education.

The Rise of Theory and Its Discontent

"It's mathematics!"

According to many educators and students I worked with, Berklee's curriculum is characterized by the overemphasis on "theory." Indeed, "theory" has played a key role in Berklee's identity and strategy of legitimation from the outset. Remember that Berklee was originally founded as the Schillinger House, named after a person described in an article in the journal *American Music* as a "Music Science Promethean," a person who "more than anything else . . . was a music scientist receptive to new technologies and experimentation related to the arts," and about whom "it is claimed that his treatise describing the mathematical basis of art was heralded by Albert Einstein and Bertrand Russell" (Brodsky 2003, 45). From the very beginning Berklee promoted the generation of musical creativity by applying mathematical principles. The celebratory book that chronicles Berklee's first fifty years (Hazell 1995) portrays its early days with many photographs that index "theory" through and through: we see educators and students analyzing together chords on a staved blackboard and music scores projected on a screen with an overhead projector. The performance of the scientification of art is evident in these photographs and in the texts that accompany them. They represent Berklee's strategy of legitimation through a modernist rhetoric. Indeed, in the sphere of academic jazz education, Berklee has come to be known, at times notoriously so, for its heavy emphasis on theory as a basis for improvisation. Some educators both inside and outside Berklee frequently refer to the school as "Chords 'R' Us," adapting the name of the giant toy retailer Toys "R" Us to express this apprehension. As one Berklee educator told me, "They don't call us the Chord Factory for nothing with all that chord-scale here."

The overemphasis on theory at Berklee has also been overdetermined by jazz's quest for cultural legitimacy, much like its eager adoption of other markers of high art. This relation finds a clear expression in the following excerpt from the introduction of a textbook for harmony classes published by Berklee's publishing press: "Some of [the] terms are not universally understood, particularly by conservatory trained professionals. Therefore, keep an open mind when it comes to other musicians' opinions about any given topic or the terminology they may use. Someone else may not be as well trained as you!" (Nettles 2002) These words represent an attempt to reclaim cultural legitimacy for jazz vis-à-vis classical music in classical music's own home court: jazz now has its own obtuse theoretical arsenal. In an ironic reversal of strategies of marginalization of jazz prevalent in the first half of the twentieth century, this textbook advises jazz students to "keep an open mind" when studying with conservatory trained musicians who may not be as well versed in jazz's own terminology as the students themselves.

This legacy of putting a premium on theory has a powerful effect on students' everyday experience in the classroom. Alex, a Berklee piano student, told me the following: "Man, in all these classes you have to play through concepts. You have to feed your intuitions through concepts. That's the way it is now. Nobody plays from the guts anymore. Today you must have a high IQ to play jazz. It's mathematics!" Alex's words invoke Branford Marsalis's characterization of the music produced by graduates of academic jazz programs as "think-tank music" that is opposed to "humanness" (Young 2006). It is crucial to emphasize that Alex's, as well as Marsalis's, discontent is not about theory per se. Theory was highly regarded by many jazz musicians from the outset, especially when it was self-determined (Monson 2007, 284–286).

Rather, their discontent is about theory that becomes the sole focus of one's craft; in other words, when theory is fetishized as if it, in itself, holds the key to creative improvisation regardless of its application and relevance to other key principles of the jazz aesthetics.

Machine-Gun Playing, One Chord at a Time

Chord-scale theory plays a key role in the overemphasis on theory at Berklee. It is a body of expert knowledge that was initially developed by various musicians and educators in the jazz world around the mid-twentieth century (Ake 2002; Monson 1998; Owens 2003). As jazz training became increasingly institutionalized in academia, this theory was more systematically codified and widely disseminated through various pedagogical aids—mainly method books. This theory is supposed to help players improvise on a given tune by spelling out for them the relationship between the chords that comprise the harmonic basis of the tune and the scales that correspond to them. Thus players can infer which notes they can use in constructing their improvisations.

In recent years, many critics have targeted chord-scale theory as a key factor in the presumed detrimental effects that academic jazz education has had on the improvisational skills of their students (Ake 2002; Nicholson 2005). They have argued that as a result of reliance on chord-scale theory, students learn how to improvise by practicing patterns and licks that they then apply to the harmonic changes, while making their point of reference the single chord. Thus, when improvising on a harmonic progression, students typically progress from one chord to the next and their improvisatory considerations are reduced to playing the "correct" notes on each chord, one after the other. This has a number of repercussions. First, some of the educators I worked with argued that students' improvisational solos become a long succession of similar patterns of improvisation that bear no relation to the tune's melody or broader form but relate solely to one chord at a time within the tune's harmonic progression. In addition, because the point of reference becomes the single chord and the scale that derives from it, students tend to play as many patterns and notes as they can during each chord's length. Many of them consider it a mark of excellence to come up with as many notes and patterns as possible for each chord. This is the reason for students' tendency to play eighth or sixteenth notes, which some of these educators referred to as "machine-gun playing."

Charlie, a high-level Berklee administrator in his midsixties who is also an accomplished musician and a graduate of Berklee, told me that in his view, in many schools,

> the methodology of teaching improvisation has improved tremendously almost to the point [that] it's not as much an oral tradition . . . but more of a written tradition: you know, the play-along, the method books, all these things. And in many ways, all these books don't stress the oral tradition as much as they stress the scale, the rhythms, the reading, so it's made improvisation more of a literacy issue. And even jazz, jazz has become a very literate art, meaning you have to be able to read really well. The improvisational techniques are very technical. It comes back to the kind of thing I've—finding programs that actually blend the oral tradition with the technique. And I think that that's where there's probably room for better methods. You know, the whole idea of call and response, keeping your melody developing, motivic development . . . a lot of the method books don't even get to that arena. They get into "These are the chord tones, these are the scales, and these are the scales that you play on the chord—*go!*" And if anything, it makes people play in a very serial, linear fashion, rather than in a very semantic kind of way: "This is what I want to express, this is what I want to convey in a tune." You know, some of the basic blues elements are sometimes lost. You hear people play and you don't hear the blues phrasing, you don't hear the call and response, you don't hear the storytelling that goes on that I think is integral for—like if you listen and say, "Man, that solo is great," it usually contains these things from the oral tradition.

Note, to begin, that Charlie argues that because of their heavy reliance on chord-scale theory, improvisation for many students has become a technical application of abstract algorithms, or rules that match chords with scales and patterns to the point where they play "in a very serial, linear fashion, rather than in a very semantic kind of way: 'This is what I want to express.'" Charlie further argues that jazz programs' heavy reliance on chord-scale theory has resulted in the fact that students' playing is missing improvisational elements that transcend the single chord as the primary unit of improvisational consideration. He refers to "motivic development" and "call and response"—key improvisational elements that transcend the single chord in that they are created by referring in real time to earlier parts of the improvisation: that is, the experienced improviser develops a motif by repeating its previous occurrences with variations. "Call and response"—the practice of playing a musical phrase and then "answering" it—is basically another version of motivic development, the most well known example of which is the blues, a form that typically consists of two four-bar "calls" and one four-bar response organized harmonically around the first, fourth, and fifth degrees of the scale. These are the conditions of possibility for poetic development and, indeed, "storytelling" (Monson 1996).[4]

Another way of articulating this critique would be to say that meaningful jazz improvisation in general relies heavily on the musician's ability to reference different aspects of the improvisation's broader context. For example, mature players often reference their own previous playing (as is the case in motivic development—Schuller 1999), the simultaneous contribution of the other players in the band (Monson 1996; Sawyer 2003), the playing of past players (through stylistic decisions and "quoting') (Berliner 1994), other famous renditions of the same tune (Walser 1997), other tunes (again through quoting), as well as the broader social context through social commentary—a practice frequently and famously utilized by bassist Charles Mingus, for example (Monson 2007; Porter 2002). Because of their heavy and exclusive reliance on chord-scale theory as the primary basis for improvisation, many students lack the skills to inform their playing with these pragmatic features.

Perhaps one of the most conspicuous ways in which many students' heavy reliance on chord-scale theory implicates their improvisational skills is their difficulty in structuring their improvisations in accordance with the broader form and melody of each standard tune. To do so is crucial for a number of reasons. To begin with, although different standard tunes may consist of the same chords, these chords are frequently not arranged in the same order. Their different order represents a different musical meaning that experienced improvisers take into account. When students improvise by taking into consideration one chord at a time they neglect a crucial resource that could make their improvisations much more meaningful and varied. Similarly, jazz standards that have the same harmonic progression have different melodies. Players who take into account those melodies are more likely to produce a different improvisation on each tune than players who improvise solely based on harmonic considerations. These insights found expression in a master class delivered at Berklee by Sam, a well-known saxophonist and one of the school's star educators. After a group of students played Wayne Shorter's tune "Yes or No," Sam told the students:

You must develop an approach where you're anticipating the harmony . . . an approach where you're not just playing on the chord that you're on. The chord that you're on is leading you to the next chord, and in some tunes the chord lasts eight bars or four bars or whatever. . . . You got to arrive to the bridge and make something out of it. The A section also: you got eight bars, then two bars, then four bars. Those last four bars—play it out. Those two bars in between make a nice entrance into those four bars. You didn't treat that at all. This record—*JuJu*—we all know that record. What made all those tunes so great was all that hookup. It wasn't just "play the head, now play on the chorus." Every chorus built from the last. And all the hits and all the things that were in the theme, you have to play off of it, build on it, not to just repeat every chorus the same. . . . [Addressing the saxophonist] The way you played the theme at the end, you have to play like that during solos so there's a hookup, so there's a thing happening . . . form-wise. That's really important. To really feel. You play on an AABA form. Each A, even though they repeat in each chorus, even with repeated hits, each A is different. The first A leads into that second A. The second A leads into the bridge. The bridge leads into the last A. You want to have a sensation of arriving within the form. Everybody has to deal with that in terms of how you're soloing, how you're playing over it, and how the rhythm section's building it.

Sam encourages the students to take the tune's melody and overall harmonic form into account in their improvisations because their current improvisations proceed from one chord to the next and hence lack a sense of development. He clarifies for them the harmonic rhythm of the A section of the tune "Yes or No" and encourages them to organize their solos in accordance with this rhythm in chunks of eight bars, two bars, and four bars. He also instructs them to have each chorus organically lead to the next one. Throughout, he articulates his points by comparing the students' playing, which lacks key improvisational considerations, with the improvisations of the past masters.

Wallace, a Berklee educator, articulated his evaluation of students' improvisational skills by comparing them more explicitly to players of previous generations:

I feel that, years ago, a lot of those cats [i.e., players of older generations], they didn't know chord changes. They knew melodies. In order to work they had to know tunes. In order to get gigs they had to know tunes. I feel that a lot of time nowadays the players know the changes before they know the tunes. Not all, but that's how it seems to me. That is how it's developed today—so they know the changes before they know the tunes. So what happened is that you created a harmonic generation, whereas before that it was a melodic generation because they were playing off the melodies.

Although Wallace exaggerates both past players' ignorance of chord changes and present players' ignorance of melodies, he articulates a wide-spread perception among the educators I worked with and commentators at large about the detrimental effects that some jazz programs' heavy reliance on chord-scale theory has had on students' improvisational skills. The overemphasis on chord-scale theory has led students to neglect pragmatic features that are crucial for making their improvisations less repetitive and more meaningful.

Legitimizing Theory and Expertise

Performing symmetrical alignment between chord-scale theory and the ephemeral discourse of the past legendary masters (i.e., the masters' recorded improvisations) can legitimize chord-scale theory. In class, during the production and analysis of transcriptions of these improvisations, some of the jazz educators I worked with constructed and mobilized the legendary musicians as agents who have always already thought through the institutionalized expert terminology that is the hallmark of academic jazz education as a field of expert practice. They did so by narrating the musical intentionality of these players during their analysis of the masters' improvisations. They authorized their own institutional expertise by presenting the jazz masters' decision-making as if it were informed by chord-scale theory. Thus, if one of the strategies of legitimizing the two jazz programs, as I suggested in previous chapters, is that of infusing the program with "unmediated" and presumably nontheoretical charisma, the strategy I describe in this chapter is that of legitimizing theory itself by constructing this charisma as if it were originally intertwined with this theory.

It should be clear from the outset that my argument does not hinge on whether or not the past jazz masters whose musical output is the subject of transcription and analysis in class were actually versed in or ignorant of the academic jazz program's institutional expert knowledge. In practice, past masters informed their improvisations by different conceptual frameworks and to different degrees. Rather, my point is that through the careful transcription and analysis of these masterpieces in class, educators rhetorically transform the past jazz masters into entities that buttress jazz education's theoretical apparatus in a way that is mostly oblivious to the specificity of each past master. They do so by voicing the masters' presumed improvisational considerations through the academic program's body of expert knowledge. In doing so, they authorize this knowledge. This process consists of four key stages.

Decontextualizing Improvisation

If students' improvisations lack many contextual features, most of the past jazz masters' improvisations are suffused with such features through and through. Indeed, this is what makes them masterpieces. Their improvisations are what linguistic anthropologists call a text-in-context, an emergent interactional event whose meaning is context-dependent (Silverstein 1998). However, the jazz transcription as it is produced in the classes I attended is decontextualized from many of these elements (Winkler 1997, 197–198). It represents the reduction of the act of improvisation into the pitch and rhythm values that were played by the soloist. It thus leaves out elements that are crucial to the ways in which a solo signifies within the tradition of jazz appreciation, such as its relation to the contribution of the other band members, or the broader contextual details that informed its production by a socially mindful musician.

Many courses in jazz transcription offered at Berklee, lower-level courses, in particular, exemplify the logical extreme of such decontextualization, which exists to a lesser degree in higher-level courses. One such lower-level course, which I attended, focused on two main exercises. One required students to notate rhythm values. The students received a music sheet that represented the pitch values of a segment of one of saxophonist Michael Brecker's solos. They were asked to add to each pitch value its rhythm value as they listened to the original recording. Because of the complexity of the piece, the educator slowed it down through use of the Amazing Slow Downer. Typically, a two-bar segment was played in a loop fifteen to twenty times until the students successfully notated the rhythm values. This exercise extended over several weeks. Another exercise cultivated students' ability to identify and notate the pitch values of a segment of one of saxophonist Cannonball Adderley's solos. In this case, the educator did not require the students to listen to the original recording while transcribing the solo. Rather, he transcribed it himself prior to class and then played the transcription with his saxophone for the students to retranscribe. The transcribed text that the students produced was thus doubly removed and doubly decontextualized from the original text-in-context.

The abstraction of solos from their pragmatic abode as well as the rationale behind this abstraction found expression in another educator's comments during a transcription exercise: "This is something for you to think about so when you're working on vocabulary stuff, that you listen for that stuff happening in the music that you're listening to. The player's doing that thing, so you're 'oh, that's this particular musical fact, this particular vocabulary, that's a pentatonic scale, that's an altered scale.'" Al, the educator, characterized the search for music vocabulary as a search for facts. Al's use of the notion of "facts" is meaningful. First, it suggests that at stake is a veritable process of decontextualization, that is, the search for extractable theoretical machinery that can be utilized across different performance contexts and hence transcend them. Second, it points to the end result of the production and analysis of the jazz transcription: as is generally the case with entities that have become "facts," the school's terminology becomes imbued with a reified and taken-for-granted status while the process of its becoming so is erased (Latour 2010).[5] Most importantly, the elimination of contextual elements from the jazz solo in the course of transcribing it renders the solo malleable to strategic recontextualization in the subsequent stages of its manipulation in class.

Inhabiting the Masters' Intentionality

When educators begin their analysis of jazz transcriptions after they have produced them or extracted them from commercial transcription books, they often weave chord-scale theory together with verbs that denote the intentionality of the players whose solos they analyze—a task made easier now that the solos have been decontextualized and reduced to their bare bones. Consider the difference between the following two takes on a transcribed solo. The first is one that I composed based on the second, which is what David, a Berklee educator, actually said in class:

> [Fictional commentary:] I can't see here any single note of a chord scale, and thus we can't tell if it's symmetric or diminished or, say, the altered scale or something like that, but you can see that the bottom portion of one of those dominant scales is there, or flat 9 and sharp 9 together.
> [Actual commentary:] He doesn't play any single note of a chord scale in there to let us know if it's symmetric, diminished, or, say, the altered

scale or something like that, but you can see that he is drawing from, you know, the bottom portion of one of those dominant scales, or using flat 9 or sharp 9 together.

Both commentaries convey the same theoretical information. However, whereas the first commentary does not imply anything about the jazz master's intentionality, the second does: the master "plays" notes from the chord scales; he is "drawing from" certain portions of the chord and is "using" specific chord tones. It is important to bear in mind the effect of this commentary when it is repeated time and again during class. By repeatedly employing action verbs to denote the intentionality of the player whose subject is supposedly this theoretical knowledge, educators construct a reality in which the jazz master's musical intentionality and the institutionalized terminology of the school imbricate one another as if the master actually thought in terms of this terminology at the time he recorded his solo.[6]

Note an additional point. According to David, the player "tries to let us know" the identity of the scale. Thus, not only did the master presumably think through chord-scale theory, but it is implied that he also tried to communicate this knowledge to the students. The casting of jazz masters and future audiences as interlocutors surfaced also in the following example of an analysis of a transcribed solo made by Ron, another Berklee educator:

Do you see that he's outlining that by playing a three up to nine [these are scale degrees]—he's outlining a B minor 7 in the arpeggio that he plays there. You know, there is a soloist who is hinting at something that you learned as a reharmonization technique at the beginning of Harmony [a specific harmony course].

Implicit in Ron's commentary is the suggestion that the player is in dialogue with his listeners about the school's institutionalized harmonic and melodic concepts. In this way, concepts produced in the context of academic jazz education become not only the mode of communication for the past player but also the topic of communication—something the player wanted to communicate to his future listeners.[7]

Bakhtin's (1996) notion of "voicing" can be useful in the analysis of the dynamics of this mutual imbrication. Bakhtin has suggested that language is stratified in the sense that it consists of many registers emerging in different social groups. Occupations, institutions, social classes, and various social strata have their own registers that are saturated with the context in which they evolved (1996, 289–292). Making a distinction between the narrating and the narrated events in the novel, Bakhtin has argued that by strategically ventriloquating registers that index different contexts and social groups when they narrate events, novelists can manipulate the relation between narrating and narrated events to achieve specific goals (299).

Educators' analyses of transcribed solos in class, on the one hand, and the past masters' original acts of creating these solos, on the other hand, can be regarded, respectively, as narrating and narrated events. In the same way that a novelist narrates the actions of a protagonist, educators narrate the soloists' musical actions and intentions as these "find expression" in the transcribed solos, measure after measure. Educators use a specific "voice" in the course of narration: the register that indexes the school's expert knowledge, namely chord-scale theory. They rely on occupational jargon to create congruence or to align role-inhabitance across the narrated/narrating universes. The institutionalized concepts belong to the narrating universe of the classroom. Yet by having the soloists "speak" through these concepts in class—a task educators achieve by deploying tropes of intentionality in the act of analysis, they create congruence between the institutionalized universe of academic jazz education and the narrated universe of the recorded solos. And because these solos and their creators are perceived to be emblems of creativity, such congruence inevitably authorizes jazz education's institutional authority.

Intentionality Made Present and to Unfold in Time

Once educators' strategies of analyzing jazz transcriptions are framed as narrating events, it becomes possible to examine them in light of genres of narration that have been traditionally the topic of sociolinguistic research such as the narration of sports events, and thus to tease out their specificity (Ferguson 1983; see also Hirschkind 2006, 160–161). A sports event can be reported on after the fact, as in printed news produced by news agencies and standardized by newspapers. Alternatively, it can be narrated in real time, as in live broadcasts. While the former mode of reporting is characterized by the past tense, the latter mode of reporting is typically dominated by the present tense. In their analysis of jazz transcriptions in class, some educators narrate events that occurred in the past (a few decades into the past, to be sure, since most of the transcribed solos that educators analyze were recorded in the 1950s or 1960s). However, educators often use the present tense to recount players' musical decisions, much as in live sports broadcasting. Thus, in the previous vignettes, David and Ron assert that a player "is drawing," "doesn't play," "is outlining," "is hinting," and so forth. Educators' analysis of the jazz solo transcription is thus different from typical referential narratives that provide information on past events (Carrard 1988). Although it is obvious to everyone in the classroom that the jazz transcription is a representation of an event that took place decades before the moment of analysis, educators' mode of narration reduces the temporal gap between this event and the classroom. If one of the effects of live broadcasting is that "the delay between the time of occurrence of the narrated events and the time of their verbal representation strives toward zero" (Ryan 1993, 139), then by narrating the past masters' intentionality in the present tense educators make it further congruent with their present expert knowledge.[8]

Furthermore, such a practice provides the basis for the production of suspense through the simulation of intentionality that unfolds in real time. In contrast to a painting of a master painter, the recorded jazz solo gives a better sense of the unfolding in time of the solo's production. The same goes for a transcribed solo, which consists of a succession of notes that typically follow each other on a stave and thus give a better figurative sense of the solo's unfolding. This, in turn, allows educators to "conjure" the soloist's intentionality much more convincingly by staging its hesitations, considerations, failures, and victories. The nature of the jazz solo thus provides unique possibilities for knowledge production and meaning-making (Knorr Cetina 2003).

More specifically, the jazz solo's unfolding in time allows educators to produce narrative emplotment—the creation of a narrative governed by a salient plot in which the soloist is a character. Narratives imbue events with a temporal and causal orderliness (Ochs 2006). A plot gives meaning to a narrative by providing it with a direction or an explanatory scheme (Ochs and Capps 1996, 26). By producing this narrative emplotment, educators are able to naturalize their suggestion that the masters' intentionality was mediated by chord-scale theory. For example, consider the way Dan analyzes a segment of a transcribed solo by trumpet player Clifford Brown on the tune "Pent-Up House" from the 1956 album *Sonny Rollins Plus 4*:

> The last eight bars or so—you know, this solo, as far as, like, the melodic accuracy, has been very meticulous. There's not, there hasn't been like a wrong note played in here. Check out this one here when I play the recording again. Here's a place where he plays E natural on the downbeat of C

minor 7.[9] I wouldn't look at this as a mistake from him. You got to take a
look at where he's coming from and where he's going to within a melodic
phrase. . . . He knows what he's done there. Because take a look at the next
note that he plays. *You know, it's almost—he realizes, you know: oops, here's
the, you know, major third on a minor chord, here's the right one* [i.e., E-flat, the
"correct" chord tone] *happening, you know, immediately after it. You know, so
here's a player, you know, completing a phrase and responding to something that
overlapped into the next chord change and correcting himself—here's the correct
third to play, and then off of that.*

Narratives are organized around available themes, schemes, or plots. Dan solidifies his mediation of the soloist's intentionality with the school's expert
knowledge by the use of a plot that is governed by what might be called the
theme of Overcoming Difficulties on the Spur of the Moment. According to
Dan, having played perfectly according to the chord changes, Clifford Brown
ends a phrase that overlaps with the next chord in a way that creates an error.
However, Brown immediately acknowledges this error and corrects himself.
Dan's ability to stage Brown's intentionality as unfolding in real time enlivens
it and makes it real. Consequently, it gives further credibility to the subtext of
Dan's analysis, that Brown indeed thought in terms of academic jazz educa-
tion's specific body of expert knowledge.

The Notion of the Immaculate Solo

Many of the educators I worked with come to the classroom with a powerful
assumption that the masters' solos cannot represent any mistake in terms of
chord-scale theory and that every aspect of a master's solo can be justified in
theoretical terms. When there is some theoretical difficulty in explaining a
particular solo, educators understand it not as the result of the soloist's shortcoming but as the result of the analyzers' own failure to perceive the theoretical justification always already present. The suspense created in such moments of theoretical difficulty and the subsequent resolution and relief that
come when the "correct" conceptual solution is identified further strengthen
the taken-for-granted status of both chord-scale theory and the past masters'
unparalleled creativity: on the one hand, such a theoretical resolution further
solidifies the masters' creativity and genius; on the other hand, when this creativity is understood to have been mediated by this expert knowledge, this
knowledge becomes further authorized and legitimized.

To achieve this desired effect, educators would frequently highlight a theoretical difficulty in a master's solo only to solve it a few minutes later. For example, in one of David's comments on a transcribed solo, he makes the assumption that a soloist was "going somewhere" even as he produced seemingly ill-fitting notes:

> The next phrase, G major 7th, the first few notes look like they shouldn't fit; he is playing a C natural and then an E-flat back to a C natural on a G major chord. Take a look to where the phrase is moving to, and then it would make a little more sense. You can see that all of this stuff here, first of all, is leading to that note at the end, the B natural, the guide tone of G major. So all this stuff in between has this destination.

This strategy invokes even more powerfully the framework of religious exegesis that I alluded to before. It is similar in its details and broader reverential orientation to a technique that emerged in medieval Jewish exegesis toward the end of the fifteenth century that one scholar termed "The Method of Doubts." This technique consisted of "beginning the discussion of a textual unit by raising a series of 'doubts' [. . .], 'questions' [. . .], or 'difficulties' [. . .], which are resolved in the ensuing exegetical treatment" (Saperstein 2003:133). One exegete who practiced this technique explained that "in raising doubts about a matter, it is not my intent to allow the doubt to remain in the mind of the listener, heaven forbid, but rather that the matter become fully explicated" (136). The purpose of raising doubts in the beginning of the discussion is not to put the religious text in doubt, but rather to dispel any potential doubt that might be associated with it by way of isolating and then knocking it down. Underlying this technique is an understanding of the religious text as truth-bearing and devoid of any mistakes and errors.

Some interactions between educators and students explicitly reveal the purpose of raising doubts about the jazz solos and then dissolving them. In the following case, Chris, a Berklee educator, points to a theoretical problem in a segment of one of saxophonist Michael Brecker's solos:

> [Chris:] Is that wrong? Did he play wrong notes?
> [Students laugh.]
> [First Student:] Highly unlikely.
> [Second Student, ironically:] He must have screwed up.
> [Chris:] What?

> [Second Student:] He must have screwed up.
> [Chris, laughing:] He must have screwed up!
> [Third Student:] He probably just wanted us to analyze it!
> [Everyone laughs.]

The suggestion that Brecker played wrong notes results in bursts of laughter because of the sheer absurdity of the suggestion. One student jokingly suggests that Brecker "screwed up," resulting in more laughter; this time, Chris laughs too. The third student's remark is the most indicative because in its hyperbolic character it points to the prevalent and powerful association between the legendary players and the expert knowledge imparted by the school—an association that is the end result of the processes I analyze here: Brecker must have "deliberately complicated" his solo so that students would have to think harder to find the theoretical justification behind his musical moves. Brecker's mastery of the school's expert knowledge is never in doubt.[10] Rather, implicitly, he and the other masters become agents who intend to disseminate it.

Later in this exchange Chris resolved the theoretical problem by determining that the "wrong" notes were actually part of Brecker's deliberate move and should be accounted for by the concept of "harmonic anticipation." He argued that Brecker had simply ignored the chord in the measure that is the focus of conversation and played according to the chord in the following measure, thus anticipating it. The suspense generated by this theoretical difficulty was resolved in the form of a concept that was waiting to be discovered by a discerning mind. Beyond their similarity to an exegetical technique, then, educators' strategies of making sense of unexpected discrepancies in jazz masters' improvisations point to one of the main functions of narratives, namely, to "offer a framework for handling unanticipated situations" (Ochs 2006, 278). Indeed, as the last vignette suggests, the role played by narratives in rendering experience coherent and logical frequently "overwhelms the desire for authenticity" that is more tolerant of ambiguity of meaning and lack of coherence (ibid.).

Educators' strategies of interpretation strengthen the link between the school's expert knowledge and the legendary past masters. By frequently demonstrating the solos' theoretical perfection, educators deify and further validate the past masters. Consequently, this deification increases the masters' role as authorizing agents for the school's institutionalized terminology when it is demonstrated time and again in class that the masters "had thought" all along in terms of this terminology in the course of their playing.

Cumulative Effects

The process I have described, when repeatedly enacted in class, has cumulative effects. To appreciate this effect, consider the following incident. It was the beginning of a class at Berklee that focused on chord-scale theory. Rick, the educator, made a list of eight different improvisational concepts, explaining each with reference to the topic of chord scales: chord tones improvisation, guide tones, upper structures, approach notes, avoid notes, chromatic approach, indirect approach, and extended chromatics to a target note. After explaining these concepts, Rick commented: "So here is a list of eight things—you know, of all of the possibilities that you could have to play on a particular harmonic form or set of changes. . . . You can use it as a means of analyzing solos of your favorite players. Looking at their soloing—considering these eight things—do they incorporate them?" This question—"do they incorporate them?"—was the beginning of the subtle and gradual process of constructing the intentionality of the past master along the four dimensions I outlined above. At the end of this class, an hour later, after the analysis of the transcribed solo had been completed, Rick concluded with these words: "OK, so here's a really nice solo for you that you can see that even though it is only one chorus in length, [the player] is drawing from just about everything that I talked about during the first hour." The master thus appears to have naturally drawn from the institutional terminology of the jazz program. Consequently, he authorizes it. When these masters are saxophonist Charlie Parker or trumpet player Clifford Brown, the implications of such symmetry for the academic jazz program's institutional authority are noteworthy. Against the backdrop of criticism against chord-scale theory in particular and the academic jazz program as a site that is devoid of creativity in general, this strategy authorizes chord-scale theory and at the same time reconciles creative agency and rule-governed, institutionalized rationality.

However, like the strategies of reconciliation I analyzed in previous chapters, educators' interpretative strategies have a flip side. Anthropologists who have studied institutional practices of inscription and recontextualization of discursive events have noted that in such instances "speaking subjects are positioned in ways that privilege not their own goals as producers of the original discourse but the goals of the institution that has taken up—or taken over—their words" (Park and Bucholtz 2009, 492). This insight also applies to the production and analysis of jazz transcriptions in the educational sites I attended.

No Race in This Place: The Politics of Decontextualization
and Recontextualization

There are a number of political dimensions to the production and analysis of
transcriptions of the recorded improvisations of the past jazz masters in class.
To begin, educators seem to reduce the creative variety that characterized the
past masters' musical output into the standardized expert terminology of the
academic jazz program. Different past jazz players came up with their own
heterogeneous and idiosyncratic theoretical systems that were often informed
by various non-Western (such as Pan-African) philosophies and frameworks
(see Gluck 2012; Lewis 2009). As Ingrid Monson puts it, "To become one's
own theorist—to have one's own concept that in turn leads to the expression
of one's own voice—was among the highest aesthetic ideals of the art form.
To become an improviser at this high level was to become aesthetically self-
determining in a world in which other forms of self-determination or agency
were more easily frustrated" (Monson 2007, 286). Past jazz musicians did not
think in precisely the same terms that the academic jazz program advances,
nor did all of them think in the same way as one another. The standardization
of this creative heterogeneity is ironic given the fact that such heterogeneity is
the creative bedrock into which educators hope to tap so they can infuse the
classroom with the past masters' charismatic creativity.

Additionally, given the fact that educators' strategies reduce the heterogeneity of the past masters' creativity, which was often embedded in social concerns that emanated from the racial politics of mid-twentieth-century United
States, and given that these strategies are deployed today in some academic
contexts by a majority of white educators, they have significant political implications. These implications are compounded by the fact that at the time of
my fieldwork at Berklee and the New School the racial politics that was part
and parcel of the history of the music almost never surfaced in class in any
explicit manner.

At the time of my fieldwork, there was one course at Berklee that could
have been potentially relevant to the broader social context of jazz in that
its focus was the history of jazz. However, Gerry, the educator teaching this
course—a white man in his early sixties, made an effort to avoid discussing
this context. The course provided a survey of the main instrumentalists of the
genre. Each week revolved around the careers of the great performers of jazz in
a particular instrument or voice: trumpet, tenor saxophone, alto saxophone,
female singers, male singers, and so forth. Gerry provided a short background

on the performers, such as dates of birth and death, short performance bios that included such details as who they played with, and reasons for their decline. He presented very little material on the broader social context of the music, eliding this context and its complications. The New School's jazz program was similar in this regard; the course on the history of jazz offered there at the time of my fieldwork was, like Berklee's, devoid of the music's political context.

Berklee in particular has been notorious for the lack of political content in its courses. For many years, a group of mostly African American Berklee educators has demanded courses that address the relation between the musical styles taught at Berklee and the African diaspora. Only in the past few years has the school's administration responded to this demand, especially following the election of the school's new president, Roger Brown. In 2006—almost sixty years after its founding—Berklee introduced Africana studies to its curriculum. Yet at the time of my fieldwork these new courses were not mandatory and were poorly attended by students who major in jazz. At the New School, no such courses were offered at the time of my fieldwork as part of the jazz program itself; students could choose to enroll into courses that address these issues in the general education program offered in other departments.

A number of white Berklee educators I spoke to provided me with a consistent justification for this elision, rooted in the assumption, common in Western modernity, that high art transcends the contingencies of life and can only find expression in the virtuosity of the stable, fixed, decontextualized, and transcendental text (Bauman and Briggs 2004; Gioia 1988b; Levine 1988). They argued that the "timelessness" of high art resides in its detachment from the contexts in which it was created. This modernistic discourse of universal high art implies indifference to factors such as time, place, and ethnicity, which connote the dreaded specter of "folk music." Given the history of jazz's upward mobility in the American cultural hierarchy, many educators are hesitant to present jazz in any way that might connote the notion of folk music. The wide circulation of this ideology is evident in the commentary provided by Gerry, the Berklee educator whose course focused on the history of jazz:

> It's not a sociology course in my mind, though I do relate to it on occasion. I try to make the course focused on the music. I mean in a sense, what does it matter that Mozart was a heavy drinker and a womanizer and killed himself by the time he was thirty-seven? What does that matter? It doesn't matter at

all. What matters is what he wrote. . . . Do we think of opera as Italian music because it was invented by Italians? I don't think so. Do we think of ballet as French dance because it was invented by the French culture? No, we think of it as an art form. And the very fact that it is an art form means that it's adaptable, that it's expressive by any culture. If it wasn't, then it wouldn't be high art. It would be folk art.

Note that Gerry emphasizes that it's all about the "music." He argues that the value of jazz, much like the value of classical music, depends on its autonomy from 'superficialities' and 'contingencies' such as character traits and ethnicity. Otherwise the music would become "folk art."[11]

However, the racial composition of the current body of jazz educators and students at Berklee might also explain their reluctance to introduce the social context of jazz into the curriculum. Jazz's entrance into academia has taken place in tandem with the increased representation of white middle- and upper-middle-class players in the jazz world. Against the backdrop of contentious American racial politics, white educators may be reluctant to introduce the history of exclusion, segregation, and bigotry that have been an integral part of jazz's own history. Consider the following argument made by Ken, a white Berklee educator in his early sixties:

I was attracted to this music because in many ways it was color-blind. It didn't matter if you were black or white—it didn't matter. It was the music that mattered. Miles Davis, I loved it when he said: "I don't care if a man has green skin and red breath as long as he can play" [laughs]. And that's always been one of the things that I loved about jazz. I mean, you know, Cannonball Adderley's band with a Jewish British piano player—Victor Feldman; and Miles's band with Bill Evans; and Bird's band with Red Rodney. And that was one of the things that were great about jazz. Not exclusivity, but inclusivity, the fact that it was inclusive of anybody if you could play. That was the only thing you needed to get in the door.

Ken argues that initiating a focus on the African American community in a survey of the history of jazz would be wrong. Jazz, he suggests, has always been about musical virtuosity. It was color-blind and nondiscriminatory.

However, scholars have convincingly argued that the rhetoric of jazz's color-blindness has often functioned to mask the social inequalities that African American jazz musicians had to cope with (Panish 1997). Note that all of the examples Ken provides to elaborate jazz's presumed color-blindness refer to instances in which African American bandleaders integrated white musicians into their bands. The reverse scenario of white bandleaders integrating African American musicians was rarer. Although Ken is right to note that Miles Davis often argued that he treated his musicians solely on the basis of their musical abilities, he forgets to mention that Davis was also an active social commentator on racial inequality in American society. According to Davis's own statements, some of his most pivotal life moments involved his being the subject of racial violence (Davis 1990, 228–230).

The contradictions and ambivalences that find expression in educators' and administrators' resistance to introducing courses on jazz's social context into the jazz program's curriculum resurface in everyday classroom reality, especially with respect to jazz pieces that were created as a direct response to American racial politics. For example, in an ensemble class I attended a few times at Berklee, the ensemble played Charles Mingus's tune, "Fables of Faubus." Mingus was one of several jazz musicians whose music explicitly functioned as social commentary and as a tool in political activism (Porter 2002). This piece was written as a response to the Arkansas governor Orval Faubus's 1957 objection to desegregation of public schools in Little Rock. Undermining a Supreme Court decision, Faubus ordered the Arkansas National Guard to prevent African American children from attending Little Rock Central High School. Mingus composed lyrics that ridiculed Faubus and other public figures. Notably, Columbia Records refused to record the piece with the lyrics; consequently, Mingus recorded the piece with lyrics for another recording company.

In class, after playing this piece, the ensemble moved on to play another of Mingus's pieces, "Remember Rockefeller at Attica." This piece, like "Fables of Faubus," emerged out of a specific historical moment: Mingus wrote it in response to the riots at Attica Prison in 1971, in which thirty-nine people died when the New York State Police took control of the prison by order of the New York governor, Nelson Rockefeller. John, a white educator in his late forties, distributed the lead sheet of the tune and then explained the piece's form and different sections. Upon arriving at the bridge section John commented that it resembled one of the main rhythmic themes in "Fables of Faubus," the piece that they had just played: "And now this is the bridge. The bridge is in two. And that's 'Fables!'—we just played it, so it's [sings], OK? So that's 'Fables' again. Because this is 'Remember Rockefeller at Attica,' so it's kind of like the same kind of political, eh, political [hesitates for seven seconds] shenanigans, going on: Rockefeller, Attica, prison riots, blah-blah-blah, OK?" John is dismissive toward the music's social commentary, perhaps because he subscribes to the modernist ideology of aesthetic value as something that is abstracted from the presumed "contingencies" of time and place—the "shenanigans." Educators are thus often caught up in the tension between the irreducible history of jazz and their desire to "cultivate" jazz in the model of a universal and autonomous high art. This ideology might also comfortably align with their preference to avoid discussing certain racially informed historical contexts, given that many of them are white.

The institutional practices of transcribing and recontextualizing the past jazz masters' musical output are thus pervaded by a powerful impulse to abstract this output from its contextual elements and past complicated history. This institutional orientation has aesthetic and political implications. We should thus pay close attention when an educator, in the middle of a class that focuses on the production and analysis of jazz transcriptions, states matter-of-factly that "something else is happening here in his [i.e., the soloist's] melodic thought," or when he declares at the end of the class, "Now you have an idea of what's in his head." As anthropologists have noted with reference to other cultural contexts, "to know others' minds" can be a matter of impinging "on each other's self-determination" and is thus political through and through (Stasch 2008, 443; see also Keane 2008, 474). Educators do not really read the thoughts or minds of the past masters. "Reading the mind of a genius," as the Berklee educator I quoted in the beginning of this chapter put it, is actually writing something different in its stead. It is a creative act of transcribing that only appears to be a straightforward act of transcribing creativity. It is another manifestation of the myriad ways in which the academic jazz program functions as a site where institutionalized rationality and creative agency coconstitute one another, and where the boundaries between them are blurred and reinstituted at the same time and on different levels.

"NOW YOU HAVE TO THINK SIMPLE!"

Improvisatory Techniques of the Improvising Body

Fingers that Move by Themselves

One late afternoon I found myself sitting with two students in a Starbucks coffee shop on Massachusetts Avenue, just across the street from Berklee. It was a cold November day. The coffee shop was bustling with students trying to get a hot drink before heading home after the school day. As we were waiting for a third student to arrive at the table, I noticed that Dan, a piano player, was moving the fingers of his right hand on the table as if he were playing the piano. This was not unusual. Whenever I spent time with students I would frequently see them moving their fingers and hands as if they were playing, although they did not have their instruments. For some of them, this was part of a conscious effort to hone their craft whenever they had the time to do so. Other students did this unconsciously. They were so immersed in the routine of practicing and playing that their fingers frequently took on a life of their own. In this particular moment at Starbucks, I asked Dan, "Hey, what are you playing there?" As if extracted from a dream, Dan looked at me with surprise. "I don't know, let me think," he laughed. He pondered. "Ah, you know," he said, and then sang a

163

common improvisation pattern of four notes that correspond to the first, second, third, and fifth degree of a major scale (1 2 3 5). Each time he finished singing one cycle of the pattern, he began to sing the same pattern again but a half tone higher. Upon hearing this, Jeremy, the second student who was sitting with us at the table, exclaimed: "Oh, man! Not that stuff again!" He then started to sing this pattern in a mocking voice, drawing laughter from both Dan and myself.

During my fieldwork at Berklee, I observed many pedagogical interactions that reminded me of this incident. It became clear to me that the playing body—especially the fingers that often functioned as a synecdoche for the body—was a site in which some of the most trenchant fears about the repercussions of the academization of jazz training found expression. Dan's quasi-automatic finger movement—the patterns articulated by his fingers—and Jeremy's response invoked those repercussions and fears. Not only were Dan's fingers moving automatically, as it were, but they also articulated one of the most cliché patterns of improvisation, one that students and educators hear ad nauseam. It is a pattern disseminated in countless jazz pedagogy method books and classes. Jeremy's reaction was indicative of many educators' and students' discomfort vis-à-vis the growing ubiquity of standardized patterns of improvisation that become incorporated in students' playing bodies. The body plays a peculiar role in this discontent over the reality of cultural standardization, as well as in the strategies educators deploy to negotiate this standardization and thus reconcile creative agency and rule-governed behavior. To unravel this role, we must begin with the bodily infrastructure of masterful jazz improvisation.

"Building muscle memory": Crafting the Normative Body

The body is implicated in numerous functions in the production of jazz and music in general. Musicians carry their instruments and interact with them through bodily manipulation that produces sound. In the case of singers, of course, the body itself is the sole instrument. Subtle relations between muscles and organs, processes such as breathing, leg posture, mental concentration, and so forth, are involved in playing. Within the jazz school, these considerations might take center stage in private instrumental courses that do not specifically concern jazz, or they might appear momentarily in improvisation classes. However, because improvisation classes are typically comprised of students who play different instruments, instrument-specific focus is not common. Rather, most of the jazz educators I worked with are more likely to discuss a limited number of aspects of bodily mastery that play an important role in the production of jazz. One of the most important of these aspects is the mastery of the "vocabulary of jazz."

Jazz improvisation is not a creation ex nihilo. Rather, as is common in many forms of improvisatory performance, the performer relies on a common stock of building blocks that she can draw from in the course of performance (Finnegan 1988; Lord 1960; Sawyer 1996). These building blocks have become conventionalized within the tradition of jazz performance and appreciation. In classes, clinics, method books, and informal conversations with students, many jazz educators often stress the importance of transcribing the recorded solos of jazz masters and then practicing them in their entirety or in selected licks and phrases in every key until the solo, or its parts, are incorporated in one's body (Berliner 1994, 97). For example, Chris, a Berklee educator of an advanced improvisation class, instructed his students to "look for turnaround vocabulary,[1] especially in the last two bars of the blues—the way he [the soloist] uses chord tones, chord scales, chromatic approach, bop scales, and symmetrical diminished [scales]. These are some of the things to look for. And what you want to do is pick them up, one that appeals to you, and practice it in every key."

When educators speak of mastery of the jazz idiom, they often index the body as the locus of such mastery by employing specific tropes. For example, after one student had transcribed, memorized, and then performed jazz legend Freddie Hubbard's trumpet solo from the tune "Birdlike," the educator exclaimed: "Yeah! Every key now, right? Just keep playing that solo for six months, all these things, just get it right in *your blood*. That's the way the week should start." The fingers frequently function as a synecdoche for the trained body because of their visibility in musical performance on most instruments. As one guest clinician told the students in a workshop, the purpose of practicing the masters' solos is to have each of their building blocks incorporated "in your fingers [so that] in the moment of truth you can manipulate it without difficulty." "The moment of truth" is the real time of jazz improvisation in which, ideally, one's fingers take charge because they have been trained in the vocabulary of jazz. Similarly, another clinician urged students to "learn as many tunes as you can—it prepares you for different situations with your fingers. [. . .] Learn it by heart as soon as you can—take it off the paper. That

way you will internalize it better—you will own it. Your fingers will own it."
Standard tunes are considered to be prototypical of the idiom of jazz with its
distinct melodic, rhythmic, and harmonic conventions. Their incorporation
in one's playing body prepares the improviser to function in "different situations" that emerge in group improvisation. The trope of the fingers is evident
below in another educator's comments on the importance of practice:

> There are a lot of notes in this class, and the way I look at this class, it's very
> comprehensive. You write it down and then summer comes along and you
> ask: "what am I going to practice?" You take one thing, like this [phrase that
> is written on the board], and you just, like that—I'm gonna pull that out, I'm
> gonna focus on that for like a few months. It takes about twenty-one days
> for a habit to happen. So you're gonna start and then after twenty-one days
> your finger muscle memory will start to take place. For it to become where
> you are like unconscious and if I woke you up [at] five in the morning and
> said, "Wow, play some shit!" [Students laugh.] That takes about six to nine
> months where you can even not think about it and do it in your sleep, you
> know—finger patterns and muscle memory.

These words suggest that "learned ignorance" (Bourdieu 1977, 19) is a crucial ideological trope in this conception of embodied practical mastery. One
should have the idiom of jazz ingrained in one's "fingers" and "muscle memory" so that he or she can improvise "automatically." The notions of "uncon-
sciousness," "sleep," and lack of "thought" that recur in this educator's words
connote the absence of deliberative agency, on the one hand, and the presence of "the body that plays," on the other hand. The player relegates his or her
agency to the body, which now acts as the sovereign agent. This meaning is
nicely figurated (Fernandez 1986) in the term *muscle memory*, which couples
the muscle—the concrete and material tissue that contracts and expands—
with the abstract and subjective quality of memory. In this account, it is the
body that remembers, not the deliberative human subject.[2] This perfection of
action, such that it bypasses the deliberative agent, is possible only through a
deliberate, meticulous, and long process of conditioning the body to "remember" so that the player can "forget."[3]

Significantly, it is precisely the incorporation of the vocabulary of jazz,
that is, the ingraining in the body of the aspect of jazz improvisation that is
most specific to this genre, which makes learned ignorance and incorporated
playing habits problematic for the educators I worked with and that provokes

their most common form of discontent about the effects of academic jazz training.

"We all tend to be button pushers": The Melancholic Normative Body

I was sitting among twenty students in an advanced-level improvisation class at Berklee. Louis, the educator, had just finished demonstrating on the piano a number of ways of generating rhythmic variety in one's solo. He paused for a moment and then said:

> Improvising in half notes is harder.[4] Try playing a line in half notes on this tune. I promise you, it will make you feel like—"I want my mommy." It will make you crawl up with tears. I promise you, half notes will kick your ass. That's because your ears have so much time to think notes, to choose notes, to select them, that often they can't make a decision: "Where do I go from here?" You have so much time to shape the melody. And when you transcribe [your solo] or listen back to the melody [of your solo], when you play in half notes, they sound so fucked up, sounds like you can't play them. Yet you can [. . .] play a pretty decent eighth-note line. Now what does that tell you about your ears? What your ears really control? Not much! Not those eighth notes! I mean, if they can't shape the half notes or the quarter notes, how the hell is it doing eighth notes? The answer is it ain't doing the eighth notes! Your mind and your fingers are playing the eighth notes. So if you really want to find out what your ears—the degree that it's in control and stirring the shit here, try playing a half-note solo or a quarter-note solo. That would be great.

Louis's words puzzled me. Why would it be a bad thing to have one's fingers "stir the shit"? After all, is not training the body and cultivating "muscle memory" and "finger patterns" one of the most important aspects of jazz training? My confusion only grew as I began noticing further commentary that reflected similar discontent. For example, during one workshop, a guest clinician scolded the students who had just finished playing, saying, "They are not thinking of things to play. They are just hoping that their fingers will bring them to a nice place." In an interview with Henry, a Berklee educator, he told me in a resigned tone that "I find that we all tend to be button pushers, you know. . . . You learn patterns that work and then you do those patterns. I know that actually all instruments do this." That which at one point is considered to be an example of perfected bodily conditioning becomes at another point an example of mere "button pushing" and "pattern playing," that is, actions that invoke the mechanical valves of an engine.

Consider the following statements made by Fred, one of the Berklee educators whose words I quoted above, in two consecutive classes:

> I don't want to turn into a factory so when we go out and play—"Oh, OK, yeah, he studied with, and he studied with, and he studied with," and it all sounds like the same automobile, you know. No, I don't want to turn into a factory. It shouldn't be that way. [...] So don't just come in trying to play stuff on chords. You know—here's the next diminished lick. I don't care! Who cares? Everybody else is going to learn it anyway. That's gonna go around the school like a virus anyway, so everybody's going to play the same shit anyway. I don't care, and the CDs don't care, because I'll listen to it once and then put it on the shelf and it will sit there for the next fifty years. It doesn't matter.

These words reveal the recurring concerns of many of the educators I worked with about the increased standardization of students' playing at Berklee, here articulated in terms of bodily playing habits. The fingers become iconic of problematic mechanization because many students educated at Berklee with the same methods play the same patterns and licks. In this framework the fingers, which represent the body as a whole, are negatively viewed as the locus of mechanical action guilty of standardization. The trope of mechanization plays a prominent role in educators' descriptions of these processes because of their concern about what might be called "The Jazz Musician in the Age of His Mechanical Reproduction," drawing on Walter Benjamin's famous essay, "The Work of Art in the Age of Mechanical Reproduction" (Benjamin 1969b). The fingers turn out to be an object of concern not because they are conditioned to play "automatically." Indeed, as I indicated above, this is a condition of possibility for jazz improvisation itself. The jazz educators I worked with stress time and again bodily perfected action as a goal of practice. They are not shy about invoking the trope of the machine to emphasize this point, as when one educator instructed his students to "program your fingers—practice slowly," thus treating the fingers as a kind of computer software. Rather, educators are concerned about the implications of such automated playing when duplicated by masses of students who rely solely on these bodily playing habits rather than on editorial considerations during their improvisations.

Fred targets students' habit of relying on the same standardized phrases and patterns—licks—in their improvisations. His reference to the "diminished lick" is not accidental. It invokes patterns that work over what is known as diminished scales and chords. Students frequently use these patterns because they can play them on many chords, especially on the dominant chords ubiquitous in jazz harmonic progressions. Learning these patterns allows students to improvise "correctly" in different playing situations. At the same time, however, students sound the same as one another.[5] Fred uses the trope of the "virus" not so much to express his negative view of the musical value of the lick; as many educators stress, these patterns are the very alphabet of the "language of jazz." Rather, the term *virus* conveys the reservations of the educators I worked with about the mode and conditions of jazz training and transmission in the present: the sheer number of students educated in the same manner is conducive to "contagious" standardization.[6] Berklee is a case in point. Among the roughly four thousand students who are enrolled in it each year, hundreds focus on jazz training as a major, while many others engage with jazz to a lesser extent. The school has played a key role in the standardization of jazz training by training thousands of players in the more than six decades of its existence, developing a curriculum that has been imitated by other jazz programs across the United States and the world, initiating exchange programs with international jazz programs, and producing and disseminating a large number of printed materials in which various aspects of jazz training are codified. To its educators, the fact that a number of Berklee's graduates went on to develop distinctive voices and successful careers is an exception to the rule. This rule entails the production of masses of players who lack a distinctive voice.

On a more general level, educators' ambivalence resonates with a cultural anxiety about mass production and mechanical reproduction, processes that have served as icons of both perfection and soullessness in US history (Batchelor 1995; Hounshell 1985). Indeed, the educators I worked with frequently reverted to culturally specific tropes of mechanization and mass production in order to articulate these concerns. Thus, in Fred's commentary, the school becomes "a car factory"—a key metaphor for standardization in American culture, invoking Fordism. Other educators at Berklee expressed fears that reverberate with the theme of the factory and mass production, referring to the school as "Chords 'R' Us" and "the Chord Factory," and thus pointing up the school's role in encouraging and perpetuating the inculcation of codified musical knowledge held to be conducive to standardized playing.

"Find your voice," "and then you will work": The Hybridity of Romantic Sensibilities and the Marketplace

To some extent, educators' ambivalence toward students' bodily playing habits is anchored in the opposition between the two narratives about modernity: as institutionalized rationality and as creative expressivity. Jazz musicians understand jazz improvisation as a cultural practice that is not concerned merely with the efficient bodily execution of conventional music vocabulary. As in other musical practices (Bryant 2005), the cultural order of jazz associates a specific kind of personhood with the mature and proficient improviser (Duranti and Burrell 2004). Specifically, the jazz educators I worked with frame jazz improvisation in terms that resonate with Romantic notions of the creative self. This conception of the creative self circulates widely in school promotional materials. The New School Admissions Information brochure distributed to prospective students declares the following: "Find your voice. Create your destiny in jazz." Similarly, the cover of a Berklee brochure distributed to prospective students reads: "Let us discover *you*" (emphasis in the original). These two slogans emphasize, first, the *discovery* of something that pre-exists such discovery and, second, the notion of something *personal* and *unique* that pertains to the prospective student and that is the subject of discovery ("your voice" and "you"). They mobilize Romantic notions that continue to influence Western ideas about art, creativity, and the individual (Taylor 1989; Taylor 1992; Wittkower 1973). These ideas highlight the importance of the imagination, emotions, and each individual's "personal nature" as a source for action, truth, and a way of life. As Charles Taylor argues, "This notion of an inner *voice* or impulse, the idea that we *find* the truth within us, and in particular in our *feelings*—these were the crucial justifying concepts of the Romantic rebellion in its various forms" (Taylor 1989, 368–369; emphasis added).

Initially, these Romantic ideals articulated the radical difference between human life and other life forms. However, they soon shifted focus to the differences between individuals, in that each person has his or her own unique nature that ought to prescribe how he or she should live his or her life. Romanticism stressed that one's inner voice and impulses are themselves one's only way of accessing one's nature; expressing them is the sole means of attaining self-understanding (Wilf 2011). Explicit in these ideas was a demand to be "in touch" with one's inner voice and a warning against surrendering to external pressures and conforming to outside models of being. It entailed the rejection of outside structures and prearranged models for action that could sever one's contact with one's inner voice.

The resonance of jazz with Romantic ideals of self-realization was clearly evident in the speech given by Berklee's president in the convocation ceremony, discussed in chapter 2, in which he encourages the students to avoid imitating other people and rather "to come back to who you are, what you were put on earth to do, what you were meant to do as a musician, as a human being." The notions of the existence of a unique voice, personality, and talent; of the danger of imitation that is bound to corrupt this voice; and of an almost moral and ethical responsibility to be true to one's voice, are interrelated and resonate with Romantic notions of creativity through and through, not only in the president's speech but also in messages with which students are bombarded during the course of their studies. To some extent, then, educators' ambivalence toward standardized patterns of improvisation is anchored in these Romantic values.

However, I suggest that the resistance to standardized playing among the jazz educators I worked with is driven not solely by the search for Romantic authenticity but also by Romantic notions of self-realization and autonomy that have been *conflated* with an orientation to success in the marketplace. This orientation is based in the understanding that given the dwindling demand for jazz and the paucity of performance opportunities, on the one hand, and the exponential increase in the number of trained musicians who graduate from academic jazz programs, on the other hand, standardized playing might decrease students' chances of securing income through playing. Success in this context means not only being a good and creative player, but also having work. These are two sides of the same coin. This orientation to the marketplace is not surprising given the fact that it has structured academic jazz education from the outset.

The conflation of Romantic notions of self-realization and success in the marketplace found a clear expression at the *Jazz Improv* conference I attended in 2007. In one panel significantly titled "Can You Make a Living in Jazz?—Yes!," the well-known saxophonist Dave Liebman, who also teaches at the Manhattan School of Music, offered the following advice:

And once you realize—you look in the mirror, it's a very objective thing, you put the tape on of what you played last night and you listen to yourself objectively. This is not good and bad, this is not I feel good and bad, you should be over that by now. And when you listen, you see what you do that is you. Now this is not something you can do in ten seconds. But when you start looking into yourself, realize who you are through other people, through influences, through influences that you absorbed and transformed, and perhaps not transformed, and you start to cut away the extra fat to get to the real heart of the meat, you start to see, slowly—it takes time—you start to see what it is that you do well. If you develop what you do well—you will work. . . . My point is that if you do something very well, if you are in the top three or five, if you're one of the great ones in that particular thing, and [this thing] can be as specialized . . . If you're the first, second, third, fourth—you know, it's a hard cold fact; if you're among the top in that particular thing in that area of the world, if you're that—you start to work.

Realizing "who you are" by cutting away "the extra fat to get to the real heart of the meat" is advice that resonates with Romantic notions of the self, which emphasize self-realization through the elimination of superfluous social layers and the discovery of one's "voice"—itself a key aesthetic principle in the cultural order of jazz (Monson 2007, 286). However, these notions are reconfigured here in that being in touch with what makes one unique becomes a means of gaining a competitive edge in the marketplace. Uniqueness is achieved by perfecting what one does well and outdoing other players in that specialization.

Another way in which the conflation of Romantic sensibilities and the marketplace finds expression within the academic jazz program is in the emphasis made by many educators on stylistic or qualitative difference rather than superiority in a specific musical dimension. This emphasis was evident when I attended a clinic at Berklee given by a well-known saxophonist in his midforties. During the clinic, this musician said:

I typically record myself when I practice, and I'll listen to these shards, these snippets, these germs of ideas. . . . *We are obligated to be as honest with ourselves as possible.* There are areas that require daily maintenance. There are areas that require specific attention not because there's necessarily a problem, but because there are points that possibly could be polished and honed, and these could become the cornerstone of your concept, of your approach. It could be your *hook*, so to speak. [. . .] So they become our signature. There are some players who have a very unusual vibrato, or tone—tonal color, or tonal *abnormality*, so to speak. This could be something that can be used to our advantage. [. . .] I'm really trying to encourage people to take note of personal differences, your *personal defects*, your personal characterizations that will set you off because [...] there are legions of great players out there in the world on a global level. And given that everybody has access to the same information, we have to raise the bar here and give ourselves the edge. [...] There are great players all over the world having a lot of chops and technique and facility. [...] So right now we have to look into what's gonna be our hook. And everyone has a hook, everyone has a hook. And if you'll give yourselves the time and the patience and discipline and honesty to evaluate what you have, we can extract that and we can make that something worthy of note. [...] And this is the thread of our discussion— identifiable characteristics in our music that will set us off. You know, in a police lineup of saxophone players, I mean, blindfolded, can you tell one guy from the next, sonically?

This musician's emphasis on "personal defects," or some form of technical deficiency that results in identifiable musical output, signifies a different orientation to the creative voice: the pressure on product differentiation equals in importance the specific quality of such differentiation. In this example, it is not instrumental excellence that matters, as in Liebman's comments, but rather musical peculiarity, a quality determined by difference from other musicians' playing.[7] However, like Liebman, this musician frames this project of understanding "what you are" as a moral obligation, an almost ethical imperative to cultivate the self whose ultimate goal is gaining a competitive edge in the marketplace against the backdrop of the "legion of players" who have access today to "the same information." As Sam, another well-known clinician at Berklee, put it in another context after making the same points, "and then you will work."[8]

I suggest that at stake is a hybridized conception of creative agency that stipulates that in the fiercely competitive jazz world, being "unique" gives a musician the cutting edge that results in gigs. In other words, the jazz program reconciles Romantic sensibilities and the marketplace via a co-translation between the notion of the "unique self" and that of "product differentiation."[9] It is crucial to highlight this conflation of Romantic sensibilities and an orientation to success in the marketplace because it is the basis for a creative orientation that emphasizes not only the quest for personal voice, as previous interpretations of jazz improvisation have put it (Duranti and Burrell 2004), but also the pressure to continuously differentiate and regenerate in case that personal voice becomes identical with the voices of other players. In other words, even if a player thinks she has found her improvising voice, she may have to further differentiate herself from other players when the specter of standardization emerges.[10]

A Challenge to the Anthropology of Embodied Practical Mastery

The body as the basis for unique creativity and regeneration has been under-theorized in anthropology. Instead, anthropologists have tended to theorize embodied practice as either the unconscious and automatic basis for agency and intentionality or as a normative practice that all group members share. Thus, in his famous essay *Techniques of the Body*, Marcel Mauss elaborated on embodied techniques such as swimming and running, arguing that "every technique properly so-called has its own form" and that "this specificity is characteristic of all techniques" (Mauss 1973, 71). The importance of techniques of the body, according to Mauss, is that they provide us with the "certainty of pre-prepared movements," thus allowing for efficient action in the world (86). Mauss thus instituted the theorization of the body in terms of unconscious and quasi-automatic functioning as epitomized by techniques of the body such as walking that are shared by all group members. Pierre Bourdieu, while introducing processuality and temporality into the discussion of practical mastery, maintained this emphasis. Bourdieu (1977) rejected objectivist explanations of social behavior as a set of discrete rules of action. He proposed the term *strategy* as a more accurate explanatory model for practice. Strategies are sets of embodied dispositions and generative schemas unconsciously acquired in childhood that account for agents' ability to improvise; these improvisations accord with and reproduce agents' positions in the social structure (Lamaison 1986). Thus, Bourdieu presumes practical mastery as overdetermined; his model allows for variation by virtue of rules of combination of a set of normative embodied dispositions rather than by virtue of individual creativity and innovation.

This emphasis has persisted even in recent anthropological studies that have rejected Bourdieu's notion of practical mastery because it ignores the role of awareness and explicit discourse in the learning process in all its stages (Bryant 2005; Hirschkind 2006; Mahmood 2005; Shannon 2003; Starrett 1995). For example, drawing on Talal Asad's contribution to the study of discipline (1993), Saba Mahmood (Mahmood 2005) has argued that anthropologists should return to an Aristotelian notion of habitus, understood as the conscious honing and cultivation of bodily dispositions and practices as a means of inhabiting specific cultural notions of personhood. From her research on the project of disciplined self-cultivation advanced by a women's piety movement in Cairo, Mahmood has suggested that the body becomes the focus of heightened collective and individual awareness and explicit rules not only in the first stages of learning but also through "constant vigilance and monitoring of one's practices" (Mahmood 2005, 139; see also Comaroff and Comaroff 1992, 70). While these studies have successfully problematized Bourdieu's assumption that practical mastery remains outside the sphere of individual awareness, they have also reproduced an analytical focus on forms of practical mastery organized around a normative set of embodied features that ought to be perfected and honed by group members. They have thus neglected culturally specific forms of embodied practice that emphasize open-endedness and unique regeneration for each member of the group.

This anthropological tradition of theorizing the body can neither account for educators' and students' ambivalence toward the bodily manifestations of the academization of jazz, which consist of unconsciously and automatically enacted embodied playing habits shared by all group members; nor can it explain the strategies I describe below, by which educators and students attempt to mitigate these expressions; nor, for that matter, can it explain how these strategies blur the distinction between rule-governed social behavior and creative agency.

To understand why such a limited analytical choice has been institutionalized within the anthropology of embodied practice, note that a number of anthropologists have turned to musical practice to theorize embodied practical mastery in general. However, they have drawn from a very specific tradition of musical practice. Consider the following words, written by the German ethnologist Richard Thurnwald in his book *Banaro Society*, first published in 1916: "The institutions of the social organization dominate the individual to such a degree that his actions become almost automatic and are generally no more considered than is his gait or *the fingers of a good piano player*. The automatization of our thinking and the prearrangement of our personal behavior by formalities saves [sic] energies and facilitates the conscious process in the reciprocal relations" (quoted in Strathern 1996, 12; emphasis added). As Andrew J. Strathern argues, Thurnwald's emphasis on the unproblematic action of the individual's body was shared by many of his contemporary European ethnologists, including Mauss. The invocation of the piano player as an exemplar of embodied practical mastery is important. Ninety years later, and from a perspective that emphasizes the importance of awareness in embodied practical mastery, Saba Mahmood explains her own perspective on embodied practice by bringing "the example of the virtuoso pianist who submits herself to the often painful regime of disciplinary practice, as well as to the hierarchical structure of apprenticeship, in order to acquire the ability—the requisite agency—to play the instrument with mastery" (Mahmood 2005, 29).[11] Now, arguably, both authors have in mind the pianist who is trained in the classical Western music tradition; in this case, mastery is evaluated in terms of the degree to which the pianist is able to execute a given, usually print-mediated piece of music. In other words, this form of embodied practical mastery revolves around a normative axis—a given repertoire and the ability to execute it with perfection according to certain criteria of evaluation.

The case of the jazz musician is radically different. Jazz students do not have a normative axis in the form of a given musical piece that they need to execute. Rather, they need to come up with their own improvisations and musical ideas. To be sure, this requires instrumental technique, and, furthermore, jazz improvisations are frequently framed by sections of notated music that need to be executed. In addition, improvisations are evaluated in terms of their adherence to certain stylistic conventions. In this respect, instrumental technique and stylistic features do, indeed, serve as a type of normative axis similar to the way they do in classical music. Yet, crucially, equally important is the requirement that students develop highly distinct improvisations different from those of other students. This requirement involves more than developing a personal style of embellishment (Bryant 2005). Now, if technical mastery and the mastery of stylistic features are embodied, then the problem of standardization of jazz students' improvisations becomes the problem of embodied playing habits that need to be constantly *reconfigured and disrupted*, not only perfected; this is a radically different cultural notion of embodied practical mastery.

The argument I advance here does not contrast the aesthetic body to the normative body. As the locus of practice that revolves around specific and definable norms that ought to be perfected by group members, the normative body might, and frequently does, have aesthetic dimensions (Hirschkind 2006). The converse is also true—aesthetic bodies might have dominant normative dimensions, as the case of the classical pianist's playing body makes clear. To give another example, bodybuilding in the United States is experienced by its practitioners in aesthetic terms, and yet it is organized around the practice of perfecting the body in accordance with very fixed norms that are definable in fine-grained, detailed, and clear terms (Linder 2007). A more fruitful distinction, then, is between different aesthetic frameworks that might inform embodied practical mastery. The peculiarity of the role played by the body within the academic jazz program results from the fact that this ethnographic context is organized around an aesthetics that requires people to differentiate themselves from one another, a Romantic-modernist aesthetics that is also grounded in the economic logic of "product differentiation." Jazz students may share the same classroom with one another, but in that classroom they are often told they need to reconfigure their embodied practical mastery so as not to sound like their classmates.

"Now you *have* to think simple!" Reconfiguring the Body

Many of the educators I worked with expressed their concern about the implications of "learned ignorance" as taught and practiced at Berklee through an ideology based on the contrast between the ear and the eye as distinct and unequal means of knowledge acquisition, production, and transmission. For example, as he wrote a number of musical examples on a staved whiteboard already cluttered with written notes, Dan, an educator of an advanced course, addressed his students:

> You should try to learn these tunes as much as you can by ear. Try to learn something once a week, some kind of a tune. You should learn a melody, something. Force yourselves to memorize. Up here [points to his ears], not on paper, because this was an ear music. You see, what's happening is that when you come into school it becomes the other way around. It becomes this: your eyes teach your hand what to play and then finally your hands are teaching your ears. With these cats [the legendary players] it was the other way around. They heard the tune, they learned a lot of these tunes on the gig, so their ears—it had to get into their ears before they could teach their fingers. That's the way it went. So you want to try to get to that point where you can hear—get it in your ear and then let your ears teach it to your fingers rather than looking at that paper and, you know, keep repeating it. You dig?

As jazz scholars have noted, notions of aurality/orality and literacy have been salient in the ideological self-understandings of jazz players (Duranti 2008). Although in practice it is impossible to define jazz as pertaining to either aurality or literacy—notions proven to be analytically problematic when considered to be mutually exclusive—some jazz players consider aurality rather

than literacy to be at the core of jazz improvisation. They are convinced that
aurality defines improvisation with its relative independence of the textual
artifact and increased reliance on the ear as a mode of communication among
players in the real time of improvisation, or they draw a connection between
aurality and jazz via the latter's African heritage (Brothers 1997). At times,
their rejection of literacy is grounded in their desire to draw a distinction between jazz and Western classical music, in which the printed artifact holds an
important role—a distinction, one must add, that has been eagerly cultivated
by the institutions of classical music (Levine 1989; Nettl 1995). Frequently,
though, jazz players hold shifting evaluations of the written score (Chevan
2001; Duranti 2008; Prouty 2006), at times viewing it as a valuable means
of studying classical music, for example, or as a marker of "high art" (Lopes
2002).

The ideological mobilization of the eye and the ear that I am pointing to
here—while still positing the ear as superior to the eye—is differently determined. Dan argues that the rise of academic jazz education has made the
eye ubiquitous as a means of accessing and producing musical knowledge at
the expense of the ear. The "eye" is a reference to the academic jazz program's
heavy reliance on printed artifacts. Students learn to improvise by incorpo-
rating into their playing bodies standardized formulas that educators write
on the blackboard or that are available in method books while they lack the
opportunities to implement and recontextualize the knowledge thus gained
in real-time performance.[12] The problem is that this mode of training does
not allow a player to inform her playing by editorial considerations, that is,
to execute novel musical ideas that arise in the course of performance, or to
respond to the musical cues produced by her band members. Dan suggests
that if jazz students used their ears more often, they would not sound like
carbon copies of one another, because they would be able to play editorially
in the course of performance. Notice that the fingers themselves, as indices of
bodily playing habits, are neutrally located within this epistemological hierarchy. They are not sources of knowledge, but only a means to its execution. In
principle, they can be conditioned by the ear, as was the case with the great
jazz masters, according to Dan. The problem is that at present the fingers and
hands are conditioned by what the eye reads. Dan's diatribe is a call for the
restoration of the "old" epistemological hierarchy, in which the ear is given its
due place as a primary source of knowledge.

This mode of understanding structures the ways in which some of the
jazz educators I worked with attempted to restore the epistemological hier-

archy that, in their opinion, is conducive to the production of great jazz, and thus reconcile rule-governed social behavior and creative agency. Thus, in the middle of a course titled "Improvisational Techniques," Hal tried to teach the students how to build solos based on the repetition of a limited number of simple melodic and rhythmic motifs. He asked the students to come up with their own well-defined motifs and develop them in the course of improvisation. However, while playing over the harmonic progression of the tune "Lady Bird," the students had trouble coming up with different motifs, especially in terms of rhythmic variety. When each of their turns arrived, they tended to play successions of eighth and sixteenth notes. Hal stopped the playing a number of times to scold them, saying, "You are playing too complicated! Simplify it! . . . Simplify it!" Despite repeated attempts, the students continued to play a series of eighth and sixteenth notes. The following exchange then took place:

[Hal:] Try not to think complicated. You want to think in rhythm. I am not even concerned with the damn melody notes. I want you to think like drummers, OK? [In an announcing voice:] Guest drummer of the day! [Pause. He looks at the students. A guitar player raises his hand] Let's go! You don't have to play any hi-hat notes [referring to the cymbal]. I just want you to play the rhythm [on the snare drum]. [The guitar player looks confused, but starts to adjust his guitar for playing]. No, you are going to the drum set, man.

[Student:] Oh, the drum set?

[Hal:] Yeah, go to the drum set over there.

[Student:] Oh. My god!

[Hal:] See that? [Laughter.] All right, you don't have to do anything but tap the snare. [Student adjusts himself behind the drums.]

[Hal:] Now you *have* to think simple!

[Student, in disbelief:] So I have to do what we were just doing?

[Hal:] Yeah! In time! In form! All you got to do is use one hand. You don't have to play all the drum set. All right, ready? OK, here we go: One, two, comp, and— [The bass and piano players play with the guitar player who plays the drums.] Good. Not bad. That's it! [Hal turns to the students again while the guitar player returns to his seat.] Guest drummers! Anybody else? Guest drummers! You want to try that, man? [Hal is addressing the vibraphone player who agrees and then goes to the drum set.] All right, some more retrograde phrases. Think in rhythm! OK, like I said, you don't need a lot of chops. All you need is to play with one

hand, all right? Here we go. You look good behind that drum set, man!
[Laughter.] You are a drum star now. All right, ready? One, two, a-one,
two, three, four! [The vibraphone player plays rhythm on the drum with
the bass and piano players.] Don't get too complicated. . . . You cats are
trying to play all this shit on a new instrument! No! Slow down. Less,
less. I'm trying to make you minimalize here!

Hal is frustrated that the students continue to take the single chord and the
scale that derives from it as a point of reference and hence play as many patterns and notes as they can during each chord's length with no distinguish-
able and memorable rhythmic figures that could serve as developable motifs
with respect to the tune's melody or broader harmonic form.[13] In response, he
asks the guitar player to sit behind the drums and to produce simple rhythmic
figures while the bass and piano players accompany him. He assures him that
he does not need to control the whole drum set, but rather hit only the snare
drum with one hand. A clue for the rationale behind this move lies in two
of Hal's phrases: "Now you *have* to think simple," and "You don't need a lot
of chops." By asking the guitar player to produce the rhythmic figures on an
instrument foreign to him, a drum, Hal achieves two goals. First, he spares the
student the need to think about adjusting the rhythmic figures to the changing
harmonic context of the tune, because the snare drum, as opposed to the guitar, is not a pitch instrument. In this respect, this action is about simplifying a
task so that the student can focus on only one of its elements, namely, rhythm.
Greg Downey (2008) describes a similar example in which capoeira teachers
reduce their students' degrees of freedom in an effort to minimize their opportunities to commit errors when they learn a new complex movement.

However, in the case that I am discussing here, Hal's request has an additional and much more important goal. He asks the guitar player to produce
the rhythmic figures on the drum because it is a way of preventing the guitar
player from relying on his standardized playing bodily habits that account for
his failure to produce anything different than successions of eighth and sixteenth notes. As soon as the student's hands and fingers are removed from the
guitar's neck, on which they have been trained to function in a certain way,
he "has to think simple"—he doesn't have a choice because he "doesn't have
the chops" on the drum. The guitar player cannot fall back on his embodied
playing habits because he does not have well-developed technique on this instrument. His body is at a loss. Now he must actually think about what to

play.[14] Under these conditions, Hal hopes that the student will be more likely to produce novel ideas.

The Phenomenological Infrastructure of Rule-Governed Creativity

Together with pragmatism, phenomenology has revealed the embodied, contingent, unintended, and emergent nature of action and the self, which individuals normalize and unify ex post facto (Csordas 1994; Dewey 2000; Joas 1993; Mead 1934; Merleau-Ponty 2002). Maurice Merleau-Ponty, in his *Phenomenology of Perception* (2002), argues that we are subjects who are conscious of the world via our bodies. The body is not simply an object in the world just like other objects. Rather, it is the medium by which there are objects for us. It is "the unperceived term in the center of the world towards which all objects turn their face" (2002, 94). Under normal conditions, the body remains marginal to, or presumed within, our perceptions. This unique positionality of the body gives consciousness and understanding a new meaning in Merleau-Ponty's schema, for consciousness becomes consciousness of an object mediated by the potentialities of our body:

Consciousness is being-towards-the-thing through the intermediary of the body. A movement is learned when the body has understood it, that is, when it has incorporated it into its "world," and to move one's body is to aim at things through it; it is to allow oneself to respond to their call, which is made upon it independently of any representation. Motility, then, is not, as it were, a handmaid of consciousness, transporting the body to that point in space of which we have formed a representation beforehand. In order that we may be able to move our body towards an object, the object must first exist for it. (Merleau-Ponty 2002, 159–161)

For Merleau-Ponty, then, understanding and intentionality are embodied— they occur via the body. They entail a "harmony between what we aim at and what is given, between the intention and the performance" (167). In this anti-Cartesian, nonrepresentational, and performative sense, consciousness "is in the first place not a matter of 'I think that' but of 'I can'" (159).[15]

Merleau-Ponty's observations are of little use in helping us understand why jazz students play in a standardized fashion. Technically speaking, they are fully capable of playing in a nonstandardized way. At stake is not the mastery of a complex technical task foreign to their playing body. The previous classroom vignette, for example, is concerned with the task of minimizing the number of notes students play. However, Merleau-Ponty's ideas can illuminate the corrective measures that some of the educators I worked with introduce to mitigate this form of standardized playing. For if one's consciousness of the world is mediated by the potentialities of the body and its habits, the act of reconfiguring the body changes its potentialities and alters one's consciousness of the world. The appropriation of new habits and instruments, such as learning to drive a car and, by implication, the renunciation of old ones, changes our "existence" (Merleau-Ponty 2002, 166). It dilates or contracts our being-in-the-world in the sense of our body's potentialities.[16]

Jazz educators have a nuanced understanding of this dynamic in that they realize the limited efficacy of discursive efforts to bring their students to play in a nonstandardized way when it concerns their bodily playing habits.[17] This is not to say that language use in the course of socialization into jazz is of no efficacy (Black 2008). Duranti, drawing on Husserl's notion of "intentional modifications," or "shifts in our ways of thinking of, feeling about, or coming into contact with the same object" (2009, 208), documents how some jazz educators use language in order to bring about modifications in students' consciousness, which ultimately involve their embodied being. However, the intentional modifications that I describe are much more radical in that the educators I worked with enact changes in their students' consciousness via a *direct* modification of students' bodies, thus proceeding to the very basis of their students' being-in-the-world. They reconfigure students' bodies so that what they used to intend musically—because "they can"—becomes impossible. The result is a stage in which students must rearrange their "corporeal schema[ta]" (Merleau-Ponty 2002, 164), that is, the unified possession of their body in which they know where each limb is and how it interacts with other limbs and with the world as "an attitude directed towards a certain existing or possible task" (114). It is precisely in such a moment of rearrangement of corporeal schemata that the creative space opens up and students have the opportunity—they don't have a choice, really—to consider other modes of improvising different from the standardized patterns they have been trained in. Whereas Merleau-Ponty turned to amputees and the phenomenon of phantom limbs in order to anchor his "existential analysis" (2002, 157), the jazz educators I worked with orchestrate a kind of metaphoric amputation in order to produce existential change.

This rationale informs the vignette I discussed in the beginning of this chapter, in which Louis, the educator, expresses his ambivalence toward his students' bodily playing habits. In that vignette, Louis advises his students to try to play only in half notes, arguing that they would discover they cannot play a "decent" solo. This means, so he argues, that it is their fingers that actually "stir the shit" rather than their ears, because playing in half notes actually gives the player more time to "think editorially" and to decide what to play. Louis's instruction to his students that they play only half notes is a way of neutralizing students' bodily playing habits, limited as they are to eighth and sixteenth notes, or "machine-gun" playing. It is a way of creating "intentional modification" through direct manipulation of one's body.

I have often observed educators utilize these tactics. These attempts are adjusted to the particularities of each instrument. For example, Tom, after failing to bring a piano player to come up with innovative melodic ideas during an ensemble class, finally instructed him to improvise only with the thumb and the little finger of his right hand. This significantly limited the student's habituated mode of playing and created more space in his playing to think about each individual note played. Similarly, Hal, the educator who requested that nondrummers play drums told me: "I used to do this with guitar players. I used to have them play only on one string, solo only on one string. Things like that. Or saxophone players—only solo with the left hand or only solo with the lower three buttons. Things like that. Just do something you never did before. Just things like that. Limit yourself—and that was what it was all about."

All of these tactics are based in the same principle of defamiliarizing the physical aspect of playing so that the "certainty of pre-prepared movements," to invoke Mauss's "techniques of the body" again (1973, 86), *becomes uncertain*. In the economy of agency which involves the eye, ear, and fingers, this action neutralizes the fingers as conditioned by the eye so that the ear can take hold and guide the fingers. It amounts to a kind of coup against what these jazz educators consider to be the tyranny of the eye within their academic jazz programs, and a restoration of the ear's sovereignty, which connotes creative agency, through rule-governed behavior. In this respect, such instances of reconfiguration should not be thought of in terms of the simple addition of skills to one's improvisation tool kit. The generation of new habits is achieved by bringing old habits into awareness via their *disruption*. Invoking the image of the boxer, which, incidentally, is mobilized by Bourdieu, following George H. Mead, to demonstrate his notion of practice as improvisation (Bourdieu 1977, 11), I suggest that these instances are not about a boxer who learns a new move but rather a boxer who learns a new move by *unlearning an old one.*

A different version of this same principle is used by educators as they attempt to reconfigure their students' playing bodies. Steve, an instructor of a performance ear training class at Berklee, frequently pulled the curtains down over the windows and turned off the lights in the beginning of each class. Only after these preparations did he begin teaching, which usually comprised playing musical phrases and chords on the piano, which the students had to match with their own instruments. In an interview, he explained to me his rationale for darkening the room:

> You guys [referring to trumpet players like me] get that. See, I find it's different with people who produce the sound. Like you guys, who have to make your own sound, you have to hear it so your body—you become part of that sound that you make. That happens less with us [Steve is a piano player] because we can just press down a key and know that we will get the right sound. We don't actually have to hear it a lot. And I find that any instrument where you can actually see the—it's laid out for you in that sort of way— that happens. Whereas trombone—who knows what this [mimicking a trombone player] is gonna do, but yet they do—before you play you have to know what sound you're going to play. If you don't hear the sound, you'll never get the note, right? So what I always tell them [the students] to do— one of the things that I learned about was practicing in the dark for improvising. When I was a kid I discovered it by accident that it became about the sound, that it was less about what the keys were, because I couldn't see the keys. It worked great for me, because I know now when I'm improvising, I'm really, especially if I'm really feeling comfortable and I'm really in that zone, I never look at my hands. I'm just like thinking of sound. It's like composing and listening to yourself and responding in the moment. So that's one of those things that I think I like to see them get—hearing an idea and kind of know where it is.

The self-imposed darkness, then, is another means of suppressing embodied playing habits, which are the product of visually mediated musical training. The purpose is to allow for aurally mediated musical production to take place, which, according to this specific epistemological hierarchy, is deemed conducive to intentional and creative musicality. Here, again, the matter of concern is not imperfect bodily mastery. Indeed, educators realize that visually mediated musical training may result in flawless technique. Rather, the problem is absence of intentionality and creative improvisation.

Garry, an educator who deliberately avoided the use of printed artifacts in his class and who insisted on teaching students "in the old style" by playing a tune's melody time and again with his trumpet until students could play it with their instruments, explained to me the rationale behind his pedagogy: "I think the benefit is that it's a different side of the brain. Learning by ear, you're learning on the . . . mystical, emotional part of the brain, and you don't really see the notes on the paper. You don't see the lines, you don't see the mathematics of it. Hopefully you're just hearing melodies which are abstract. . . . Because it's easy to read. You can learn how to read. Anyone can learn how to read music. But whether you can hear it or not is another question." These words make it clear why the image of the classically trained piano player mobilized by a number of anthropologists as a model of embodied practical mastery is of small use in understanding the creative embodied practice of jazz music in this context, and why this image is culturally specific and partial. Garry distinguishes between practical mastery that is visually, as opposed to aurally, mediated. He associates the danger of mechanical playing with the former form of music production by invoking terms like *mathematics, analytical,* and the *lines* (i.e., the stave). He uses the adjectives *mystical* and *emotional* to denote the creative experience that is the added value of aurally mediated musical training and production within this epistemological hierarchy. He suggests that restoration of the latter is the key to overcoming standardized embodied playing habits and producing stylistic differentiation.

Note, too, the way Steve, the educator who commented on the pedagogical value of darkness, superimposes the epistemological hierarchy that places aurality above literacy on top of what I call "an instrumental hierarchy." At the bottom of the instrumental hierarchy are those instruments that allow for visually mediated playing to a greater extent than those instruments in which the visual is of little use. The guitar and the piano belong to the former, while the trombone and the trumpet belong to the latter. Steve explains that the piano player has all the keys in front of him and thus can produce sounds mechanically without necessarily hearing the sounds prior to producing them. The trumpet player, on the other hand, has only three valves at his disposal and thus must rely on subtle bodily actions (pushing a specific valve, using a certain amount of air, manipulating the embouchure in a certain way) that require synchronization through inner hearing to a greater extent. Note, finally, that in the darkness, players of pianos and other "suspect" instruments surely orient themselves on the instruments through tactile and propriocentric means rather than through full reliance on their ears (a modality that probably does not exist at all), yet such means of orientation are considered acceptable by the educators I worked with when they are conditioned and guided by the ear.

The Imperative to Self-Differentiate

Educators' strategies of cultivating creative agency through rule-governed social behavior that reconfigures the playing body suggest that embodied practical mastery might consist of *techniques of generating temporary bodily habits* in addition to specific bodily practices that ought to be routinely honed and perfected by all of the group members. While the jazz educators I worked with inculcate their students with "the idiom of jazz," which indeed entails normative, well-defined bodily practices, they also teach them techniques of generating shifting bodily practices. The manipulation of the body during the attempted "intentional modification" that is supposed to mitigate the threat of standardization is meant to be temporary. The student who plays the piano is not supposed to continue to play only with his thumb and little finger indefinitely. Rather, it is a means of generating new musical ideas that ideally will culminate in new bodily practices in the sense of the embodied capacity and inclination to execute these ideas in the real time of improvisation. These newly incorporated musical ideas are good as long as they are not played by too many students. When they do become standardized, the student ought to revert to a similar technique of generating new ideas through reconfiguration of the playing body. In this specific conception of embodied practical mastery that is characterized by the dialectic of learned ignorance and learned awareness, the constant problematization of embodied practical mastery is a condition of possibility for acquiring such mastery.

On one level, the strategies devised by educators to help their students achieve this mastery are precisely a form of negotiating creative practice and institutionalized rationality. They are a means of cultivating creative agency via rule-governed social behavior. On another level, however, these strategies are structured by the rhetorical reproduction of the dichotomy between aurality and literacy. This means that these strategies sustain the basic opposition between creativity and institutionalized rationality by constantly associating aurality with the former and literacy with the latter. This duality of simultaneous reconciliation and polarization of creative agency and institutionalized rationality has been a constant feature in the strategies discussed in previous chapters. It also recurs in the strategies devised by students to negotiate and reverse the various implications of their academic training for their improvisational competence. These strategies are the focus of the next chapter.

THE GAMES STUDENTS PLAY

Technologies of the Listening Self

"What did you whistle?" Recalibrating the Ears

It is a cold February night. Sarah, a Berklee vibraphone student, and I are approaching Inman Square in Cambridge when a person sitting in a parked car next to us suddenly honks twice. In response and in complete synchrony with one another, Sarah and I whistle. We attempt to imitate the exact pitch of the car horn. However, each of us whistles a different pitch. Sarah abruptly stops walking. She turns to me and asks: "What did you whistle?" I whistle the exact pitch that I whistled a minute ago. Sarah then repeats her whistle. Mine is a few steps below hers. Sarah looks at me for a second and says in a flat voice: "Go and ask them to honk again." At first I think she is joking; it is an extremely cold night and I am eager to be indoors. I look at the car. The engine is running and there are three people sitting inside. I look again at Sarah and I realize that she is serious and is not going to take no for an answer. Reluctantly, I walk to the car and knock on the window. The two men in the front seats and the woman in the back seat look at me. The driver has a cell phone in his hand and appears to be calling someone to come downstairs to meet them in the car. The window rolls down.

"Can you honk again, please?" I ask, hesitatingly. "You see," I continue, trying to figure out what to say, "we had a bet." I do not explain any further. As I say these words I point with my head toward Sarah, who watches me. The passengers look at me with dismay. After a moment of silence the driver, almost hastily, honks again and rolls up the window. "Thanks," I manage to say before the window is completely sealed again. I turn around to face Sarah who is standing motionless, an almost unperceivable smile on her lips. She says: "Let's go?"

This interaction illustrates well the kind of reflexive cultural work on the senses that has become increasingly prevalent among a number of students with whom I formed close friendships during my fieldwork at Berklee (Wilf forthcoming). While spending time with these students, I recorded and participated in various interactional games in which they and other students negotiated their concerns about their improvisational skills in the context of their academic training. These games were an inseparable part of the institutionalization of jazz training. Although they took place in the shadow of the more formal pedagogical strategies deployed by educators in the classroom, they addressed some of the same challenges that educators were preoccupied with, and they were often informed by the same discourses and practices of creativity endorsed by educators.

Consider the interactional game between Sarah and me. What triggered this interaction and what was its logic? On the surface, the attempt to match the car horn by whistling was motivated by a kind of a competition. However, note that Sarah's and my initial reactions to the car horn were synchronous with one another, and I assure you that we did not walk Cambridge's streets waiting to hear random sounds so that we could compete with one another over who could best match it by whistling. Certainly not during the cold winter! In other words, competition was not the initial organizing principle that triggered this interaction. Rather, it was only after realizing that the other person whistled, too, and, more importantly, that there was a discrepancy between our sonic reactions to the pitch of the car horn, that the situation was transformed into a competition or a game. As I will suggest, our attempts to match the car horn were motivated first and foremost by our desire to retrain our ears in a cultural context pervaded by concerns about the shift in students' aural skills. It is precisely these concerns that have led educators to manipulate their students' playing bodies with the hope of replacing visually mediated with aurally mediated modes of knowledge production.

At the same time, although the competitive aspect was secondary to Sarah's and my initial responses, it certainly did structure the interaction that ensued. It made this and the other interactions I describe below effective as training ground for the formation of a specific self defined by its ability to engage with the surrounding world through listening and aurally mediated playing. After Sarah and I discerned a discrepancy in our reactions to the car horn, there emerged a heightened collective focus on and exploration of the various dimensions of the culturally valued skill of listening. The agonistic nature of this framework motivated us to enact an elaborate verification process—asking the driver to honk again—that had a dual purpose.[1] First, when students engage in this kind of interaction, such verification processes heighten their awareness of the different dimensions of the culturally valued skill of listening. Second, these processes allow students to ascertain whether or not they are mastering this skill. By putting themselves in situations where their performance authenticity—defined by listening—is tested, students both learn about this experience and aim for it.

Thus the particular interactional game in which Sarah and I participated targeted a key dimension of listening as a normative ideal in the jazz tradition, namely the ability to vocalize one's musical ideas (and, as we shall see below, to respond with one's instrument to the external sonic cues produced by one's group members in the course of improvisation). Many of the educators I worked with view whistling and singing as ideal forms of expressing one's musical ideas, which musicians should strive to attain with their instruments, because these forms involve a more direct connection between a musical idea and its expression. Consider what Sam, a well-known saxophonist, said in a master class he gave at Berklee:

> You see, this is what I'm talking about. Singers—they have a direct connection. They're not pressing keys. Every tone is about the energy and dynamics and the song and that connection with how you're speaking and making statements. That's what I'm talking about. On the piano, if you're playing forte, you gotta feel that energy [yells], and if you play pianissimo [whispers]—the same. Especially on the piano, guitar, bass, drums—instruments that you're not actually blowing into. And then with cats that are really blowing into the horn it's easy to just play in one dynamic all the time. So that connection is in there too: you have to feel the speed of the air, but especially on instruments like the piano, where people a lot of the time hold their breath and just play notes. That's why it's important to vocalize

yourselves all the time. I'm always singing to get a direct connection with
what I'm trying to play. All the time.

Sam argues that singing is a medium that allows a person to be in direct connection with her "musical" self and to articulate it. According to his reason-
ing, the musical instrument might interfere with such articulation: players can
learn "to press keys" without actually having any musical ideas they want to
express or without having the skills to express them with their instruments.
Hence it is crucial for students to maintain this ideal of immediate expression
epitomized by singing so that, eventually, they can model their playing after
this ideal. Sam invokes the "instrumental hierarchy" I discussed in the previous chapter, within which instruments that approximate this ideal of singing
are ranked higher in comparison with instruments that are more distant from
it. The latter should be approached with care, because they are more conducive to nonintentional or noneditorial playing.

    The game I played with Sarah was one of a number of interactional games
played by the students I worked with, with which they addressed the academization of their training and its implications for their improvisational competence, especially the shift in their aural skills and sensitivities. Before unpacking each of these games, however, I want to describe an analytical framework
within which these interactional games can be theorized and their logic, reasons, and intended effects can be clarified. This framework relies on Michel
Foucault's notion of "technologies of the self" (Foucault 1997), which I appropriate and transform to the notion of "technologies of the listening self."

Technologies of the Listening Self

Foucault developed the notion of technologies of the self late in his career
after providing a history of various discourses that originated in the West
and that objectified the self as an object of study and control (two examples
discussed by Foucault are psychiatry and statistics). Following this analysis
of "regimes of truth," Foucault explored technologies of the self, or ways in
which individuals constitute themselves as subjects via the enactment of such
discourses (see Rabinow 1997). He offered a history of Western technologies
of the self beginning from antiquity, and in the process emphasized a number
of methods and principles of self-cultivation that have persisted throughout
this history. Although Foucault's notion of "technologies of the self" is often featured in anthropological research to designate work that individuals

perform on themselves, the notion he originally developed has a number of dimensions that often remain unspecified in such discussions. These dimensions make explicit the notion's relevance for theorizing the strategies devised by the students I worked with to cultivate their improvisational skills in response to the challenges produced by the academization of jazz training.

First, inasmuch as they are defined as "the procedures, which no doubt exist in every civilization, suggested or prescribed to individuals in order to determine their identity, maintain it, or transform it in terms of a certain number of ends, through relations of self-mastery or self-knowledge" (Foucault 1997, 87), technologies of the self are about the possibility of self-fashioning in view of specific ends. Thus, they suggest the possibility of sensory self-fashioning in accordance with normative ideals such as listening.

Second, Foucault makes it clear that "if I am now interested in how the subject constitutes itself in an active fashion through practices of the self, these practices are nonetheless not something invented by the individual himself. They are models that he finds in his culture and are proposed, suggested, imposed upon him by his culture, his society, and his social group" (Foucault 1997, 291). Thus, in arguing for the possibility of students' sensory self-fashioning, I am not postulating the existence of some kind of an autonomous space in which students fashion themselves in any way they want, within the presumed oppressive sphere of the academic jazz program. Rather, the students I worked with embrace a discourse of listening-oriented performance authenticity that they learn from their educators. The latter frequently convey to their students their understanding of what the production of "real" jazz consists of—an understanding that is grounded in an epistemology that has a long history in jazz.

Third, while technologies of the self are linked to institutions of power, this does not mean they have no basis in reality (Foucault 1997, 296). Accordingly, concerns about students' sensory and improvisational skills as a result of the academization of jazz training, while shaped by a regime of truth, are grounded in experience. In other words, this academization, coupled with broader changes in the conditions of existence of jazz, has had real effects on students' improvisational skills, which cannot be reduced to and dismissed as fiction or "ideology."

Fourth, most importantly, Foucault postulates the existence of technologies of the self that are concerned with a notion of ethics understood as embodied dispositions that are conducive to the performance of culturally sanctioned actions (Foucault 1997, 209; for the use of a similar notion of ethics, see Asad 1993; Mahmood 2005; Hirschkind 2006). The purpose of these techniques is to incorporate, absorb, and assimilate a specific notion of truth into one's body so that it becomes part of one's self as a "permanent principle of action" (Foucault 1988, 35; Foucault 1997, 99–103). Foucault describes various technologies of the self that focus on embodied dispositions used in antiquity, such as abstinence and physical exercises. This suggests that techniques of the self can be concerned with the honing of sensory skills that are defined as the seat of one's moral agency in a culturally specific context. Hence students' cultivation of their listening skills, which are often enacted through embodied playing habits, nicely accords with Foucault's notion of technologies of the self.

Fifth, Foucault argues that the self is not a single unitary entity. Rather, it is heterogeneous in accordance with the multiplicity of contexts in which one acts: "You do not have the same relationship to yourself when you constitute yourself as a political subject who goes to vote or speaks at a meeting and when you are seeking to fulfill your desires in a sexual relationship" (Foucault 1997, 290). Thus, the games played by the students I worked with are concerned with a specific model of the self that circulates in the jazz world and that emphasizes listening to oneself and to other players in one's group as a moral imperative (Black 2008; Duranti and Burrell 2004). This self exists side by side with other models of the self that students hold in their various capacities other than as aspiring jazz musicians.

Sixth, there may be various forms of technologies of the same self, from thought experiments to real situations where one has to demonstrate that he or she has the discursive truth incorporated within him or her (Foucault 1997, 102–103; Foucault 1988, 35). The games I discuss belong to the second type of training. Students often put themselves in situations in which they have to display their listening skills in real time in front of their friends. Such micropractices form the backbone of technologies of the self.

Seventh, technologies of the self need not be a solitary activity. Rather, they can involve teachers, private counselors, family relations, friends, and so forth (Foucault 1997, 97–99). Similarly, the games I discuss are a form of technologies of the self that are enacted among a number of friends who perform for one another a quasi "soul service" (ibid.). They help one another hone the desired model of selfhood that is based on listening.

Finally, it is perhaps not accidental that Foucault calls technologies of the self "games of truth," that is, "a set of rules by which truth is produced. It is not a game in the sense of an amusement; it is a set of procedures that lead to a certain result, which, on the basis of its principles and rules of procedure, may be considered valid or invalid, winning or losing" (Foucault 1997, 297). This is a quite adequate definition of the interactions I am concerned with, in which students negotiate with one another a set of rules for the purpose of ascertaining whether they are endowed with the skill of listening or not, and for cultivating this skill at the same time.[2]

These various dimensions give analytical thickness to the study of the ways in which the students I worked with attempted to negotiate some of the concerns about their improvisational skills by devising micropractices of sensory self-fashioning that focus on different dimensions of the "listening self." In addition to vocalizing one's musical ideas, these dimensions included the execution of sonic cues by means of one's instrument, listening and responding to one's band members in the course of performance, identifying the unique sounds and styles of the great past masters, and informing one's improvisation with tunes' melodies and broader contextual meanings.

"Nail it on the trumpet": Cultivating Listening on One's Musical Instrument

I meet Pierre for our weekly playing session in one of the offices in Berklee's guitar department. This time Sarah and Carla—a Berklee singer—are present too. We all play a few tunes together: I on trumpet, Pierre on guitar, Sarah on percussion, and Carla singing. After an hour of playing we take a break. I go to a corner and play some random lines. One note that I play at the end of a phrase is cracked. I stop and try to play it properly a few times. Upon hearing this, Pierre, who is sitting quietly with his guitar, tries to play the exact same pitch. He misses my note by two whole steps above. He then hesitantly descends in a glissando until he finds the correct pitch. I can't help myself and laugh, saying "Man, that was funny!" I then imitate his glissando with my voice. As I am about to continue with my playing, Carla interjects. She stands up and says: "Oh yeah? Let's see you do better than him!" "What do you mean?" I ask. Carla goes to Pierre and pulls him toward me. "Come, you stand here," she says, directing him with her hands. Pierre is laughing. "And you," she says to me, turning me around with her hands, "you stand with your back to him." Pierre and I are now standing back to back. "Pierre, play some notes. I don't want him to remember what you just played," Carla says. Carla then moves Pierre's hand randomly over the neck of the guitar, plucking the strings with her other hand and producing a cacophony of sounds. She thus hopes to disorient me so that I will not remember what Pierre played when he tried to match the cracked sound I had produced earlier. "Now play one note," she tells Pierre, "and you," she turns to me, "you need to nail it on the trumpet. Let's see you do better than him!" There is silence. Sarah looks at us attentively from her seat. I stare forward, trying to focus, preparing myself. Do I know my trumpet that well? My thoughts are abruptly cut short: Pierre plucks a string and a note sounds in the air. I ponder for a split second, trying to figure out where to place it on the trumpet. What note on my trumpet is identical to it? I play a D, then immediately, with the same urgency of a reflex reaction when one pulls one's hand away from fire, I change it a whole step below to a C only to realize that Pierre actually played a C-sharp, which I then quickly play. "It doesn't count, it doesn't count," Carla exclaims, waving her hands in dismissal while Sarah, shaking her head, mutters "No, no, no."

As I went back to my corner, licking my wounds, I thought to myself that I would have probably done better had I been asked to match with my voice or by whistling the note that Pierre played. But I knew this was not a good excuse. While the students I worked with often reverted to singing and whistling to cultivate their listening, it was clear to everyone that ultimately it was one's ability to exercise listening with one's musical instrument that really mattered. Accordingly, they devised interactional games like this one that focused precisely on this ability.

The imperative to exercise listening with one's musical instrument has many subtle dimensions. In the previous chapter I discussed the argument made by a number of educators according to which the musical instrument can pose a problem if approached in the wrong way. While educators understand that the instrument is an inevitable component of playing, they insist that it must be approached via one's "ears" so that it may become an unproblematic medium for the expression of the player's musical ideas in the real time of improvisation, much as in singing or whistling. In an interview, Charlie, a Berklee educator, described this ideal of symbiosis between musicians and their instruments, as well as a technique for developing it, in the following way:

> When you're starting playing things in every key every day, you start recognizing the difference between the key of A and the key of C and the key of B-flat on the instrument. You feel it. It's a strange thing. I can't explain it but you start developing a relative pitch from your fingers to your ears,

you know. So if I hear somebody playing in a certain key, I'll relate [it] to my instrument—whatever it is—tenor or alto [saxophone] and say: "That key feels like that note on my horn." You know what I mean? So I'll relate [it] to maybe the tenor and say: "Yeah, that sounds like it's in the key of A" because I can feel . . . actually the fingering in my fingers of the horn. It's really a strange thing, but it does work, but only if you do it every day. If you only play like in three keys—[for example] C, F, and B-flat all the time— you won't get it. But if you do all the keys . . . you kind of feel it in your hands. . . . You hear something on the radio and it's like: "Oh yeah, that's in the key of E" . . . I can actually feel that note. The color, yeah, you get the color right. That's what that's like. But it takes time, don't get me wrong.

Charlie describes a delicately achieved association between the sounds one hears and the way their production with one's instrument "feels." The pro-duction of each note with an instrument involves the combination of numer-ous bodily actions and sensations such as pressing *this* finger, breathing *this* amount of air, tightening the lips to *this* degree, and so forth. Each note pro-duced with an instrument, therefore, entails a distinct configuration of bodily actions and sensations, what I would call its "bodily signature." As Charlie clarifies, how one makes oneself familiar with the instrument is crucial. One does not want to breed the "wrong" kind of familiarity by relying exclusively on visually mediated modes of knowledge transmission and production. He describes one technique of cultivating the desirable symbiosis with the instru-ment that consists of repeatedly playing a pattern in each of the twelve keys without the mediation of a written score. After practicing in this way for a long time, the player begins to form an association between each of the notes that she *hears* as she produces it with her instrument and the note's "bodily signa-ture," that is, how it feels like to produce each of these notes.[3] When Charlie refers to "the color, yeah, you get the color right," he points to this bodily signature. Feeling it "in my fingers," "in your hands," is a way of describing this subtle conditioning.

This kind of mastery is important in jazz because of the music's improvisa-tory basis, which requires players to respond to the constantly changing music on the spur of the moment, which is one of the conditions of possibility for group creativity and the production of a groove (Monson 1996). If a player is able to locate on his instrument the musical ideas that form in his head and the sounds that his band members produce as they improvise, he can execute the former and respond to the latter in real time, thus contributing to the music in a way which makes musical sense. The game that Pierre and I played in front of Carla and Sarah was concerned precisely with the ability to match an external (or imagined) sound with our instruments, a skill that requires prolonged practice. Upon hearing the note that Pierre played, I had an embodied sensation of what that sound "felt" like on the trumpet. I was close—a half step above—but not close enough. Part of the epistemological crisis that the educators and students I worked with are preoccupied with revolves around the realization that because students do not use their ears in the same way that players of previous generations used their ears, they have harder time executing their musical ideas and responding to the musical cues produced by their band members in the course of performance. This severely compromises the emergent structure of group improvisation and makes it repetitive and predictable.

Students are exposed at school to different versions of this "game of truth"—to use Foucault's notion—which are meant to mitigate these implications. Thus, in one of the few courses at Berklee that were dedicated to the cultivation of listening with one's instrument, Ron, the educator, would often play a note or a chord on the piano and the students would have to match what he played with their instruments. Significantly, he would not allow them to slide toward the right note when they missed it as I did in the game of truth I described above. In an interview I conducted with him, Ron explained to me the rationale behind this restriction in the following way:

> To me they are just digging around. I want them to actually hear it first. If they do that [search for the note], then they don't trust their ears. I want them to trust their ears. . . . I think it develops your inner ear so that you can hear things without actually having to play them. You can hear ways to approach tunes. Like if you get to know what's the sound of a certain chord progression, if you hear that progression in your ear then you can know where to find it [on the instrument].

Ron explains that allowing a student to slide toward the correct pitch after he missed it the first time is not as conducive to the development of listening as forbidding him to do so. Once a student plays a note with the instrument it is fairly easy for him to slide to the correct pitch that the educator played. Nailing it the first time, however, is a totally different story. It demonstrates that one has achieved the kind of symbiosis with the instrument that allows him or her to play intentionally and editorially in the real time of improvisation. The truth game that Pierre and I played was concerned with displaying, but also providing the opportunity to cultivate, this skill.

Note that these games allow students to collectively recalibrate their ears in unexpected times and places, thus cutting across prescribed and regimented learning processes found in the school that focus mostly on visually mediated modes of learning. In the previous game I described it was a car horn that prompted such a game, but in other examples I observed it was the ringing of a cell phone, the sound of an airplane passing in the sky, and other external auditory stimuli that prompted similar competitive attempts between students to match the sonic stimuli either by singing or whistling or with a musical instrument. Perhaps the most conspicuous example of this type of interaction took place at the New School while a number of students waited for the educator to arrive. When the sound of an ambulance siren infiltrated into the classroom from the busy street outside, three students immediately began to try to top one another in their imitation of the siren with their instruments. These attempts were immediately followed by elaborate verification processes of various sorts—attempts to ascertain which student imitated the siren in the best way. Such verification processes forced students to engage in an exploration of what the normative ideal of listening is and thus to better understand and internalize it.

"Fresh milk": Cultivating Listening with Joint Musical Interaction and Chance Objects

Carla, Sarah, Pierre, and I are sitting in Carla's living room. We spend a number of hours talking and arguing about music, exchanging information about classes, and listening to music. Suddenly, Pierre addresses us. "You know," he says, his eyes fixed on the table, "I understood something today." "Oh, here it comes," Carla laughs, referring to Pierre's habit of unexpectedly delivering quasi-existential musings. Pierre, still looking at the table, continues undeterred, taking his time between each word. "I understood that music is not about skills and [chord] changes and hexatonics and pentatonics and all this stuff.[4] It is not about that. You can know all this and it still won't mean a damn thing. It's about something else, about what you put in it, about playing with guts. Playing with guts, with what you feel." Sarah interjects: "Yeah, but what do you mean, playing with guts? That's the question, no? What do you mean 'guts'? It's easy to say 'guts.'" "Playing with guts is playing from the inside, it's about forgetting all these things," Pierre answers. He pauses. "It's so funny," he shakes his head. "The reason Wes Montgomery's music is so killing is not because he had all this knowledge and technique, but because he played with feeling. Listen to his music! Every note has so much swing and soul!" We remain silent, watching him. "We need fresh energy instead of thinking about all the technique and knowledge; to go back to basics. We need fresh milk!" At this point Carla, Sarah, and I burst into laughter, but Pierre remains still. He does not mean this as a joke. "The milk they're giving us stinks. We need fresh milk," he insists. "It doesn't matter anymore if it's good, if it's correct, as long as it's fresh." Still laughing, Carla says to him, "Oh yeah? So prove to us that you don't have to have all these skills and knowledge to be great." At this point, I expect the matter to be put aside. Pierre doesn't have his guitar with him, and I can't envision how he can "prove" his point. But I am wrong. Raising his hands and moving them rhythmically as if he were milking a cow or a goat, Pierre begins to sing a line to the rhythm of his hands. We stare at him for two minutes in disbelief, bursting into laughter time and again, but he continues. Soon enough, we all join him: singing, hitting the table with pencils or hitting our chests with our hands. We continue like this for about twenty minutes, each of us continuously changing his or her part in accordance with the changing parts of the other people, hypnotized by the rhythmic movement of Pierre's hands, which slowly but surely extract from us, for us, "fresh milk."

The distinction between "theory" and "feeling" that organizes Pierre's words surfaced in previous chapters. Pierre invokes "theory" with "[chord] changes," "hexatonics and pentatonics," and "knowledge and technique"; he invokes "feeling" with "feeling," "guts," "playing from the inside," and the "fundamentals" of the music. In doing so, he articulates the epistemological hierarchy that places listening above seeing, as well as the opposition between theory and humanness that was featured in the doctoral honoree's speech. By invoking legendary guitar player Wes Montgomery, Pierre reverts to the familiar rhetorical strategy of pointing to allegedly "intuitive" players who produced jazz masterpieces regardless of the sophisticated theoretical knowledge imparted by educators in jazz programs.

Pierre's call to "return to basics" was performed in this game-like interaction in three ways. First, by appropriating chance objects that seem to have nothing to do with musical production, Pierre performed the trope of unmediated creativity, a kind of "pure" creativity unencumbered by the school's institutionalized theory and any convention in general. Perhaps the most memorable example of such performance took place one Saturday night as I stood in the company of six Berklee students in the backyard of an old house. We were in the midst of a conversation when John, a saxophone player, started to kick the wooden fence of the balcony in a repetitive rhythmic pattern. He was immediately joined by Pierre, who contributed his own rhythm with a spoon and a fork. Sarah joined John by hitting the fence with her hands, adding a different pattern. Carla started to scat. The most inventive of all, Sebastian, a Spanish trumpet player, took a folding chair and unfolded and folded it, producing an interesting squeaking sound in a way that contributed beautifully to the evolving groove. I joined in by clapping my hands. In a matter of seconds we created a dense groove that dynamically shifted as participants constantly changed their parts in subtle ways. Soon enough, other students came out of the house and watched this performance of seemingly unmediated creativity.[5]

Second, the appropriation of chance objects supports Pierre's call to "return to basics" and to clear a space for listening in another way that is free from the program's institutionalized theory and its codification in printed artifacts. Students often appropriated chance objects as a way of making sure and demonstrating that they use their ears rather than fall back on the visually mediated embodied playing habits cultivated with their musical instruments in class—habits that are often framed as more conducive to standardized playing. The appropriation of chance objects *forces* students to use their ears and places them in a situation in which they must be creative.

The philosopher Martin Heidegger's description of our attitude toward an instrument before and after it malfunctions sheds some light on this aspect. According to Heidegger, as long as an instrument functions properly, it remains within our taken-for-granted framework of action. Only when it malfunctions does it become a problem that attracts our attention, because it needs to be creatively resolved (Heidegger 1996, 68–71; for commentary see Dreyfus 1994, 70–83; Knorr Cetina 1997, 10). The students I worked with often appropriated chance objects rather than their musical instruments in such game-like interactions for the purpose of music making because doing so transformed these objects into problems in need of a solution: how to creatively appropriate them into meaningful improvisation. This practice constitutes a technology of the listening self because it makes sure that visually mediated bodily playing habits cultivated on one's instrument through learning from standardized method books become less dominant. Indeed, at times students appropriated chance objects even though their own musical instruments were readily available. The reason, as Pierre so aptly put it, is that it doesn't matter if it's "correct" as long as it's "fresh."[6] Freshness means listening to one's musical ideas and articulating them accordingly, or responding to the sonic cues provided by one's band members even if these articulations and responses do not reach "professional" standards. The creative appropriation of chance objects is a way to demonstrate for others that one can use one's ears, as well as to cultivate this use.

Finally, and perhaps most importantly, such interactions provided a site in which students could practice listening to one another in the context of a real-time musical interaction. The increased abstraction generated by the theory codified in printed artifacts that has become ubiquitous in the jazz programs in which I did fieldwork, coupled with the fewer opportunities available to students to implement this theory in live performance, greatly impacted students' improvisational skills, especially with respect to their ability to interact with other musicians in real time. This impact was compounded by mounting evidence that new pedagogical devices have reduced students' willingness to play together even outside of school, as well as jeopardized their ability to listen to one another when they do happen to play together. One pedagogical device in particular, which has played a key role in the academization of jazz training, is frequently invoked in the context of such discussions.

Blowin' Alone: The Virtualization and Atomization of Music Sociality

At the time of my fieldwork, concerns revolved around what is known as "play-along" devices. These are educational aids that usually include a recording of a rhythm section that typically consists of a piano, a bass, and drums playing over the harmonic changes of standard tunes. These changes are written in a booklet that accompanies the recording. The student can improvise on a specific tune with the recording. Usually the rhythm section features well-known players, a fact that increases the appeal of these devices to neophyte jazz musicians who seek the experience of playing with well-known musicians. Since their introduction a couple of decades ago, these devices have become immensely popular among students. Significantly, the inventor of the most popular play-along products, Jamey Aebersold, correlates their success with the rise of institutionalized jazz education. A *New York Times* article on jazz education noted:

> If the mass commercialization of jazz instruction has a decisive moment, it would probably be the arrival in 1967 of a play-along album and guidebook

called "How to Play Jazz and Improvise." The recording featured a rhythm section only, leaving room for anyone to fill in the blanks. Though not the first effort of its kind—a company called Music Minus One was already in business—it was quickly the most successful, and influential. Jamey Aebersold, the man behind "How to Play Jazz," was no stranger to formal study, having received a master's degree in saxophone from Indiana University, one of the few colleges in the country with a jazz department at the time. He originally conceived of his target audience as hobbyists playing at home. "Until I got up to about Volume 25 or so, I wasn't thinking this was going to be a foundation for jazz education," Mr. Aebersold said recently from his home in Indiana. But he acknowledged that the Aebersolds, as his play-along kits are now widely known, have become a regular part of jazz's training arc. "If they haven't heard of me, they're probably not doing jazz," he said, sounding not boastful but matter-of-fact. The series is now up to Volume 118. (Chinen 2007)

The popularity of these devices has been fueled by many jazz programs' increased reliance on them as pedagogical tools. Berklee itself has endorsed these devices in various ways, as it became clear to me one day early in my fieldwork when I went to Berklee's library hoping to ascertain how often and in what ways students make use of it. Upon entering the library I noticed Avishai, an Israeli guitar player with whom I had become acquainted a few days earlier. Avishai was leaning against a counter next to the circulation desk and turning the pages of what appeared to be a reference booklet. When I approached him he showed me the CD he was holding in his hand: *Favorite Standards*, volume 22 of Jamey Aebersold's play-along devices. He told me, "You see, anytime I go to the library I check out one of these!" He then showed me the booklet he was perusing. It was a reference booklet that comprehensively catalogued the library's collection of play-along CDs, with standard tunes arranged alphabetically. When a student wishes to practice a specific tune, he consults the catalogue and then checks out the relevant CD and practices alongside it.

In at least ten of the courses I attended at Berklee, educators recommended and sometimes mandated the use of play-alongs. Students were instructed to practice with play-along devices to prepare for their exams in improvisation classes and to familiarize themselves with tunes that would be played in class. Often, when members of a rhythm section failed to show up to class, educators would use play-along CDs as a substitute. When students showed me the contents of their music hard drives, they inevitably contained a file comprised of dozens of play-along volumes.

To a great extent, the enormous success of these devices has resulted from the same factor that propelled the expansion of academic jazz education: the disappearance of viable jazz scenes in which students can experience and benefit from real-time musical interactions. Academic jazz education, established in part as an attempt to reconfigure rapidly disappearing jazz scenes, adopted these devices precisely because they enable a recorded rhythm section to substitute for a live one.

However, although these devices have been useful as a way of compensating for the significant shifts in the conditions of possibility for the cultural reproduction of jazz, they have also made it increasingly unnecessary for students to pursue collaborative musical interactions with their peers. After all, if these recorded rhythm sections are so handy, why bother coordinating a practice session with real musicians, finding the practice space that will be available at a time convenient to all, making sure there is a drum set and amplifiers, and so forth? It is much easier to use a play-along and proceed immediately with practicing.

Many of the educators and students I worked with confirmed this effect of the devices. When I asked Tim, an African American Berklee educator in his midforties, how the jazz scene had changed since his days as a student at Berklee some twenty five years ago, he replied:

That's easy. It's [i.e., the music] not visible. We all wanted to be the next jazz thing. How many young musicians want to be the next jazz thing? There is no next jazz thing. There was more activity, more clubs. There were clubs all over the place. It was in the culture. And you would hear it. You would be walking down to the dorms—kids have on iPods now. When we were in school here you heard kids playing music. Padadududaliyabim [scats]. Drumming and singing, people scatting, that's what you heard when you walked down Boylston street or any other street that circles the New England Conservatory of Music and Boston Conservatory and Berklee. Students would be singing outside their dorm rooms and their apartments and playing, and you heard that. Now everything is programmed. They're just hearing that on their iPods or their computer. They are not participating and music-playing as much. I mean, they are, but what was different is that visually you didn't have people making music in a box.[7] Now you have more people making music in a box. There are musicians who are playing, too. But there is a greater number of musicians who can produce all their music on their iPods, on their computer, and realize it that way without needing any other musician around. They themselves are not singing, because all the responses they need to get artistically and musically can be gotten by pushing a button. It's devastating. Everybody recognizes it. Now the question, educationally, is how to get it back towards the other direction a little more. Not that you want to totally wipe out the things that are of value in terms of electronics and modern conveniences—Finale, Pro Tools [music software]—all these are great things, but the balance is off-kilter now. We want more musicians dealing with music, playing the guitar, hitting the drums, singing out loud, trying to make dance steps in time with the drummer—those are the things you want more of, and that's our challenge right now.

As I listened to Tim, I was reminded of an essay written by the political scientist Robert Putnam (1995), entitled, "Bowling Alone: America's Declining Social Capital," which has provoked significant debate. In this essay, Putnam argued that Americans are becoming less and less likely to participate in civic organizations, especially those that are political in nature. Based on extensive statistical data, Putnam provided evidence for his claim: a decrease in voting rates, a decline in attendance at public meetings, and plummeting rates of recruitment to party work. These trends, he suggested, signify a general decline in the social capital so essential to democracy. Putnam argued that the causes for this trend are rooted in the atomizing force of technologies such as television that have encouraged dissociation from civic engagement. Using the metaphor of bowling, he argued that while in the past Americans were more likely to bowl within the context of bowling leagues, today they are more likely to bowl alone. As I collected more evidence for the discontent with the growing virtualization and atomization of jazz training, I asked myself, are we having here a case of "Blowin' Alone"?

To be sure, the two jazz programs in which I conducted fieldwork offer ensemble classes that are supposed to provide students with contexts in which they can apply and test their knowledge in collaborative playing. However, students get to benefit from only a few hours a week of ensemble time for a number of reasons. First, ensemble classes are expensive because they pair only a limited number of students with one educator. Second, the explosion in the number of students at Berklee sometimes forces administrators to assign a number of students who play the same instrument to the same ensemble, so an ensemble might have two bass players, two piano players, and so forth.

This means that students get to play less even in those contexts dedicated to real-time performance. Lastly, the paucity of rehearsal space means that students have limited options to organize their own ensemble settings at school. As Pierre noted, "There is a facility problem. There is not enough room—it's really difficult to get a room to rehearse. It was less of a problem for me because I worked in the guitar department and I could book a room. But before that, if you wanted to book a room you had to wake up at seven in the morning and wait in line for two hours." Another student, Alex, argued similarly that "they don't have enough rehearsal rooms. With several thousands of students they have so few rehearsal rooms. And half of them are closed because of the BPC shows" (i.e., because of rehearsals for performances that take place at the Berklee Performance Center, the school's main performance venue). Both Berklee and the New School face significant challenges in light of the exorbitant real-estate prices in Manhattan and Boston, which make it harder to expand. Although Berklee has managed to open a new student-run music venue in an attempt to address these issues, and the New School frequently collaborates with music venues in Manhattan in which student ensembles can play, the dearth of rehearsal space and performance opportunities continues to constitute a problem. Students, then, still play together, but they do so less than before because they must compete over limited rehearsal space or hold sessions in their apartments, which poses significant practical limitations.

A number of the educators I worked with had no doubt that, coupled with such practical difficulties, the ubiquity of devices such as the play-along has increased students' isolated practice when compared to the mode of training experienced by players of previous generations. And they were convinced that this isolated practice has compromised students' skill of responding to one another in the real time of improvisation, which is a basic feature of this art form. Consider an incident that took place during a clinic at Berklee given by Randy, a well-known jazz trombone player. At a certain point when Randy played a blues tune with a group of students there was miscommunication with the rhythm section. The rhythm section stopped playing after Randy had played a phrase that remotely resembles a standard phrase used in many play-along devices to designate the ending of a tune. The students thus played automatically, thinking Randy was about to end his solo. However, he did not mean to end his solo and continued playing. This resulted in a prolonged confusion while the rhythm section attempted to resume its playing and catch up with him. At the end of the tune Randy turned to the audience and asked:

"What's just happened?" After trying to elicit a response for about two minutes to no avail, he said:

> Well, what happened up here is real life. What I hear a lot of times when
> I hear jazz performances, especially in schools, is an attempt to not create
> real life. Because this is how life is. Your life cannot ever be like a computer
> program without communication. All those who have computers know:
> you have a deadline and then the computer is going to crash—that's real life.
> [Laughter.] And when you're improvising—one of the greatest travesties
> in music is the play-along record. Now the play-along records started in the
> 1950s and [their purpose] was to provide you guys a chance to play with a
> rhythm section if you needed one and that was the idea. It was called Music
> Minus One. Nowadays the play-along records have taken over. And . . . it
> affects—it's a way for you to sit there with your headphones and your speak-
> ers and you just do what you want to do, and you don't have to worry about
> the fact that in real life the rhythm section thinks that I'm taking the melody
> out and we have to figure out what's going on. In real life the drummer's
> usually playing too loud and you have to fight against that. With these play-
> along records you adjust the volume, and you decide, and it's just stagnant; it
> stays the same. No matter what you do. You try to push something different
> and it's going to be the same right there.

In commenting on the miscommunication, Randy makes the distinction between "real life" and playing with play-along devices to emphasize the repercussions of the increasing virtualization and atomization of jazz training as a result of the use of these devices by a growing number of students. He hints at the standardizing impact of these pedagogical devices by saying that they transform jazz improvisation into something that is "stagnant; it stays the same." When students do not listen to one another, but rather play as if they were isolated atoms, their improvisations become monotonous and standardized, because they do not feed off the ongoing musical input contributed by their band members and generated by the contingencies of live performance. This is why when it turned out that Randy did not want to end his solo the students did not know what to do. They did not have the skill to follow him and respond accordingly once they understood they had made a mistake, which itself was the result of their following the stagnant conventions institutionalized by play-along devices.

Ironically, the play-along devices' ubiquity has also affected the jam session, the site where musicians have traditionally learned how to musically interact with one another. When I asked Carl, a Berklee student bass player, why he does not attend the Sunday afternoon jam sessions held at a venue located next to Berklee, he responded: "Are you crazy? Why should I go there? Go and see for yourself: one saxophone player after another going up on stage, each one of them taking seventeen choruses and playing their shit. No interaction with the rhythm section, as if we were their play-along. Is this jazz? Excuse me, but I have better things to do with my time." In Carl's view, students come to the jam session with an atomistic orientation that thwarts the possibility of interactive playing. He points to the play-along as a pedagogical device responsible for and epitomizing this kind of orientation.

I do not want to argue that prior to its academization jazz was characterized by a mythically unified community as opposed to its present modern atomistic form of sociality. As I noted earlier, jazz students still play with one another. Yet there is little doubt that the culture of jazz prior to and in the earlier stages of its academization was characterized by denser musical sociability among aspiring musicians, which fed directly into their improvisational skills. Jam sessions functioned as laboratories for creating new musical forms and ideas, exchanging professional information, maintaining contacts, negotiating the tenuous economic reality of the performing jazz musician, and, most importantly, learning how to musically interact with other players (DeVeaux 1997, 202–235). One need only recall the 1950s-era Philadelphia jazz community that produced legendary trumpeter Lee Morgan and other masters to realize that jazz was an interactive cultural phenomenon that implicated associations of people larger than the single player:

> The musically supportive environment of mid-century Philadelphia provided a complex positive feedback system that routinely produced experienced musicians of the highest caliber. . . . Public school programs, interaction with professional musicians, numerous performance venues, and a civic emphasis on the performing arts combined to nurture talent in the city's youth and encourage them to pursue a creative life in the arts. For jazz musicians like Lee Morgan, these elements were further complemented by the proactive attitude of many of the city's families, club owners, disc jockeys, and most of all, musicians, to provide the city's aspiring young players with an invaluable foundation. (McMillan 2001, 160)

It is this kind of dense sociality that provided the context for the production of the musical masterpieces whose aesthetics was based to a large degree on artful real-time musical interaction between players.[8] In contrast, the present atomization of jazz training in some academic contexts is highly conducive to atomized playing and hence the standardization of the music.

Truth games in which students use chance objects in the course of musically interacting with one another represent students' strategies of cultivating crucial interactive skills. These games provide the context in which listening can be discerned and evaluated based on the contribution to group improvisation made by each participant. By initiating "improvised improvisations," as I call these interactions that appropriate chance objects, students hone the skill of listening and responding to one another in the course of performance. The fact that each of the students can only contribute a small piece—usually a short rhythmic or melodic figure—to the larger whole because they play on chance objects with limited possibilities for music making and of which they have limited mastery, encourages them to cultivate these listening skills rather than sink again into mechanistic and noneditorial playing.

"Who is playing this?" Identifying Distinct Timbres and Styles

Carla, Sarah, Pierre, and I sit in Sarah's living room. On a table littered with glasses, plates, an open box of cookies, and an ashtray, is Sarah's laptop. It plays track after track of jazz, randomly chosen by the iTunes player. Suddenly, Pierre raises his head from his guitar and asks "Who is playing this?" Sarah looks at him, then at the computer, and then back at him. "OK," she declares, "let's see who can guess who the player is on each track!" She stands up, approaches the table, and then sits next to the computer, not looking at it yet. We listen to the music carefully. I recognize the sound of the sax player. The smooth attacks, the behind-the-beat and laid-back approach to the meter, the bending of the notes, and the light tone—I have no doubt. "Lester Young," I say. Sarah searches for the title of the track on the iTunes. She looks at me with a poker face: "Are you sure?" Pierre and Carla remain silent. "Yes," I say. "And it's 'I'm Confessin' That I Love You.'" Sarah looks again at the laptop's screen. "Correct," she says. We listen to the tune until it ends.

Then another tune begins. It is a fast-tempo blues number that opens with a saxophone solo. Every note is crystal clear. I am familiar with this sound, too. Though I am certain I heard it hundreds of times before, I simply cannot come up with the name. "It's Cannonball," Pierre declares. The moment he says it I know he is right. It is Cannonball Adderley. Sarah once again engages in the "Are you sure?" routine, but Pierre insists. However, there is a problem. It appears that Cannonball is a sideman on this recording, and because the tune is played through the iTunes player, Sarah cannot verify whether it is Cannonball or not. Neither the sidemen nor the album's title are specified. I support Pierre by saying that of course it is Cannonball, but this does not satisfy Sarah. To be on the safe side she calls her roommate, Jonathan, a gifted saxophone player who is also a Berklee student. She asks him to listen to the recording and tell us who the saxophone player is. She replays the track. Jonathan listens for only three seconds before declaring: "Cannonball." "Well," Sarah says, closing the laptop with both hands, "I guess that's settled."

In many of the student parties and gatherings I attended, jazz often played in the background and stimulated all kinds of reactions. Sometimes students would sing or tap rhythm with their hands or simply engage in commentary about the music; this ranged from the simple "It's so cool" to extended debates about the musicians, albums, and tunes. Their most common reaction, however, was to compete over their ability to accurately identify key musicians and performances.

These games of "recognition" are embedded in a particular cultural, technological, and social context. To begin with, they are made possible by the technology of digitized music. Many times students would set their music players so that tracks from different albums followed each other randomly. This constant shuffle of musicians and styles is conducive to games of recognition, because the identity of the musicians constantly shifts, almost asking to be identified.

However, the fact that a practice is made technologically possible does not explain why people actually engage in it. I suggest that students initiate this game of truth as a response to those features of print pedagogy prevalent in the academic jazz program that erase unique timbre or personal sound as a key aesthetic principle in jazz improvisation. Many students fail to develop a personal style and an identifiably unique sound or timbre because of the program's heavy reliance on printed artifacts, coupled with the paucity of live performance opportunities in which students could implement this abstract knowledge in playing. The game of truth I just described is a technology of the listening self that sensitizes students to the importance of cultivating such a style, sound, and timbre. Learning to recognize the masters' unique timbral identities, as well as key performances and recordings in the history of the genre, exposes students to the importance of producing similar identities and identifiable moments in and through their own playing. In this way, students learn about and also strive to reproduce a key normative ideal in jazz improvisation, which their playing currently lacks due to their institutionalized modes of training. This game allows participants and observers to tap into students' collective "mind"—a wealth of knowledge that is the sum of the partial knowledge of each of them, in order to retrain themselves in a particular dimension of the listening self that is crucial to this art of improvisation.

"Goodbye Pork Pie Hat": Of Tunes, Titles, and Tales

It is evening. Sarah, Carla, Pierre, and I are walking back from school to Carla's place to "chill" for the rest of the night. We walk quickly, trying to minimize our exposure to the cold in this cloudless winter night. The streets are empty. I am engulfed in my own thoughts when I suddenly hear Sarah's voice: "Hey guys, look at the moon!" I lift up my head. We have arrived at a clearing in the forest of buildings and we can now see more of the sky. We stop for a second to admire the full and perfectly round moon. "Can anyone come up with a name of a jazz standard with a moon in it?" Sarah asks. "How High the Moon," Pierre says. "It's Only a Paper Moon," I add. I start to hum the melody of "How High the Moon." I hum the first four bars and then stop. The moment I stop, Carla continues the melody into its next four bars. We quickly establish a pattern: Carla stops after four bars, Pierre takes it into the next four bars, and Sarah concludes with the last four bars of the first half of the tune. All this doesn't take more than a few seconds.

We continue to walk and resume our conversations. I walk with Sarah, while Carla and Pierre walk ahead of us. Sarah points to a rundown grocery store whose old neon sign reads in blue letters: "Punjab." "You know," she says to me softly, "in Lyon, where I come from, there is also a supermarket with the same name right next to my home, just like here. It's strange, no?" I agree. "Punjab" is a standard tune written by Joe Henderson. To have two supermarkets whose namesake aligned with a jazz tune's title next door on two different continents as a jazz musician is a strange coincidence. Sarah then starts hesitantly to sing Punjab's melody. I, too, am not sure of the melody although I have heard it dozens of times. We try to reconstruct it, each of us contributing what he or she knows, serving as a crutch to the other. Thus, our melody is limping but walking nonetheless until we reach the house.

The evening progresses lazily in Carla's living room. At about 3:00 a.m. I decide it is time to go home. I prepare myself for the long walk in the cold night and deserted streets. Carla walks me to the door. Outside I turn around to face Carla. "OK," I say, "Goodbye." Carla smiles at me. "Goodbye, Pork Pie Hat," she says.[9] I start to walk. It is not so lonely and cold now that I have this beautiful tune to keep me company on my way home.

The game-like interaction I just described might give the reader the impression that students at Berklee have ample knowledge of the standard tunes that comprise much of the jazz repertoire. Yet this interaction actually emerged against the backdrop of the concern over students' lack of such knowledge and as an attempt to address it. Indeed, during my fieldwork at Berklee and the New School, I was often surprised by the fact that many students had scant knowledge of standard tunes or jazz history. This lack of knowledge was not immediately evident in class because students could function moderately well in ensemble settings even without this knowledge by playing on the chord changes that would usually be available to them in printed form. Yet, sometimes evidence of large-scale shifts in musical competence would become apparent. This always caught educators, especially veteran musicians with impressive performance history, by surprise. They would usually respond with disbelief.

For example, in a class at the New School, an educator instructed the students to improvise on a standard tune of their choice. It took the students more than five minutes to decide on a tune, because it was difficult for them to find one tune they all knew even though the suggested tunes were all relatively well-known.[10] At one point the educator lost his patience and said to a student who confessed that he did not know a certain tune, "You don't know this tune? What the hell DO you know?" When educators probed deeper, they realized that the fact that many students do not know some basic tunes is indicative of a much more significant shift in their musical taste.

Thus in one class at the New School, Benny, an educator in his early seventies, spent a long time trying to teach the drummer to play softer while other students waited and listened. Then the following conversation ensued:

[Benny:] This is something that you have to work on.
[Drummer:] It's hard when I have people telling me to hit even harder.
[Benny:] You have people who tell you, who tell you to hit even harder?

Who tells you? Is that the way you want to play the drums? Let's answer
   that first. Do you want to play them harder?

[Drummer:] Sometimes, yeah. I like it.

[Benny:] You like hitting the drums harder?

[Drummer:] Yeah, that's why I started from the beginning. I guess anyone
   would like hitting the drums harder.

[Benny:] Of course.

[Drummer:] But the people I am involved with, you know, outside of
   school, sometimes they ask me to hit—

[Benny:] You're talking about jazz-wise or funk-wise?

[Drummer:] No, no, not even funk. I don't play any funk bands.

[Benny:] What do you play then?

[Drummer:] Like Indie Rock.

[Benny:] Oh.

[Drummer:] And alternative.

[Benny:] Yeah, right, so that's bash-crash.

[Drummer:] Yeah, so I'm used to bash-crash.

[Benny:] So you're not playing that many jazz gigs, so you don't have a
   chance to use this [i.e., the material taught in class].

[Drummer:] Here and there I do, and when I do play those gigs I really
   consciously try to play as soft as I can.

[Benny:] All right, yeah, so you have a problem that the gigs that you make
   to pay the rent don't allow you to work on this. All right. [Turning to the
   second drummer:] Come over. Same with you, man? Is that the same
   situation with you? Do you play more jazz gigs? Because you play softer.

[Second drummer:] Yeah. I mean, no. I don't play more jazz gigs.

[Benny:] Really? [Benny looks at the floor in what appears to be despair and
   emits a long sigh].

Only in the fourth week of the semester did Benny become aware of the fact
that some of his students play jazz only infrequently. He was amazed and sad-
dened by the fact that some of the students would not use most of the knowledge he taught them. He exhibited the same reaction (gazing at the floor in
silence and sighing) whenever he called a standard tune and one or several of
the students did not know it.

   Some of the educators and students I spoke to argued that students are to
blame for their ignorance. Itai, an Israeli student at the New School explained:

I think that most of the students who come to the New School do not
come to study jazz in terms of what you and I would define as jazz. They are
not interested in the tradition—they are not interested in connecting to it
and in playing it. [. . .] The older generation is much more used to mutual
respect. The reason that jazz thrived so much was because information was
shared. [. . .] But if a person doesn't know who Junior [i.e., pianist Junior
Mance] is, there is a problem. He will say, "Wait a minute. Why should I sit
in this classroom with this man—an eighty-year-old man—giving me this
stuff and playing all the time? Wait a minute, let me play, let me play some
hip shit." I can understand that, but I come from a very different place. I
come from a place where this is exactly the experience I want. What ruins
my experience, though, is that not all students have the same frame of mind
as mine. Most of the students who come to schools today want to know how
to play the stuff that is in *now*, but this is not the place where the old cats are
coming from, especially at their age.

Indeed, when asked, some students explained their lack of knowledge of the
tradition by referring to historical transformations and broader cultural shifts
that have taken place in the past few decades in the jazz world. They argued
that what the jazz program identifies as "jazz music" is an archaic cultural form
no longer relevant to the present moment. Consider the following commentary given by Dan, a New School student pianist who managed to perform in
prestigious jazz venues and with leading veteran jazz musicians by reluctantly
mastering the tradition:

I feel it's not fair to expect me to know all these standards. For these guys
[the past jazz masters], it was part of the culture. It was in the air: it was the
popular music of the day. But this is not my culture, man. It's not today's
culture anymore. No one knows any standards. Whenever I go to one of
these gigs I need to do historical research to play that. I need to go online.
Fuck that. I don't want to play museum music. I don't care about Wynton
[trumpeter Wynton Marsalis]! I want to play my music through the influence of the tradition. I don't want to play the tradition. And in the school
it's the same. They call it Jazz and Contemporary Music [referring to how
the New School brands itself], but there is no contemporary music in the
school. It looks backwards, not forwards, and partly because of all those
teachers that they bring here just because they were in the scene and played
with all those big names. And when a student brings to class some funk bits

and two chords, Paul [a veteran New School educator] will tell him to get the fuck out of the classroom because it's not jazz to him. Well, where's the contemporary music here? And this is why people drop out: they don't want to play this music. They prefer to play improvised music in bars in Brooklyn rather than to play straight-ahead jazz at Dizzy's.

Dan points to larger shifts in the taste for and trends of jazz music. He observes that what educators consider "jazz music" is anachronistic with contemporary music. In the words of some of the other students I discussed this with, jazz has become akin to Western classical music, presumably a museum exhibit that has little to no relation to the present musical scene. Dan invokes the aesthetic agenda of the trumpeter and director of Jazz at Lincoln Center, Wynton Marsalis, as an epitome of this approach. Within the jazz world, Marsalis is often criticized for his classicist approach, because he has pushed for the canonization of a very specific body of music that he considers "the jazz tradition" and has presumably excluded styles not aligned with it (Nicholson 2005; Stewart 2007; see also Prouty 2004). Usually, the canonized tradition includes music produced until the late 1960s, especially in its acoustic, as opposed to electric, forms. Dan spatializes the opposition between this approach and his search for more contemporary artistic expressions by distinguishing between Dizzy's—a reference to Dizzy's Club Coca-Cola at the mainstream Lincoln Center in Manhattan, and "bars in Brooklyn" where young musicians explore new musical directions for low or no pay. For Dan, jazz as it is taught at the New School has ceased to be part of contemporary "experience," certainly not an invalid observation given the paucity of jazz venues and the small market share of jazz. He is willing to engage with the jazz tradition only as something that can inform contemporary music and only if he has to do so in the context of specific gigs, not as something in and for itself.

However, for many students, the jazz of the past has little relevance to much of the contemporary music they want to play. They prefer to "move on" and explore other musical directions. One person who graduated from the New School wrote the following on his MySpace web page:

I'm a graduate of the Jazz & Contemporary Music Program at the New School. I like to think of myself as more "Contemporary Music" than "Jazz." No disrespect to the tradition, or the masters of it (whom I've listened to thoroughly).... They've already played the best bop lines ever, swung the hardest, played the ting ting ta-tingiest. Musicians in my generation have no real point of reference for this music, and for me it seems illogical to retrace the paths that have already been cut when there's still so much out there to explore.

Against the backdrop of these transformations, the game of truth I described above functions as a site in which students attempt to make the jazz tradition part of their contemporary experience. They weave the music into the fabric of their everyday reality by invoking tunes' titles and melodies with reference to what they experience. In this way they resist isolating or sequestering jazz to the space of the academic jazz program as if it were a rarefied and obsolete object in a museum.

This way of organically integrating the jazz tradition into students' daily life can feed back into their playing, because tunes' melodies and even titles are an important source of variety in jazz improvisation. Different standard tunes are frequently based on similar harmonic progressions, and some tunes even have identical harmonic progressions. Hence, improvising only by taking into consideration a tune's harmony and chord changes, as is often done by students in the jazz program, leads to standardized improvisation. This is why veteran jazz performers have always emphasized the importance of knowing tunes' lyrics and titles as a way of individuating one's improvisation. One venerable New School educator told his students about what he had learned directly from four past jazz masters:

> What's the first thing you gotta do before you learn a ballad? Learn the lyrics. What I usually do, I have everybody learn the lyrics before they play the tune in class. The lyrics tell what the composer had in mind. It sort of makes you use your phrasing more as improvisation. Some people think improvisation is just playing a whole bunch of notes. But this is not the case. Four people that I worked with told me the same thing, and I was surprised that these four told me to learn the lyrics first. One was Charlie Parker. Even though he just plays bebop, if you listen to him play a ballad you'll always hear that thread through it. Like if you listen to his string albums [i.e., a number of albums that Parker recorded with string orchestras], he plays the melody with his own phrasing. The second one was Coleman Hawkins, same thing. He advocated learning the lyrics first. As did Ben Webster. Ben Webster will not record until he knew the lyrics. Clark Terry once told Ben Webster—this was years ago—"Ben, I got a great tune for you to play." Ben said, "What's that?" Clark said, "My Funny Valentine." Ben said, "Ah,

no." Clark said, "Why? It's a great tune, everybody plays it." [Ben responded:] "I don't know the lyrics." However, he learned the lyrics and he played it, probably the best version ever. The other one, which was a guy I worked with for two years, Lester Young. But he was different, though. . . . When I was on the road with him—this was in the forties before they had LP's, you know— he carried stacks of 78s, all singers, and he would listen to the vocalists' version rather than listen to somebody else playing it on their horn or instrument. That surprised me, man. All singers—Billie Holiday, of course; Frank Sinatra; and a lot of singers I never heard of. But that's how—he says—that's how you learn a tune: listen to the lyrics, what the composer had in mind.

I suggest that when students tap time and again into tunes' titles and melodies in the course of their everyday life, they do so in response to such discourses. They individuate tunes in a number of ways. First, tunes have different subjects: one is concerned with the moon; a second with an Indian state; a third with a type of a hat worn by a jazz master. Second, when students integrate these titles into the flow of their everyday lives, tunes acquire a personal meaning: one tune is about a huge moon seen on a specific cold night spent with friends; the second is about a supermarket in one's hometown; the third is about saying farewell to a friend in the middle of the night. Tying different tunes to unique personal experiences is a way of making these tunes meaningful and thus the basis for different improvisations. On yet a third level, each tune is explored with regard to its melody. If, as one Berklee educator told me, today's jazz students belong to a "harmonic generation" as a result of jazz programs' emphasis on harmony, whereas players of previous generations informed their improvisations much more by tunes' melodies, the students who engage in this game learn how to take melodies into consideration when constructing improvisations. This game of truth tests students' mastery of, and also provides them with the training ground to develop, these skills.

The Transformation of Performance Authenticity into a Scarce Resource

The technologies of the listening self or games of truth designed by the students I worked with are micropractices by means of which students actively negotiate shifts in their improvisational competence and at times manage to reverse them. Students get exposed through their educators to critical reflexive discourses on some of the problematic aspects of their academic jazz training and what performance authenticity in jazz should consist of. They tap into these discourses and fashion technologies of the listening self accordingly.

The nature of such technologies as micropractices suggests that the full implications of the academization of jazz training cannot be studied only through the "official" and most visible social practices, but must be complemented by exploration of so-called informal practices that take place in their shadow.[11] Much of the academization of jazz training takes place in the context of these invisible, mundane, and spontaneous interactions and events that reveal the complexity of the cultural reproduction of jazz in academic jazz programs— complexity that challenges reductive accounts that present these programs as sites in which jazz slowly but surely approaches its end. In its commitment to remain close to practice and everyday life, anthropology is well situated to explore these microlevel interactions and events. If, as Foucault argues, part of what makes the analysis of technologies of the self difficult is that they "do not require the same material apparatus as the production of objects; therefore they are often invisible techniques" (Foucault 1997, 277), anthropology is well equipped to unearth these techniques to better explore the ways in which individuals participate in the production of their selves vis-à-vis institutional affordances and limitations.

At the same time, it is important to note that these truth games are agonistic in nature and result in the construction of listening as a scarce resource. To participate and to invite other students to participate in the last game of truth I described is to ascertain who among the students can individuate jazz tunes and who can only treat them as abstract and decontextualized harmonic progressions. To sing a melody is an invitation that is also a challenge for other students to display their knowledge of the melody by taking it from one place and continuing it. The practice of creatively integrating tunes' titles in episodic moments is a similar challenge. The same applies to the previous games I discussed: to nail a note with one's instrument; to imitate an outside sound by whistling or singing; to creatively improvise with chance objects; to correctly identify canonical players as quickly as possible—while these games function as a training ground that allows students to develop and cultivate crucial skills, they are also competitive sites that emphasize the emergent nature of listening as a scarce resource in some contexts of academic jazz education. The inevitable production of winners and losers suggests that performance authenticity as defined in this context remains a scarce resource to some extent. Hence, at the same time that these games allow students to negotiate creative agency and institutionalized rationality, they also keep them opposed to each another, because, as competitions, they inevitably frame some students as lacking in listening skills as the result of the academization of jazz training.

Yet above and beyond these unintended implications, the students I befriended viewed these game-like interactions as an intimate space in which they could help one another fashion an ethical self in the sense I outlined above: to become a musician who commands the multiform skills of listening that can be implemented with mastery in real-time improvisation. Taking their inspiration from the critical discourses voiced by their educators, but also fashioning their practices against the pedagogical practices of the classroom, these students took jazz pedagogy back to "the street." This was not the mythical and gritty street invoked by some veteran educators as a legible sign of their presumed indigeneity, but rather the space of lived experience, of everyday life, a space in which jazz becomes once again the contemporary music of its time if only briefly and for a few dedicated individuals who collaboratively orchestrate this powerful alchemy of time travel.

And powerful it is. Even now, a few years after the end of my fieldwork at Berklee, whenever I listen to the lonely and sorrowful melody of "Goodbye Pork Pie Hat," I am immediately reminded of Carla's smiling face before my departure in that cold night, and I am immediately taken back to the many wonderful moments I spent with my friends, now dispersed all over the globe. This tune has indeed become part of the fabric of reality for me, similar to no other jazz tune, and whenever I improvise on this tune I try to imbue my improvisation with the unique experience now associated with it in my mind. I cannot think of a better outcome for such strategies of collective self-fashioning.

CONCLUSION

It is my hope that this book has succeeded in developing a number of theoretical points.

First, the opposition between creative agency and institutionalized rationality is historically specific, the product of two key narratives about modernity: modernity as increased rationalization (mostly associated with the Enlightenment), and modernity as the expansion of normative ideals of creative agency (mostly associated with Romanticism). The first narrative assumes a view of modernity as an increasingly cold, rationalized, and technical Iron Cage, whereas the second narrative understands modernity as the opening up of new horizons of human creativity, where emotions take the center stage as sources of action. This opposition is a key feature in the cultural logic of Western modernity. It is neither universal nor inevitable.

Second, in practice there are many institutional sites in which the two narratives and the practices they entail are brought together under one roof. The academic jazz program in particular, and the academic art program in general, are two exemplary forms of such sites because their logic entails the rationalization of creative practice.

Third, when these two opposing narratives are brought together—including the normative ideals and sets of practices unique to each—the result is the production of many tangible challenges, which, in the case of the academic jazz program, include how to reconcile seemingly opposing forms of authority (rational versus charismatic), expertise (accreditation-based versus experiential-performative), mediation of knowledge (abstract knowledge versus immersion in real-time performance), sensory agency (visually oriented versus aurally oriented), and sociality (modes of speaking, etiquette, gender relations).

Fourth, these numerous challenges notwithstanding, when one looks closely at the everyday reality in such institutions it becomes clear that the individuals who have to operate within these tensions often find various ways to reconcile and resolve them. Taking the academic jazz program as an example, educators, administrators, and students recruit charismatic performers to teach alongside educators who derive their authority mainly from their academic training; they take advantage of advanced technologies of sound mediation to immerse their students in the sounds of the past jazz masters' creative improvisations against the backdrop of the gradual disappearance of vibrant jazz scenes; they imbue the past masters' improvisations with the institutionalized terminology of the academic jazz program through acts of translation, interpretation, and narration that bring the two closer together; they use rule-governed techniques to reconfigure their students' playing bodies and thus to open up new creative horizons in their improvisations; and they devise routinized strategies of sensorial self-fashioning that increase the role played by aurality in students' improvisational competence. Throughout, elements from one narrative are interwoven with elements from the other narrative such that the very infrastructure of the institutional environment of the academic program becomes a condition of possibility for forms of cultivation of creative practice.

Fifth, although the everyday reality in such institutional sites reveals the many ways in which individuals are able to reconcile the two narratives with one another on one level, it also reveals that such practices of reconciliation reproduce the opposition between the narratives on another level. Taking the academic jazz program as an example, the strategies administrators, educators, and students deploy to reconcile institutionalized rationality and creative practice frequently *sustain* certain dimensions of the basic opposition between these poles. Their strategies reproduce purist binary oppositions such as aurality/literacy, blackness/whiteness, past/present, intuition/theory, lowbrow/ highbrow, associating creativity in jazz with the terms occupying the left side of these oppositions, and institutionalized rationality with those on the right side. That these sites function as sites of reconciliation that is productive of opposition is perhaps the most important, and certainly the most ironic, theoretical point of this book. It is important because it explains why the opposition between the two narratives about modernity persists despite the fact that the fabric of everyday reality consists of strands of both narratives. Attempts to reconcile the two narratives create situations in which the differences between the narratives and the sets of normative ideals and practices they entail become salient for people, compelling them to highlight these differences and to make them even more salient. Think again of the doctoral honoree's speech and the ways in which it crystallized in an almost inimitable way a number of key oppositions that typically remain more subtle. Think of all the instances in which educators and students felt the need to divide, to dichotomize, and to separate even as they were busy reconciling and bridging.

This finding is also ironic because critics who argue that the academic jazz program is a contradiction in terms and hence doomed to failure depend on the very basic opposition or idea that is the product of these programs. To some degree, had there been no academic jazz programs and other sites that provoke people (and critics) to make salient the differences between the two narratives, these differences might not have been reproduced to begin with, and critics might not have had any reason to believe that creative practice and institutionalized education are oppositional to one another. Severe critics of academic art programs are thus also their products.

The sixth and last theoretical point is that in assessing the question of the conditions of possibility for cultural reproduction we need to move beyond the surface level of cultural forms and consider the often invisible experiential dimensions of culture. These dimensions are invisible not in the sense that with some effort they can be made visible, but in the sense that they cannot be made visible at all because they do not pertain to the realm of the visual—that dimension that has too often been the focus of anthropological research. At stake are cultural modalities that involve the body and its sensorium beyond the modality of the visual (Erlmann 2004; Geurts 2003; Hirschkind 2006; Howes 2006). This point relates to a key dimension of the story told in this book: the transformations in the role of aurality following the academization of jazz training. It can be best unpacked in the context of a current debate in the anthropological literature that is directly relevant to these questions.

Beyond the Dichotomy of Cultural Continuity and Loss

In the past two decades, anthropologists have argued that we need to rethink notions of cultural change that emerged from traditional anthropology, globalization theory, and modernization theory (Appadurai 1996; Greenblat 1991; Hannerz 1990; Hirschkind 2006; Mahmood 2005; Jackson 1995; Rosaldo 1989; Trager 1988). A programmatic articulation of this view has been provided by Marshall Sahlins (1999) in an article that I would like to draw on in detail. In this article, Sahlins criticizes a number of assumptions about cultural change that traditional anthropology has inherited from the Enlightenment, such as viewing indigenous cultures as historyless entities that have existed in a kind of pristine state prior to cultural contact with the West; or conceptualizing cultural change as "adulteration" and "cultural loss" when it concerns indigenous societies, and "progress" when it concerns the West. Drawing on recent anthropological research, Sahlins argues that indigenous societies the world over have responded to modernity by indigenizing it. This does not mean that these societies returned to some kind of a pristine and fetishized identity, but rather that they appropriated elements associated with modernity to develop *their own* cultural orders. Northern Eskimo hunters who use snow machines, radios, all-terrain four-wheelers, rifles, fishing vessels, and airplanes to perfect their culturally specific subsistence practices are a case in point. These hunters have managed to survive not because they isolated themselves from modern means of production, but rather because they incorporated these means to further their own cultural order, that is, to have "more and better of what they consider good things" (Sahlins 1999, x). Sahlins concludes that "the struggle of non-Western peoples to create their own cultural versions of modernity undoes the received Western opposition of tradition vs. change, custom vs. rationality—and most notably its twentieth century version of tradition vs. development" (xi). As for anthropology's reaction to these developments, Sahlins observes that rather than taking these changes as an opportunity to renew itself, current anthropology has remained in a state of a postmodern panic over the assumed impossibility of culture as we have come to know it, characterized by "coherent logics and definite boundaries" (xx). Sahlins maintains that anthropologists have preferred to mourn the "disappearance" of culture precisely when culture is everywhere to be found in new forms and configurations. They have entrenched themselves in the "culture of resistance" paradigm while remaining myopic to the possibility of the "resistance of culture" (xvi).

On the one hand, Sahlins's points lend themselves nicely to the ethnographic material and theoretical points I have presented in this book. Many commentators have reacted to the rise of academic jazz education in the same way that the anthropologists Sahlins criticizes reacted to various instances of the modernization of indigenous societies: they have assumed in advance that such academization signals the disappearance of the allegedly "pristine" cultural order of jazz, its adulteration by the academic environment, and its transformation into a pale shadow of its glorious past due to increased rationalization and bureaucratization. Similarly to Sahlins's suggestion that the inventive ways in which indigenous societies appropriated the forces of modernity have allowed them to survive and advance their cultural orders, it is possible to argue that jazz's entrance into academe did not signal jazz's destruction but has allowed the reproduction of its cultural order against the backdrop of adverse extracurricular conditions. Jazz educators and musicians have inventively appropriated academe to sustain and reproduce myriad dimensions of the creative cultural order of jazz.

On the other hand, the story is not so simple. Although both the persistence of "old" cultural orders within the "new" and the appropriation of "new" by "old" cultural orders are signs of the resilience and "resistance of culture," there are paradoxical social contexts in which "new" cultural orders are appropriated by "old" ones to announce the latter's own death. During the sixteen months of my fieldwork at Berklee and the New School I recorded many incidents in which educators reverted to what seemed like culturally specific and "traditional" modes of knowledge transmission only to articulate what they considered to be the differences between academic jazz training and the modes of socialization into jazz that predated it, and which some of them experienced firsthand. For the most part, they portrayed academic jazz training as a flawed structure of socialization that leaves out valuable knowledge that can only be learned pragmatically when transmitted by experienced performers in live performance situations outside of the normative environment of institutionalized higher education. They further argued that the result of the rise of academic jazz education has been the production of musically incomplete musicians. Many of these educators, then, used the infrastructure of academe to reproduce "traditional" cultural forms of jazz knowledge production and transmission but only to argue that academic jazz training has resulted in a "cultural loss."

This paradox is precisely what puzzled me about the incident with which I opened this book, which involved T.K., the educator who scolded Pierre during one of our joint playing sessions. Although T.K. argued that in the academic jazz program knowledge is not transmitted anymore by seasoned musicians in the form of stories and lived experience, he conveyed this argument precisely as a seasoned musician who imparts knowledge via stories and lived experienced. He told Pierre what he had experienced when he played with Art Taylor—a legendary jazz master—in a nonacademic setting. Thus, on the one hand, T.K. appropriated the academic classroom to further one dimension of the traditional order of jazz—storytelling. On the other hand, he used this traditional mode of imparting knowledge to declare that such a mode has been rendered obsolete because of the academization of jazz: students are not taught valuable knowledge in appropriate ways anymore.

Thus one of the significant challenges I faced during my fieldwork was not how to overcome the myopia that prevented me from taking into account reconfigured cultural forms and practices, as Sahlins would suggest. Rather, the problem I experienced was how to *interpret* these reconfigured cultural forms and practices. I could find everywhere around me evidence of what appeared to be educators' and students' inventive appropriation of the infrastructure of academe to reproduce the traditional cultural order of jazz. Yet this evidence was paradoxical through and through. How should we consider incidents where "old" cultural forms persist within and through new ones, yet at the same time explicitly index and announce their own precariousness and possible demise? Why should we take seriously only the "traditional" form of T.K.'s mode of teaching that points to cultural continuity—his use of storytelling about his own apprenticeship with Art Taylor, while bracketing off the fact that he does so to explicitly argue that the case of the academic jazz program is one of cultural discontinuity?

I suggest that as long as we stay within the Manichean framework of the "culture of resistance" and the "resistance of culture" we will continue to lack the analytical tools and models that can account for these ambiguities. On a more concrete and straightforward level, we need to move beyond the visible dimensions of cultural reproduction and assess the variety of its experiential dimensions. It may not be enough to point out hunters who use rifles instead of bows and arrows to suggest cultural continuity or loss. What is needed is an understanding of the shifts in the experiential dimensions of using each technique and whether or not these shifts and dimensions are culturally salient for group members. The rise of academic jazz training *was* accompanied with experiential changes manifested in neophyte musicians' skills and in the music they produce. The meaning and function of aurality as a traditionally key modality of knowledge production and transmission in the cultural order of jazz have shifted among the jazz students I worked with. This does not mean that students stopped listening as a result of enrolling in academic jazz programs. In fact, many of the pedagogical practices I have discussed, such as the production and analysis of transcriptions or the manipulation of advanced media technologies, involve intricate hearing practices. Rather, these practices have become oriented to, and organized around, the growing role played by the typographic medium and literacy practices of various kinds in the curriculum, which, coupled with the disappearance of extracurricular performance opportunities, has had specific implications as to the ways in which aurality informs students' improvisations. These changes have taken place at the same time that many individuals from within the two academic jazz programs have turned to traditional forms of knowledge transmission and production in an attempt to negotiate the academization of jazz training. If one is not tuned to the experiential dimensions of academic jazz pedagogy, one might miss the fact that their inventive forms of appropriating academe are a strategy of mitigating the various forms of experiential changes ushered by academic jazz training *itself* as well as by the various macrosocial forces within which such a form of training exists. Rather than simply being signs of cultural revival or resistance, then, the persistence and renewal of "traditional" modes of knowledge production and transmission in the two academic jazz programs point to the complexity of cultural reproduction that involves cultural continuity and loss at the same time and on different levels.

On a metatheoretical level, the very idea of an opposition between "old" and "new" cultural orders is often also the rhetorical and discursive product of sites of explicit cultural reproduction such as the academic jazz program in which attempts are made to reconcile these orders. In this case, we should treat the very theoretical question of cultural continuity and loss as not only historically determined (as Sahlins does by pointing out the relevance of the legacy of the Enlightenment), and empirically determined (e.g., by pointing out the shifting role of aurality as the result of the academization of jazz training), but also as internally generated by the very sites that are the focus of our study. These sites polarize such cultural orders at the same time that they reconcile them, and in doing so, they provide the discursive basis for the questions anthropologists ask.

Future Questions and Applications

To conclude, note that the above theoretical points and cautionary notes have implications for future research and questions whose scope is wider than the sphere of the socialization into jazz education in particular, and other art forms in general, in institutions of higher education. They also apply to the flip side of this form of radical conflation of institutionalized rationality and creative practice in the present historical moment. I refer to increasingly prevalent attempts to model the management and operation of the modern, rational organization after forms, practices, and normative ideals of the creative arts in an attempt to increase the organization's productivity and revenues (Wilf 2013; see also Florida 2003). Thus if the academic jazz program is an example of the organizational cultivation of creativity, its flip side is the creative cultivation of the organization.

Indeed, consider the ironic fact that scholars and practitioners of organizational research have recently turned to no less than jazz music in an attempt to find organizational models that would be better suited to the fluctuating and changing conditions of the postindustrial economy, which require an improvisatory approach to decision making. This is how one of these scholars begins an article titled "Creativity and Improvisation in Jazz and Organizations: Implications for Organizational Learning," published in 1998 in the journal *Organization Science*, in a special issue titled "Jazz Improvisation and Organizing":

> At the dawn of the twenty-first century, we are in the midst of a revolution that has been called variously the post-industrial society . . . , the third wave . . . , the information revolution . . . , and the post-capitalist society. . . . We do not yet perceive the entire scope of the transformation occurring, but we know that it is global, that it is based on unprecedented access to information, and that since more people have access to information than ever before, that it is potentially a democratic revolution. . . . Given the unprecedented scope of changes that organizations face and the need for members at all levels to be able to think, plan, innovate, and process information, new models and metaphors are needed for organizing. Drucker has suggested that the twenty-first century leader will be like an orchestra conduc-

tor. However, an orchestral metaphor—connoting pre-scripted musical scores, single conductor as leader—is limited, given the ambiguity and high turbulence that many managers experience. Weick . . . has suggested the jazz band as a prototype organization. This paper follows Weick's suggestion and explores the jazz band and jazz improvising as an example of an organization designed for maximizing learning and innovation. (Barrett 1998, 605)

Recent organizational theory has consistently emphasized the importance of "improvisation" and nonhierarchical interactional norms to organizational productivity in specific sectors. This emphasis has led theorists and practitioners to draw from forms of interaction and praxis in jazz music. Managers seek to have their organization function like a jazz group and their employees think and interact with one another like jazz musicians. Theorists hold that jazz can inform managers' decisions about product innovation (Kamoche and Cunha 2001) and entrepreneurial self-efficacy (Hmieleski and Corbett 2008), and that it can provide a general mindset for organizational analysis (Weick 1998; see also Sawyer 2007).

This form of creative cultivation of the organization is further evidence for the increasing number of contemporary hybrid institutional forms in which institutionalized rationality and creative practice are conflated, in which long-held and taken-for-granted oppositions are reproduced and resolved, and in which nothing is what it appears to be at first glance. But now that we have cultivated our listening skills and sensitivity to the harmonic form, melody, and broader contextual history of what is fast becoming a standard, late-modern tune, we are better equipped to embark upon research-improvisations of our own and to account for these hybrid forms' complex nature and intricate workings.

NOTES

Chapter One

1. Herbie Hancock was a pianist in one of Miles Davis's most renowned quintets.

2. Jazz aligns with Benjamin's example of storytelling also in terms of the ways in which both art forms are understood to be meaningful. One of the key aesthetic principles within the cultural order of jazz is that of "telling a story" or "saying something" with one's improvisation, namely, building a "narrative" structure (Monson 1996).

3. Throughout the book, I use "jazz music" to refer to a fluctuating entity that is constantly being negotiated by critics, music producers, musicians, educators, collectors, and other actors within the jazz art world. Broadly defined, jazz is a prototypical set of formal aspects that include distinct patterns of improvisation, harmony, rhythm, orchestration and voicing, execution (e.g., phrasing, timbre manipulation) (Berliner 1994; Jackson 2003), and modes of interaction between performers (Monson 1996), to name but a few factors. In addition, it is informed by a canon of repertoire and great performers, a historical narrative, and various ideologies (DeVeaux 1991; Gennari 2006) that pertain to the music's "meaning" for experienced and inexperienced listeners and for practitioners (Townsend 2000).

4. The International Association for Jazz Education has since then filed for bankruptcy, mostly due to poor attendance at the 2008 annual meeting held in Toronto. See Ratliff (2008). Its place has been filled by other initiatives.

5. This trope references Max Weber's influential idea of modern rationality as an "Iron Cage," which I address below.

6. For ethnomusicological studies that give some space to both the continuities and discontinuities that structure academic jazz education with respect to previous modes of jazz training, see Ake (2002; 2012) and Prouty (2011). A different strand of research not over-determined by pessimism about academic jazz education has focused on the nuts and bolts of academic jazz training but has tended to leave out the broader cultural context and social forces within which such training takes place (e.g., May 2003; Watson 2010). It is the relation between these different levels and how they intersect with and impact one another that is the focus of this book.

7. Juilliard's jazz studies program was established in 2001.

8. The history of jazz has been riddled with concerns about standardization even prior to the music's full-blown academization. One early example centers on alto saxophonist Charlie Parker's innovative musical style, also known as bebop, in the 1940s, a style that departed in a number of ways from the swing style. Other musicians attempted to learn bebop by studying Parker's live and recorded improvisations. Soon enough, as critics noted, "every-one" was imitating Parker. Lennie Tristano, a pianist who played with Parker, was one of the critics who, in 1951, targeted this mimicry when he said: "If Charlie Parker wanted to invoke plagiarism laws he could sue almost everybody who's made a record in the last 10 years. If I were Bird, I'd have all the best boppers in the country thrown into jail!" (Shim 2007, 75). Twenty-two years later, Tristano was still preoccupied with the mass imitation of Parker's style: "Bird enjoyed playing with me. Because I was not imitating him and everybody in the world was. [. . .] See, if you went down the Street [52nd Street in Manhattan] and walked into a club and heard a ten-piece band, everybody stood up and took about 50 choruses of Bird's licks [improvisational formulae]. And it stayed that way until, say maybe the middle fifties. And it finally caught up to Bird. It really bugged the shit out of him. Because he told me so" (Shim 2007, 42).

9. See Latour (1993, 78) for an analysis of this kind of duality.

10. Following standard ethical practice in anthropological research, I have used pseud-onyms and other means to anonymize my interlocutors at Berklee and the New School save for some interlocutors who spoke at public events outside of these programs or at mass events within these programs, which were attended by representatives of the news media and mem-bers of the general public.

11. Only a small share of these students actually focus on jazz performance, however.

12. Online jazz courses, which are playing an increasingly important role in academic jazz education, will not be covered in this book. For an analysis of this aspect of jazz education, see Prouty (2011).

13. This second caveat is especially important given the fact that more than six years have passed since my fieldwork at Berklee and the New School, a time during which these programs might have changed in ways not reflected in this book.

14. Because this book is addressed to a wide range of both academic and nonacademic audiences, I have abstained from including music charts and have made limited use of music terminology.

15. As are the days when anthropologists hesitated to conduct ethnographic research on the acoustic infrastructure of culture (Erlmann 2004; Feld 1982; Hirschkind 2006).

Chapter Two

1. The following historical outline of jazz's marginalization is limited to the North American context. A very different history is that of jazz's reception in Europe, where jazz was received with much more consistent enthusiasm. However, some of this enthusiastic reception was motivated by various racial ideologies (such as noble-savage tropes) and romanticizing approaches based in misunderstandings of the nature of improvisation (Gioia 1988a; Nettelbeck 2005; Ramshaw 2006). One might argue, then, that this form of reception was a subtle mirror image of the more explicit forms of essentialization of jazz in the American context. Ironically, as one of the reviewers of this book has correctly observed, jazz musicians themselves were prone to romanticize European understanding and appreciation of jazz, thus turning a blind eye to the darker undercurrents of the appreciation they received in Europe.

2. Although the following cursory history is built around the polarity of classical music and jazz, it goes without saying that the field of music in the US throughout the twentieth century was much more complicated than that, with various musical genres occupying midlevel positions and often bridging between different genres, including jazz. See, for example, Fellezs (2011) for the case of fusion and its bridging between jazz, rock, and funk.

3. For other bibliographical items from this period, in which debates about jazz as a potential object of institutionalized pedagogy took place, see Caswell and Smith (2000); Prouty (2008).

4. For another ethnographic study of a classical music conservatory, in which various notions such as talent are used to naturalize and mask specific social formations, see Kingsbury (1998).

5. A number of well-known musicians such as Benny Goodman, Tommy Dorsey, Glenn Miller, and George Gershwin studied with Schillinger or were influenced by his ideas at that time (Brodsky 2003).

6. To reiterate, the story is not so simple, because Schillinger's theory-informed pedagogy and persona represent Berklee's love-hate relationship with "theory" as both a legitimizing trope and a trope that connotes jazz's own marginalization by classically trained musicians.

7. In 2000, jazz accounted for little more than 1 percent of the retail value of global sales of recorded music, while classical music accounted for about 7 percent (Laing 2003, 328).

8. This distinction found expression in the writings of the early philosophers of modernity such as John Locke and Francis Bacon, who invested a lot of rhetorical energy in associating modernity with the normative ideal of literacy as the sphere of rationality and in dissociating it from forms of orality/aurality that presumably perpetuate irrationality (Bauman and Briggs 2004).

9. These data were derived from a conventional random sample of jazz musicians belonging to the American Federation of Musicians.

10. Invoking Pierre's words at Winthrop House, John, a Berklee saxophone student, told me during an interview: "In New York there are a lot of places where you can play. They don't pay, but you can play. For a jazz musician, that's what we do. A classical musician wouldn't play for free, but a jazz musician would."

11. Http://www.apimages.com/metadata/Index/Associated-Press-Domestic-News-New-York-United-/41ed9a7360e5da11af9f0014c2589dfb/2/0, accessed July 21, 2013.

12. Indeed, several educators at Berklee acknowledged to me that in the absence of gigging opportunities and venues where they could play regularly, the school provides them, too, with much-needed experience in the form of playing with students during ensemble classes.

13. Compare with Myers (1993), who argues that the professionalization of the field of creative writing in the United States was, in part, the result of poets' attempt to increase their financial security amid minimal commercial demand for poetry.

14. Drummer Chico Hamilton and trumpeter Jimmy Owens served as educators at the New School at the time of my fieldwork.

15. Beefsteak Charlie's was a well-known hangout for jazz musicians in Midtown Manhattan—see Josephson (2009, 84).

16. Most of the students I interviewed argued, too, that one of the best things their jazz program provided them with was the opportunity to join a community of fellow jazz musicians. Furthermore, students find the rehearsal spaces provided by the jazz program to be a great benefit. As one New School student told me, many students who graduate from this program keep in touch with currently enrolled students to maintain access to the rehearsal rooms.

17. On the recruitment of students by big bands, see Collier 1994.

Chapter Three

1. All figures were obtained from the National Association of College and University Business Officers (2013).

2. Although Berklee grants various student fellowships, most students are of middle-class background as a result of the relatively high tuition (approximately $24,000 for two semesters in the degree program at the time of my fieldwork; in the 2013–2014 academic year tuition is expected to be approximately $36,000) and the exorbitant costs of living in Boston and its environs.

3. See Porter (1989, 138) on the prioritization of enrollment rates in academic jazz education. The international students I interviewed were not unaware of the function of the scholarships they received. As one of them told me, "Berklee gives almost everybody something, everybody who applies—the international students. They send you a letter, saying: 'Congratulations! You received the scholarship, we opened the door for you, now you're going to be part of the Berklee community, it's going to be fantastic.' And of course it's a way to attract people who are going to spend all the thousands of dollars they miss for the tuition." As another international student put it: "They send you a letter—'Congratulations, you just won 10,000 dollars, yoo-hoo! Please come to our place and give us 10,000 more.'" Later we shall see that these students' cynicism targets a very specific cultural logic operative at Berklee, namely, the commodification of the markers of higher education.

4. Http://en.wikipedia.org/wiki/Esse_quam_videri, accessed December 14, 2011.

5. Indeed, the hiring of this president was a source of some anxiety at Berklee, because unlike many other administrators, he was neither a former graduate of the school nor a professional musician. To emphasize that he is not entirely foreign to the school's culture, he and his team kept emphasizing the fact that he is an amateur drummer. A drum set was displayed in the vestibule of his office for everyone to see.

6. Recall again the claim made by Berklee's treasurer that Berklee's ambition is to become "the M.I.T. of music" (Hornfischer 2004).

7. To be sure, this general orientation is not particular to academic jazz education, as

was recently demonstrated by the concern resulting from Harvard's decision to substantially increase its financial aid for undergraduates, a fact that in the commodified field of higher education forced Yale and Princeton to figure out ways to match Harvard (Glater 2007; Rimer and Finder 2007). However, I suggest that this dynamic has a specific manifestation and intensity at Berklee.

8. To be sure, this was not the case at the convocation event that is the focus of this chapter.

9. See http://www.berklee.edu/about/honorary.html, accessed June 30, 2013.

10. Kenny G. is a highly successful saxophonist who is often associated with "smooth jazz."

11. The honoree is referring to Chamberlayne Junior College, which was located on Commonwealth Avenue in Boston. The college eventually merged with Mount Ida College of Newton, MA.

12. Thus, referring specifically to academic jazz education, the saxophonist Branford Marsalis said in a *Boston Herald* article: "The times are different now. The talent level is severely diminished and that stuff that has replaced it has really put jazz in a bind because the music seems to lack any kind of substance in regard to humanness or humanity. It's very professional, like think-tank music" (Young 2006).

13. Jazz was historically associated in the public imaginary with uninhibited sexuality, and this in turn indexed African American culture in the context of dominant racial ideologies (Entman and Rojecki 2001; Jones 2005). In addition, theory has long been coded as white in American culture because of racial ideologies with a long history (Gioia 1988a; Monson 2007; Torgovnick 1990).

Chapter Four

1. At the same time, one must not overestimate these educators' ability to assert their authority in class and simulate forms of authority they associate with the past. To begin with, most educators cannot "fire" their students. They may retaliate against students for unprofessional behavior or lack of dedication by giving them low grades, but the status of the student as a (high) tuition-paying client grants him or her immunity from harsh measures, except for extreme cases of disobedience. Furthermore, not only does the jazz program deprive educators of means of retaliation against students, it provides students with the means to retaliate against educators in the form of student evaluations, a feature that it shares with many other academic programs. Many of the criteria by which students are supposed to evaluate educators are in complete opposition to the traditional model of jazz mentorship. Statements such as "The instructor presented course materials in a clear way," "The instructor created a class environment which encouraged questions and free exchange of ideas," "The instructor's interactions with students were helpful and respectful," are simply irrelevant to the highly hierarchical social relationship between a bandleader and his sidemen, and to the often ambiguous ways in which bandleaders would impart knowledge and give instructions to their sidemen (Smith 1998).

A last factor that undermines these educators' charismatic authority is many students' lack of knowledge of the history of jazz, which would allow them to associate these educators with the past masters and thus to recognize their charismatic power. As we shall soon see, Weber argued that the charismatic leader depends on the recognition of his audience. These educators face many students who do not recognize and acknowledge their powers because they lack the basis to do so. Consequently, the educators' charismatic power ceases to exist—indeed, sometimes it has never been successfully asserted to begin with. This situation results in frequent clashes between the educators I worked with who come to the jazz program with the certitude that they possess complete authority over the situation by virtue of their lineage charisma and the knowledge it entails, and students who challenge and question that authority because they are not aware of its basis. In these moments, rather than authority emanating "naturally" and "self-evidently" from charisma, the educators need to verbally assert it; indeed, they need to remind students that they possess authority. In point of fact, they ask students to remember something that the latter never really knew to begin with.

2. A play-along is a pedagogical device that includes a recording of a rhythm-section accompaniment for jazz tunes; the jazz student can improvise with the recording.

3. Thus the pattern 1 2 3 5 becomes 8 2 3 5. The educator then asked the students to treat the second degree as a ninth degree such that the pattern 8 2 3 5 became 8 9 3 5, and so forth.

4. Throughout this chapter, I make a distinction between "professional educators" and educators who have had significant performance experience with the past masters. In doing so, I am tapping into my interlocutors' identification of the first group with academic credentials rather than with "experiential knowledge," and with education rather than performance as the focus of one's career. The term "professional" is thus used in a purely formal way, i.e., regardless of pedagogical efficacy. Although many of my interlocutors presented these categories as mutually exclusive, in practice they are very porous. Some so-called professional educators have achieved legitimacy due to their performance competence, while many of the charismatic educators attended standard conservatories and the first schools for jazz in addition to acquiring significant performance experience with the past masters. See Ake (2012) for a discussion of these issues.

5. One can take this suggestion one step further and point out that Art Blakey named his band the Jazz Messengers. Thus his sidemen, much like the selected group of Jesus's disciples, are themselves "messengers" who are entitled and obliged to spread "the word," not only about jazz, but also about their charismatic master's extraordinary and unique powers and revelations.

6. These associations are powerful. I remember that when I studied with a trumpet player who had studied with Red Rodney in the late 1980s, I was truly excited about the fact that I was "two links" from Charlie Parker, since Red Rodney played with Parker in the late 1940s.

7. Note that some students, too, attempt to imbue the classroom and their educational experience with tropes of a past, mythical "street." They mobilize specific forms of dress, speech, and interaction that connote for them jazz's heydays.

8. See Grazian (2005) for a similar dynamics in the case of the Chicago blues scene.

9. See Monson (2007, 77) for additional examples.

Chapter Five

1. One example is the Jamey Aebersold Jazz Studies Program at the University of Louisville, Kentucky, which is named for Jamey Aebersold—currently one the most important publishers of jazz pedagogy material in the United States. The program was named for Mr. Aebersold in 2000.

2. Similar erasure of pragmatic elements has been noted in efforts to represent spoken or

other aural/oral phenomena with various notational systems, such as the transcription of languages by linguistic anthropologists (Bucholtz 2000; Ochs 1979) or the transcription of trial proceedings in the American legal system (Woolard 1998, 23). Paralinguistic features such as stress are frequently omitted in transcription due to the limitations of available notational systems (Haviland 1996, 74; Urban 1996).

3. Significant scholarship has been devoted to debunking purist conceptions of aurality (or orality-aurality) and literacy, as well as "great divide" theories in general. Theories of "great divide" received their boost in the 1960s, when a number of scholars claimed that the advent of literacy implied a great shift in human history (Goody and Watt 1963; Goody 1987; Olson 1977; Ong 1982). According to their argument, literacy, in the sense of alphabetical writing systems accompanied with technologies of text production and circulation, results in major changes on several levels. It supposedly allows for the rise of "a fully developed logic," a scientific attitude, the codification of law, the depersonalization of social relations conducive to modern bureaucratic forms, and democracy by virtue of making knowledge available to the masses, to give but a few elements of this argument. Starting in the 1980s, however, new studies of specific ethnographic contexts have made clear that the meanings of orality-aurality and literacy and the uses to which they are put are highly varied, and that literacy practices are intertwined with supposedly aural-oral communicative practices such that it is impossible to make a clear-cut distinction between these categories (Besnier 1995; Bledsoe and Robey 1993; Collins and Blot 2003; Duranti and Ochs 1986; Finnegan, 1988, chap. 6; Heath 1986; Knorr Cetina 2003, 106; Kulick and Stroud 1993; Latour and Woolgar 1986; Mehan 1996; Rockhill 1987; Schieffelin 1999; Shuman 1986; Street 1984; Street 1993; Thomas 1991; Vincent 1993).

4. Educators' strategies of distancing themselves from print pedagogy can be compared to attempts to overcome the mediation of the written word and arrive at a "direct" communication with God in some religious spheres (Engelke 2004).

5. Of course, Benjamin understood the revolutionary potential of such features in a more directly political sense.

6. For further details, see http://www.ronimusic.com/, the website of this program's manufacturer.

7. Indeed, it seems that students who witness such replications performed in class by their classmates often experience a ritual transformation, too, in which they inhabit the original moment of a master's improvisation as spectators. I do not have the space to pursue this point. I thank Robert Moore for this suggestion.

8. This can change with future technology. It is possible to imagine a technology that will record the gradual process of a painting being painted, brushstroke after brushstroke, by a great contemporary painter and then "play" this process on an interactive pad upon which a novice painter would be able to laminate a synchronous iconization of the same process of painting with paint.

9. Indeed, Adorno's (1982) problematic criticism of the very form of jazz revolved around this argument. See Wilf (2010, 579n16).

Chapter Six

1. Note, though, that from the mid-1930s, specialized trade magazines began to appear, such as *DownBeat*, which published transcribed solos from key recordings with commentary.

2. The album was recorded in 1954 but released three years later.

3. Here and throughout this chapter I occasionally use "discourse" to denote the past masters' solos as the subject of transcribing and recontextualizing although these solos do not consist of language properly defined.

4. Charlie also emphasizes stylistic features that can be learned only via an aural mode of producing and transmitting knowledge, for example, "blues elements" or modes of articulation in which the concept of "pitch" is much more flexible and involves bending notes and approaching them via glissando. In doing so, Charlie invokes the critique of print pedagogy that I discussed in the previous chapter.

5. It is crucial to note that my point is not that the transcriptions produced in these classes are partial representations of the solos. Indeed, all transcriptions are necessarily partial representations. My point is that acts of transcription can and should be informed with the awareness of their partiality. Such reflexivity is mostly absent from the sites I worked in; indeed, this absence is almost a necessary condition for the naturalization of chord-scale theory. As this chapter also relies on transcribing interactions (between educators and students in class) for making its arguments, I ought to adhere to the same criteria and hence point up the limitations of my own argument and the elements it necessarily leaves out, especially with respect to the fact that Berklee and academic jazz education at large are informed by diverse pedagogies, not all of which are characterized by the decontextualization and abstraction I emphasize in this chapter.

6. Note that educators' interpretative strategies are based in the understanding that it is both possible and permissible to "read other minds." This understanding is culturally specific. Scholars of societies in the Pacific have recorded a widespread claim "that it is impossible or at least extremely difficult to know what other people think or feel" (Robbins and Rumsey 2008, 407–408). Some of these anthropologists have stressed that at stake is not so much the impossibility to impute intentions to others but rather the fact that doing so would be to infringe upon that person's right to be the one who verbalizes his or her thoughts (Stasch 2008; Schieffelin 2008). In any case, at stake are assumptions that are highly different from those that underlie the educators' interpretative strategies.

7. I bracket the question of whether Ron or any other educator, when explicitly prompted, would actually say that the past jazz masters thought in terms of, or wanted to communicate to their audience, the principles of chord-scale theory. Rather, educators' modes of production and analysis of jazz transcriptions in class support these assumptions and hence have practical implications and rhetorical force for the many students who are exposed to them time and again, as is evident in the latter's eager adoption of chord-scale theory, a stance which, to be sure, is also determined by various other factors.

8. In itself, then, this type of narration is not unique to the jazz educators I worked with. It is ubiquitous in other forms of narration, such as sports broadcasting, the interpretation of the compositional "intentions" of a classical music composer as inferred from a musical score, and my own analysis of the pedagogical practices at Berklee and the New School. Rather, what is significant is the ways in which educators' mode of narration combines with the other stages I describe in this chapter to produce a distinct interpretative configuration that has specific implications.

9. This represents a "mistake" according to chord-scale theory because C minor 7 has E-flat as its chord tone, not E natural.

10. To be sure, the assumption of such mastery is probably not so far-fetched in Brecker's

case, since he was trained at Indiana University, albeit only for a short while. Nevertheless, the importance of the classroom vignette transcends this fact, as the third student's comment makes clear.

11. Gerry's emphasis on the importance of the "music" and his disregard for the broader social context that surrounds it are reminiscent of the formalist approach in twentieth-century art criticism, which held that art works should be analyzed in terms of their internal formal features such as composition and texture rather than in terms of their ideational content and broader contextual circumstances such as the artist's biography (see Tekiner 2006 for a short history and critique of formalism). However, as I will soon argue, Gerry's stance is probably motivated by considerations that are highly different from the considerations that motivated the rise of formalism.

Chapter Seven

1. The term *turnaround* refers to conventional harmonic progressions.

2. Note that the educator suggests that building a strong muscle memory is a condition of possibility for bypassing deliberative agency. He does not suggest that it necessarily results in such bypassing.

3. Recent studies in music cognition have demonstrated that it is impossible to make a neat division between body and intellect in music execution. See, for example, Iyer (1998).

4. The length of a note can be divided in various ways. For example, in Western classical music notation, notes might have the lengths of whole, half, quarter, eighth, sixteenth, and so on, in which each value is half of the preceding one. A half note is thus a longer note than an eighth note.

5. Educators argue that standardization is evident also within the frame of each student's playing in the sense that it is highly monotonous and lacking in variety.

6. To reiterate a point made in the introduction, concerns about the "contagious" imitation by novices of a few jazz masters are nothing new—the case of copycatting Charlie Parker in the 1950s through the avid learning of his records is an example. What is different is the historical-specificity of each case, including their institutional conditions of possibility and their implications.

7. That this notion of "product differentiation" resonates with Romantic ideologies of creativity becomes clear when the last vignette is compared with the opening lines of Jean-Jacques Rousseau's *Confessions*, one of the main prophets of the Romantic pursuit of the unique self: "I am resolved on an undertaking that has no model and will have no imitator. I want to show my fellow-men a man in all the truth of nature; and this man is to be myself. Myself alone. I feel my heart and I know men. I am not made like any that I have seen; I venture to believe that I am not made like any that exist. If I am not more deserving, at least I am different" (Rousseau 2000, 5). "If I am not more deserving, at least I am different"—Rousseau, too, condones personal defects because of their potential to produce difference and because they are what makes each person unique.

8. Pierre Bourdieu (1980; 1993) argues that the field of cultural production and consumption is based on a somewhat similar logic of differentiation. However, for Bourdieu, individuals' capacities for differentiating themselves from one another, whether as consumers or producers, are severely limited by their position in the social structure and their embodied habits that result from this position, which are hard to overcome and change. Differentiation

in Bourdieu's schema, then, is highly "impure" and overdetermined. Some of the clinicians at
Berklee endorse the notion of pure differentiation, while some of them endorse the notion of
overdetermined differentiation.

9. The confluence of Romantic sensibilities and the marketplace has been documented
elsewhere. For example, Colin Campbell, in his *The Romantic Ethic and the Spirit of Modern
Consumerism* (1987), has suggested that in response to the erosion of meaning due to over-
production of standardized objects, the Romantic self has become a key source of authenticity
and meaning in modern consumer culture.

10. Jazz scholars have documented the ways in which musicians produce in real-time
performance distinct identities that their audiences would be more likely to notice (Berger
1999, 119–149). The classroom vignettes I discuss suggest that players' orientation to an
imagined audience, i.e., in abstraction from an actual performance situation, plays a key role in
musicians' stylistic considerations, too.

11. There is no doubt that here, too, Mahmood draws heavily on Asad, who argues that
when Mauss spoke about techniques of the body he "wanted to talk, as it were, about the way
a professional pianist's practiced hands remember and play the music being performed, not
about how the symbolizing mind 'clothes a natural bodily tendency' with cultural meaning"
(Asad 1993, 76).

12. Note, however, that some of the more advanced students write their own phrases precisely in an attempt to escape this standardization. Thus Alex, an advanced saxophone player,
told me in an interview: "I haven't really practiced patterns that I haven't written for myself in
a long time. I write patterns for myself—I have books of phrases that I wrote. . . . I have like
three books of phrases, hundreds of phrases."

13. This is the "machine-gun playing" discussed in the previous chapter.

14. As will soon become clear, at stake is the relative place given to fully conscious, editorial considerations, not the separation between body and mind. As ample phenomenological
research has demonstrated, all thinking is embodied, and many forms of embodiment are
forms of thinking.

15. David Sudnow (2001) [1978] explored this phenomenological basis in his own
process of learning to play the piano, and jazz improvisation in particular.

16. Of course, Merleau-Ponty was aware of the possibility of persistence of body schemata despite such changes, as is evident from his analysis of the phenomenon of phantom
limbs (2002, 90–94).

17. See Csordas (1990) for the nondiscursive element of embodiment.

Chapter Eight

1. Scholars familiar with the cultural order of jazz would recognize the interactional genre
that this game is based on as the agonistic exchange of the "jam session." In the jam session, a
number of musicians take solos one after the other to the accompaniment of a rhythm section.
Jam sessions have had a number of functions in the history of jazz. One of the most important
of these has been to establish hierarchies among musicians. Musicians participated in these
sessions to display their musical prowess in the course of performance by trying to outdo one
another's solos. The highly agonistic nature of these musical interactions received expression
in the phrases musicians used to describe them. These interactions were referred to as "hand-
to-hand combat"; "the best man wins"; to "embarrass" one's opponent; having no "mercy";

to "take shots"; "sharpening your [musical] knife"; and "ceaseless warfare for mastery and recognition" (DeVeaux 1997, 208–213).

2. This might suggest that Foucault has added an important dimension to the history of the theorization of play and games in social theory in the context of which, at least as far as anthropology is concerned, play has been viewed as either pure waste that does not deserve consideration, as in Marxist approaches, or as an affirmation of an already existent meaning, as in hermeneutic approaches informed by the writings of Clifford Geertz (Malaby 2009). According to Foucault, playing games of truth, whose logic often incorporates open-endedness and contingency (Foucault 1997, 300), is a process of productive self-formation, i.e., it is neither waste nor the necessary affirmation of an already existing meaning.

3. This skill is probably more complicated than that. To begin with, I would hypothesize that the "bodily signature" of each note also varies according to the notes that precede and follow it. For example, the bodily signature of a single A note played on any instrument might be different from the bodily signature of an A note that is part of an A major triad. In other words, it would be simplistic to consider the bodily aspects of the production of music through the analytic category of the single note.

4. These terms refer to types of music scales.

5. I qualify by "seemingly" because this performance of immediation depended on the mediation of these chance objects.

6. Pierre's argument resonates with the jazz standard "It Don't Mean a Thing If It Ain't Got That Swing," composed by the pianist and bandleader Duke Ellington in 1931. One section of the tune's lyrics is: "It doesn't matter if it's sweet or hot as long as you give it everything you've got," a line that invokes the tension between mediation and immediation that has played a key role in the cultural order of jazz from its early days.

7. Tim is referring to a software program called Band-in-a-Box, which allows players to generate an accompaniment with which they can play along. See http://www.pgmusic.com/, for the website of this program's manufacturer.

8. See Sawyer (2003) for a semiotic analysis of group creativity in improvisation-based art forms, including jazz and improvisational theater. See also Monson (1996) for a similar orientation that focuses exclusively on jazz.

9. "Goodbye Pork Pie Hat" is a tune written by Charles Mingus as an elegy for Lester Young, who used to wear this type of a hat.

10. For an analysis of the ways in which jazz musicians collectively navigate the vast jazz repertoire, including the decision of what tune to play, see Faulkner and Becker (2009).

11. For an argument that challenges the distinction between formal and informal learning, see Strauss (1984).

WORKS CITED

Abbott, Andrew. 1988. *The System of Professions: An Essay on the Division of Expert Labor*. Chicago: University of Chicago Press.

Adler, Judith E. 1979. *Artists in Offices: An Ethnography of an Academic Art Scene*. Piscataway, NJ: Transaction Books.

Adorno, Theodor W. 1982. "On the Fetish-Character in Music and the Regression of Listening." In *The Essential Frankfurt School Reader*, edited by Andrew Arato and Eike Gebhardt, 270–299. New York: Continuum.

Agha, Asif. 2007. *Language and Social Relations*. Cambridge: Cambridge University Press.

Agrama, Hussein A. 2010. "Ethics, Tradition, Authority: Toward an Anthropology of the Fatwa." *American Ethnologist* 37 (1): 2–18.

Ake, David. 2002. "Jazz 'Traning: John Coltrane and the Conservatory." In *Jazz Cultures*, 112–145. Berkeley: University of California Press.

———. 2012. "Crossing the Street: Rethinking Jazz Education." In *Jazz/Not Jazz: The Music and Its Boundaries*, edited by David Ake, Charles Hiroshi Garrett, and Daniel Goldmark, 237–263. Berkeley: University of California Press.

Americans for the Arts. 2007. "Why Some People Think Duke Ellington Is a Member of the Royal Family." Accessed May 1, 2013, http://www.americansforthe arts.org/public_awareness/images/the_ads/duke_large.jpg.

Appadurai, Arjun. 1986. "Introduction: Commodities and the Politics of Value." In

The Social Life of Things: Commodities in Cultural Perspective, edited by Arjun Appadurai, 3–63. Cambridge: Cambridge University Press.

———. 1996. *Modernity at Large: Cultural Dimensions of Globalization*. Minneapolis: University of Minnesota Press.

Asad, Talal. 1993. *Genealogies of Religion: Discipline and Reasons of Power in Christianity and Islam*. Baltimore: Johns Hopkins University Press.

Bakhtin, Mikhail M. 1996. "Discourse in the Novel." In *The Dialogic Imagination*. Translated by Caryl Emerson and Michael Holquist, 259–422. Austin: University of Texas Press.

Barrett, Frank. 1998. "Coda: Creativity and Improvisation in Jazz and Organizations; Implications for Organizational Learning." In "Jazz Improvisation and Organizing," Special issue, *Organization Science* 9 (5): 605–622.

Batchelor, Ray. 1995. *Henry Ford: Mass Production, Modernism and Design*. Manchester: Manchester University Press.

Bauman, Richard, and Charles L. Briggs. 2004. *Voices of Modernity: Language Ideologies and the Politics of Inequality*. Cambridge: Cambridge University Press.

Belgrad, Daniel. 1998. *The Culture of Spontaneity: Improvisation and the Arts in Postwar America*. Chicago: University of Chicago Press.

Bell, Daniel. 1978. *The Cultural Contradictions of Capitalism*. New York: Basic Books.

Benjamin, Walter. 1969a. "The Storyteller: Reflections on the Works of Nikolai Leskov." In *Illuminations*, edited by Hannah Arendt, 83–110. New York: Schocken Books.

———. 1969b. "The Work of Art in the Age of Mechanical Reproduction." In *Illuminations*, edited by Hannah Arendt, 217–252. New York: Schocken Books.

Berdahl, Daphne. 1999. "'(N)Ostalgie' for the Present: Memory, Longing, and East German Things." *Ethnos* 64 (2): 192–211.

Berklee College of Music. 2004. "The Inauguration of Roger H. Brown." Accessed May 1, 2013, http://www.Berklee.Edu/Sites/Default/Files/Pdf/President/Images/Inauguration/Program.Pdf.

Berger, Harris M. 1999. *Metal, Rock, and Jazz: Perception and the Phenomenology of Musical Experience*. Middletown, CT: Wesleyan University Press.

Berlin, Isaiah. 1999. *The Roots of Romanticism*. Princeton: Princeton University Press.

Berliner, Paul. 1994. *Thinking in Jazz: The Infinite Art of Improvisation*. Chicago: University of Chicago Press.

Besnier, Niko. 1995. *Literacy, Emotion, and Authority: Reading and Writing on a Polynesian Atoll*. Cambridge: Cambridge University Press.

Black, Steven. 2008. "Creativity and Learning Jazz: The Practice of 'Listening.'" *Mind, Culture, and Activity* 15(4): 279–295.

Bledsoe, Caroline H., and Kenneth M. Robey. 1993. "Arabic Literacy and Secrecy among the Mende of Sierra Leone." In *Cross-Cultural Approaches to Literacy*, edited by Brian Street, 110–134. Cambridge: Cambridge University Press.

Boas, Franz. 1955. *Primitive Art*. London: Dover.

Boellstorff, Tom. 2003. "Dubbing Culture: Indonesian *Gay* and *Lesbi* Subjectivities and Ethnography in an Already Globalized World." *American Ethnologist* 30 (2): 225–242.

———. 2008. *Coming of Age in Second Life: An Anthropologist Explores the Virtually Human*. Princeton: Princeton University Press.

Boon, Marcus. 2010. *In Praise of Copying*. Cambridge, MA: Harvard University Press.

Born, Georgina. 1998. *Rationalizing Culture: IRCAM, Boulez, and the Institutionalization of the Musical Avant-Garde*. Berkeley: University of California Press.

Bourdieu, Pierre. 1977. *Outline of a Theory of Practice*. Translated by Richard Nice. Cambridge: Cambridge University Press.

———. 1980. "The Aristocracy of Culture." *Media, Culture and Society* 2: 225–254.

———. 1993. *The Field of Cultural Production: Essays on Art and Literature*. New York: Columbia University Press.

Briggs, Charles L., and Richard Bauman. 1992. "Genre, Intertextuality, and Social Power." *Journal of Linguistic Anthropology* 2 (2): 131–172.

Brodsky, Warren. 2003. "Joseph Schillinger (1895–1943): Music Science Promethean." *American Music* 21 (1): 45–73.

Bronson, Po, and Ashley Merryman. 2010. "The Creativity Crisis." *Newsweek*, July 10.

Brothers, Thomas. 1997. "Ideology and Aurality in the Vernacular Traditions of African-American Music (ca. 1890–1950)." *Black Music Research Journal* 17 (2): 169–209.

Bryant, Rebecca. 2005. "The Soul Danced into the Body: Nation and Improvisation in Istanbul." *American Ethnologist* 32 (2): 222–238.

Bucholtz, Mary. 2000. "The Politics of Transcription." *Journal of Pragmatics* 32: 1439–1465.

———. 2009. "Captured on Tape: Professional Hearing and Competing Entextualizations in the Criminal Justice System." *Text and Talk* 29 (5): 503–523.

Campbell, Colin. 1987. *The Romantic Ethic and the Spirit of Modern Consumerism*. Oxford: Blackwell.

Carey, Joseph K. 1986. *Big Noise from Notre Dame: A History of the Collegiate Jazz Festival*. Notre Dame, IN: Notre Dame University Press.

Carr, Summerson E. 2010. *Scripting Addiction: The Politics of Therapeutic Talk and American Sobriety*. Princeton: Princeton University Press.

Carrard, Phillippe. 1988. "Telling the Game: Baseball as an AP Report." *Journal of Narrative Technique* 1: 47–60.

Caswell, Austin B., and Christopher Smith. 2000. "Into the Ivory Tower: Vernacular Music and the American Academy." *Contemporary Music Review* 19 (1): 89–111.

Cattelino, Jessica. 2008. *High Stakes: Florida Seminole Gaming and Sovereignty*. Durham: Duke University Press.

Cherbo, Joni M., and Margaret J. Wyszomirski. 2000. *The Public Life of the Arts in America*. New Brunswick, NJ: Rutgers University Press.

Chernoff, John M. 1979. *African Rhythm and African Sensibility*. Chicago: University of Chicago Press.

Chevan, David. 2001. "Musical Literacy and Jazz Musicians in the 1910s and 1920s." *Current Musicology* 71–73: 200–231.

Chevigny, Paul. 2005 [1991]. *Gigs: Jazz and the Cabaret Laws in New York City*. New York: Routledge.

Chinen, Nate. 2007. "Jazz Is Alive and Well; In the Classroom, Anyway." *New York Times*, January 7.

———. 2008. "Jazz World Confronting Health Care Concerns." *New York Times*, February 21.

Cicero, Marcus T. 1909. *On Friendship*. New Rochelle, NY: Knickerbocker Press.

Collier, Graham. 1994. "The Churchill Report on Jazz Education in America." *Jazz Changes Magazine* 1 (1).

Collins, James, and Richard K. Blot. 2003. *Literacy and Literacies: Texts, Power, and Identity*. Cambridge: Cambridge University Press.

Comaroff, John L., and Jean Comaroff. 1992. "Bodily Reform as Historical Practice." In *Ethnography and the Historical Imagination*, 69–91. Boulder: Westview Press.

———. 2009. *Ethnicity, Inc.* Chicago: University of Chicago Press.

Csordas Thomas J. 1990. "Embodiment as a Paradigm for Anthropology." *Ethos* 18 (1): 5–47.

———. 1994. *Embodiment and Experience: The Existential Ground of Culture and Self.* Cambridge: Cambridge University Press.

Dance, Stanley. 1980. *The World of Count Basie*. New York: Scribner's.

Davidson, Joanna. 2010. "Cultivating Knowledge: Development, Dissemblance, and Discursive Contradictions among the Diola of Guinea-Bissau." *American Ethnologist* 37 (2): 212–226.

Davis, Miles. 1990. *Miles: The Autobiography*. New York: Simon and Schuster.

Deloria, Philip J. 2004. *Indians in Unexpected Places*. Lawrence: University Press of Kansas.

DeVeaux, Scott. 1991. "Constructing the Jazz Tradition: Jazz Historiography." *Black American Literature Forum* 25(3): 525–560.

———. 1997. *The Birth of Bebop: A Social and Musical History*. Berkeley: University of California Press.

Dewey, John. 2000. *Experience and Nature*. London: Dover.

DiMaggio, Paul. 1982. "Cultural Entrepreneurship in Nineteenth-Century Boston: The Creation of an Organizational Base for High Culture in America." *Media, Culture and Society* 4 (1): 33–50.

Douglas, Mary. 2002. *Purity and Danger: An Analysis of Concepts of Pollution and Taboo*. London: Taylor.

Downey, Greg. 2008. "Scaffolding Imitation in Capoeira: Physical Education and Enculturation in an Afro-Brazilian Art." *American Anthropologist* 110 (2): 204–213.

Dreyfus, Hubert L. 1994. *Being-in-the-World: A Commentary on Heidegger's "Being and Time," Division I*. Cambridge, MA: MIT Press.

Duranti, Alessandro. 2008. "L'oralité avec impertinence: Ambivalence par rapport à l'écrit chez les orateurs samoans et les musiciens de jazz américaines." *L'Homme* 189 (1): 23–47.

———. 2009. "The Relevance of Husserl's Theory to Language Socialization." *Journal of Linguistic Anthropology* 19 (2): 205–226.

Duranti, Alessandro, and Kenny Burrell. 2004. "Jazz Improvisation: A Search for Inner Harmonies and a Unique Self." *Ricerche di Psicologia* 27 (3): 71–101.

Duranti, Alessandro, and Elinor Ochs. 1986. "Literacy Instruction in a Samoan Village." In *The Acquisition of Literacy: Ethnographic Perspectives*, edited by Bambi B. Schieffelin and Perry Gilmore, 213–232. Norwood, NJ: Ablex.

Eisenlohr, Patrick. 2010. "Materialities of Entextualization: The Domestication of Sound Reproduction in Mauritian Muslim Devotional Practices." *Journal of Linguistic Anthropology* 20 (2): 314–333.

Elkins, James. 2001. *Why Art Cannot Be Taught: A Handbook for Art Students*. Urbana: University of Illinois Press.

———. 2009. *Artists with PhDs: On the New Doctoral Degree in Studio Art*. Washington, DC: New Academia Publishing.

Eliade, Mircea. 1998. *Myth and Reality*. Long Grove, IL: Waveland Press.

Engelke, Matthew. 2004. "Text and Performance in an African Church: The Book, 'Live and Direct.'" *American Ethnologist* 31 (1): 76–91.

Entman, Robert M., and Andrew Rojecki. 2001. *The Black Image in the White Mind: Media and Race in America.* Chicago: University of Chicago Press.

Erlmann, Veit. 2004. *Hearing Cultures: Essays on Sound, Listening, and Modernity.* New York: Berg.

Espeland, Wendy N., and Mitchell L. Stevens. 1998. "Commensuration as a Social Process." *Annual Review of Sociology* 24: 313–343.

Faulkner, Robert R., and Howard S. Becker. 2009. *"Do You Know . . . ?": The Jazz Repertoire in Action.* Chicago: University of Chicago Press.

Feld, Steven. 1982. *Sound and Sentiment: Birds, Weeping, Poetics, and Song in Kaluli Expression.* Philadelphia: University of Pennsylvania Press.

Fellezs, Kevin. 2011. *Birds of Fire: Jazz, Rock, Funk, and the Creation of Fusion.* Durham: Duke University Press.

Ferguson, Charles A. 1983. "Sports Announcer Talk." *Language in Society* 12 (2): 153–172.

Fernandez, James. 1986. *Persuasions and Performances: The Play of Tropes in Culture.* Bloomington: Indiana University Press.

Finnegan, Ruth. 1988. *Literacy and Orality.* Oxford: Basil Blackwell.

Florida, Richard. 2003. *The Rise of the Creative Class: And How It's Transforming Work, Leisure, Community, and Everyday Life.* New York: Basic.

Foucault, Michel. 1988. "Technologies of the Self." In *Technologies of the Self: A Seminar with Michel Foucault,* edited by Luther Martin, Huck Gutman, and Patrick Hutton, 16–49. Amherst: University of Massachusetts Press.

———. 1997. *Michel Foucault: Ethics, Subjectivity, and Truth,* edited by Paul Rabinow. New York: New Press.

Gates, Henry L. 1988. *The Signifying Monkey: A Theory of African-American Literary Criticism.* New York: Oxford University Press.

Gennari, John. 2006. *Blowin' Hot and Cool: Jazz and Its Critics.* Chicago: University of Chicago Press.

Geurts, Kathryn Linn. 2003. *Culture and the Senses: Bodily Ways of Knowing in an African Community.* Chicago: University of Chicago Press.

Gioia, Ted. 1988a. "Jazz and the Primitivist Myth." In *The Imperfect Art: Reflections on Jazz and Modern Culture,* 19–49. Oxford: Oxford University Press.

———. 1988b. "The Imperfect Art." In *The Imperfect Art: Reflections on Jazz and Modern Culture,* 50–69. Oxford: Oxford University Press.

Glater, Jonathan D. 2007. "Harvard's Aid to Middle Class Pressures Rivals." *New York Times,* December 29.

Gluck, Bob. 2012. *You'll Know When You Get There: Herbie Hancock and the Mwandishi Band.* Chicago: University of Chicago Press.

Goodman, Jane E. 2002. "Writing Empire, Underwriting Nation: Discursive Histories of Kabyle Berber Oral Texts." *American Ethnologist* 29 (1): 86–122.

Goody, Jack. 1987. *The Interface between the Written and the Oral.* Cambridge: Cambridge University Press.

Goody, Jack, and Ian Watt. 1963. "The Consequences of Literacy." *Comparative Studies in Society and History* 5 (3): 304–345.

Grazian, David. 2005. *Blue Chicago: The Search for Authenticity in Urban Blues Clubs.* Chicago: University of Chicago Press.

Greenblatt, Stephen. 1991. *Marvelous Possessions: The Wonder of the New World.* Chicago: University of Chicago Press.

Handman, Courtney. 2010. "Events of Translation: Intertextuality and Christian Ethnotheologies of Change among Guhu-Samane, Papua New-Guinea." *American Anthropologist* 112 (4): 576–588.

Hannerz, Ulf. 1990. "Cosmopolitans and Locals in World Culture." In *Global Culture,* edited by Mike Featherstone, 237–251. London: Sage.

Haviland, John B. 1996. "Text from Talk in Tzotzil." In *Natural Histories of Discourse,* edited by Michael Silverstein and Greg Urban, 45–78. Chicago: University of Chicago Press.

Hazell, Ed. 1995. *Berklee: The First Fifty Years.* Boston: Berklee Press.

Heath, Shirley B. 1986. *Ways with Words: Language, Life, and Work in Communities and Classrooms.* New York: Cambridge University Press.

Hechinger, Fred M. 1983. "About Education: New Study Finds Lack of Creativity." *New York Times,* March 29.

Heidegger, Martin. 1996. *Being and Time.* Translated by Joan Stambaugh. New York: SUNY Press.

Heilbrun, James, and Charles M. Gray. 2007. *The Economics of Art and Culture.* Cambridge: Cambridge University Press.

Helmreich, Stephan. 1998. *Silicon Second Nature.* Berkeley: University of California Press.

Hirschkind, Charles. 2006. *The Ethical Soundscape: Cassette Sermons and Islamic Counterpublics.* New York: Columbia University Press.

Hmieleski, Keith M., and Andrew C. Corbett. 2008. "The Contrasting Interaction Effects of Improvisational Behavior with Entrepreneurial Self-Efficacy on New Venture Performance and Entrepreneur Work Satisfaction." *Journal of Business Venturing* 23: 482–496.

Ho, Karen. 2009. *Liquidated: An Ethnography of Wall Street.* Durham: Duke University Press.

Hobsbawm, Eric. 1983. "Introduction: Inventing Traditions." In *The Invention of Tradition,* edited by Eric Hobsbawm and Terence O. Ranger, 1–14. Cambridge: Cambridge University Press.

Hornfischer, David. 2004. "Know Your Niche: Berklee Set Out to Be the MIT of Music; Now the Trick Is to Keep the Focus without Straying." *University Business,* February 1.

Hounshell, David. 1985. *From the American System to Mass Production, 1800–1932: The Development of Manufacturing Technology in the United States.* Baltimore: Johns Hopkins University Press.

Howes, David. 2006. *Sensual Relations: Engaging the Senses in Culture and Social Theory.* Ann Arbor: University of Michigan Press.

Ingold, Tim. 2000. *The Perception of the Environment.* London: Routledge.

Ingold, Tim, and Elizabeth Hallam. 2007. "Creativity and Cultural Improvisation: An Introduction." In *Creativity and Cultural Improvisation,* edited by Elizabeth Hallam and Tim Ingold, 1–24. Oxford: Berg.

Iyer, Vijay. 1998. *Microstructures of Feel, Macrostructures of Sound: Embodied Cognition in West-African and African-American Musics.* PhD Diss., University of California, Berkeley.

Jackson, Jean E. 1995. "Culture, Genuine and Spurious: The Politics of Indianness in the Vaupés, Colombia." *American Ethnologist* 22 (1): 3–27.

Jackson, Travis A. 2003. "Jazz as Musical Practice." In *The Cambridge Companion to Jazz*, edited by Mervyn Cooke and David Horn, 83–95. Cambridge: Cambridge University Press.

———. 2012. *Blowin' the Blues Away: Performance and Meaning on the New York Jazz Scene*. Berkeley: University of California Press.

Jaffe, Alexandra. 2009. "Entextualization, Mediatization and Authentication: Orthographic Choice in Media Transcripts." *Text and Talk* 29 (5): 571–594.

Jay, Martin. 2005. "Lamenting the Crisis of Experience: Benjamin and Adorno." In *Songs of Experience: Modern American and European Variations on a Universal Theme*, 312–360. Berkeley: University of California Press.

Jeffri, Joan. 2003. *Changing the Beat: A Study of the Worklife of Jazz Musicians*. NEA Research Division Report 43.

Joas, Hans. 1993. *Pragmatism and Social Theory*. Translated by Jeremy Gaines, Raymond Meyer, and Steven Minner. Chicago: University of Chicago Press.

Jones, Marvin. D. 2005. *Race, Sex and Suspicion: The Myth of the Black Male*. Westport, CT: Praeger.

Josephson, Sanford. 2009. *Jazz Notes: Interviews across the Generations*. Westport, CT: Praeger.

Kamoche, Ken, and Miguel P. e Cunha. 2001. "Minimal Structures: From Jazz Improvisation to Product Innovation." *Organization Studies* 22 (5): 733–764.

Keane, Webb. 2008. "Others, Other Minds, and Others' Theories of Other Minds: An Afterword on the Psychology and Politics of Opacity Claims." *Anthropological Quarterly* 81 (2): 473–482.

Kingsbury, Henry. 1998. *Music, Talent and Performance: A Conservatory Cultural System*. Philadelphia: Temple University Press.

Knorr Cetina, Karin. 1997. "Sociality with Objects." *Theory, Culture, and Society* 14 (4): 1–30.

———. 2003. *Epistemic Cultures: How the Sciences Make Knowledge*. Cambridge, MA: Harvard University Press.

Kopytoff, Igor. 1986. "The Cultural Biography of Things: Commoditization as Process." In *The Social Life of Things: Commodities in Cultural Perspective*, edited by Arjun Appadurai, 64–94. Cambridge: Cambridge University Press.

Kulick, Don, and Christopher Stroud. 1993. "Conceptions and Uses of Literacy in a Papua New Guinean Village." In *Cross-Cultural Approaches to Literacy*, edited by Brian Street, 30–61. Cambridge: Cambridge University Press.

Kuper, Adam. 2003. "The Return of the Native." *Current Anthropology* 44 (3): 389–395.

Laing, Dave. 2003. "The Jazz Market." In *The Cambridge Companion to Jazz*, edited by Mervyn Cooke and David Horn, 321–331. Cambridge: Cambridge University Press.

Larson, Magali S. 1977. *The Rise of Professionalism: A Sociological Analysis*. Berkeley: University of California Press.

Lamaison, Pierre. 1986. "From Rules to Strategies: An Interview with Pierre Bourdieu." *Cultural Anthropology* 1 (1): 110–120.

Lamont, Michèle, and Virág Molnár. 2002. "The Study of Boundaries in the Social Sciences." *Annual Review of Sociology* 28: 167–195.

Latour, Bruno. 1993. *We Have Never Been Modern*. Translated by Catherine Porter. Cambridge, MA: Harvard University Press.

———. 2010. *On the Modern Cult of the Factish Gods*. Durham: Duke University Press.

Latour, Bruno, and Steve Woolgar. 1986. *Laboratory Life: The Construction of Scientific Facts*. Princeton: Princeton University Press.

Lavie, Smadar, Kirin Narayan, and Renato Rosaldo. 1993. "Introduction: Creativity in Anthropology." In *Creativity/Anthropology*, edited by Smadar Lavie, Kirin Narayan, and Renato Rosaldo, 1–8. Ithaca: Cornell University Press.

Leach, James. 2007. "Creativity, Subjectivity, and the Dynamic of Possessive Individualism." In *Creativity and Cultural Improvisation*, edited by Elizabeth Hallam and Tim Ingold, 99–116. Oxford: Berg.

Levine, David O. 1986. *The American College and the Culture of Aspiration, 1915–1940*. Ithaca: Cornell University Press.

Levine, Lawrence. 1988. *Highbrow/Lowbrow: The Emergence of Cultural Hierarchy in America*. Cambridge, MA: Harvard University Press.

———. 1989. "Jazz and American Culture." *The Journal of American Folklore* 102 (403): 6–22.

Lewis, George E. 2009. *A Power Stronger Than Itself: The AACM and American Experimental Music*. Chicago: University of Chicago Press.

Linder, Fletcher. 2007. "Life as Art, and Seeing the Promise of Big Bodies." *American Ethnologist* 34 (3): 451–472.

Lloyd, Richard D. 2005. *Neo-Bohemia: Art and Commerce in the Postindustrial City*. London: Routledge.

Lopes, Paul. 2002. *The Rise of a Jazz Art World*. Cambridge: Cambridge University Press.

Lord, Albert. 1960. *The Singer of Tales*. Cambridge, MA: Harvard University Press.

Lukács, Georg. 1999. "Reification and the Consciousness of the Proletariat." In *History and Class Consciousness: Studies in Marxist Dialectics*. Translated by Rodney Livingstone, 83–222. Cambridge: MIT Press.

Mahmood, Saba. 2005. *Politics of Piety: The Islamic Revival and the Feminist Subject*. Princeton: Princeton University Press.

Malaby, Thomas. 2009. "Anthropology and Play: The Contours of Playful Experience." *New Literary History* 40 (1): 205–218.

Marquis, Alice G. 1998. "Jazz Goes to College: Has Academic Status Served the Art?" *Popular Music and Society* 22 (2): 117–124.

Martin, Randy. 2004. Introduction. *Social Text* 79 (22): 2–11.

Mauss, Marcel. 1973. "Techniques of the Body." *Economy and Society* 2 (1): 70–88.

May, Lissa F. 2003. "Factors and Abilities Influencing Achievement in Instrumental Jazz Improvisation." *Journal of Research in Music Education* 51 (3): 245–258.

Mazzarella, William. 2009. "Affect: What Is It Good For?" In *Enchantments of Modernity: Empire, Nation, Globalization*, edited by Saurabh Dube, 291–309. London: Routledge.

McDaniel, William T. 1993. "The Status of Jazz Education in the 1990s: A Historical Commentary." *International Jazz Archives Journal* 1: 114–139.

McGurl, Mark. 2011. *The Program Era: Postwar Fiction and the Rise of Creative Writing*. Cambridge, MA: Harvard University Press.

McMillan, Jeffery S. 2001. "A Musical Education: Lee Morgan and the Philadelphia Jazz Scene of the 1950s." *Current Musicology* 71–73: 158–178.

Mead, George H. 1934. *Mind, Self and Society*. Chicago: University of Chicago Press.

Mehan, Hugh. 1996. "The Construction of an LD Student: A Case Study in the Politics of Representation." In *Natural Histories of Discourse*, edited by Michael Silverstein and Greg Urban, 253–276. Chicago: University of Chicago Press.

Merlan, Francesca. 2009. "Indigeneity: Global and Local." *Current Anthropology* 50 (3): 303–333.

Merleau-Ponty, Maurice. 2002. *Phenomenology of Perception*. Translated by Colin Smith. London: Routledge.

Monson, Ingrid. 1994. "Doubleness and Jazz Improvisation: Irony, Parody, and Ethnomusicology." *Critical Inquiry* 20 (2): 283–313.

———. 1995. "The Problem of White Hipness: Race, Gender, and Cultural Conceptions in Jazz Historical Discourse." *Journal of the American Musicological Society* 48 (3): 396–422.

———. 1996. *Saying Something: Jazz Improvisation and Interaction*. Chicago: University of Chicago Press.

———. 1998. "Oh Freedom: George Russell, John Coltrane, and Modal Jazz." In *In the Course of Performance: Studies in the World of Musical Improvisation*, edited by Bruno Nettl and Melinda Russell, 149–168. Chicago: University of Chicago Press.

———. 1999. "Riffs, Repetition, and Theories of Globalization." *Ethnomusicology* 43 (1): 31–65.

———. 2007. *Freedom Sounds: Civil Rights Call Out to Jazz and Africa*. Oxford: Oxford University Press.

Muehlebach, Andrea. 2003. "What Self in Self-Determination? Notes from the Frontiers of Transnational Indigenous Activism." *Identities: Global Studies in Culture and Power* 10 (2): 241–268.

Murphy, Daniel. 1994. "Jazz Studies in American Schools and Colleges: A Brief History." *Jazz Education Journal* 26 (3): 34–38.

Muther, Christopher. 2004. "Berklee Professor Takes DJ Class Out for a Spin." *Boston Globe*, February 17.

Myers, D. G. 1993. "The Rise of Creative Writing." *Journal of the History of Ideas* 54 (2): 277–297.

Myers, Fred. 2002. "Introduction: The Empire of Things." In *The Empire of Things*, edited by Fred Myers, 3–64. Santa Fe: School of American Research Press.

National Association of College and University Business Officers. 2013. "U.S. and Canadian Institutions Listed by Fiscal Year 2012 Endowment Market Value and Percentage Change in Endowment Market Value from FY 2011 to FY 2012." Accessed July 5, 2013, http://www.nacubo.org/Documents/research/2012NCSEPublicTablesEndowmentMarketValuesFinalJanuary232013.pdf.

NEA. 2008. *NEA Jazz Masters*. Washington, DC: National Endowment for the Arts Office of Communications.

Nettelbeck, Colin. 2005. *Dancing with de Beauvoir: Jazz and the French*. Melbourne: Melbourne University Publishing.

Nettl, Bruno. 1995. *Heartland Excursions: Ethnomusicological Reflections on Schools of Music*. Urbana: University of Illinois Press.

Nettles, Barry. 2002. Introduction. *Harmony 3*. Boston: Berklee Press.

Nicholson, Stuart. 2005. "Teachers Teaching Teachers: Jazz Education." In *Is Jazz Dead? (Or Has It Moved to a New Address)*, 99–127. London: Routledge.

Ochs, Elinor. 1979. "Transcription as Theory." In *Developmental Pragmatics*, edited by Elinor Ochs and Bambi Schieffelin, 42–72. New York: Academic.

———. 2006. "Narrative Lessons." In *A Companion to Linguistic Anthropology*, edited by Alessandro Duranti, 269–289. Malden, MA: Blackwell.

Ochs, Elinor, and Lisa Capps. 1996. "Narrating the Self." *Annual Review of Anthropology* 25: 19–43.

Ogren, Kathy J. 1992. *The Jazz Revolution: Twenties America and the Meaning of Jazz*. New York: Oxford University Press.

Olson, David R. 1977. "From Utterance to Text: The Bias of Language in Speech and Writing." *Harvard Education Review* 47: 257–281.

Ong, Walter J. 1982. *Orality and Literacy: The Technologizing of the Word*. London: Methuen.

Owens, Thomas. 2003. "Analyzing Jazz." In *The Cambridge Companion to Jazz*, edited by Mervyn Cooke and David Horn, 286–297. Cambridge: Cambridge University Press.

Panish, Jon. 1997. *The Color of Jazz: Race and Representation in Postwar American Culture*. Jackson: University Press of Mississippi.

Park, Joseph S. 2009. "Regimenting Languages on Korean Television: Subtitles and Institutional Authority." *Text and Talk* 29 (5): 547–570.

Park, Joseph S., and Mary Bucholtz. 2009. "Public Transcripts: Entextualization and Linguistic Representation in Institutional Contexts." *Text and Talk* 29 (5): 485–502.

Parmentier, Richard J. 2007. "It's About Time: On the Semiotics of Temporality." *Language & Communication* 27 (3): 272–277.

Passaro, Joan. 1997. "'You Can't Take the Subway to the Field!': 'Village' Epistemologies in the Global Village." In *Anthropological Locations: Boundaries and Grounds of a Field Science*, edited by Akhil Gupta and James Ferguson, 147–162. Berkeley: University of California Press.

Peirce, Charles Sanders. 1998. "Sundry Logical Conceptions." In *The Essential Peirce: Selected Philosophical Writings*, 2:267–288. Bloomington: Indiana University Press.

Pelican, Michaela. 2009. "Complexities of Indigeneity and Autochtony: An African Example." *American Ethnologist* 36 (1): 52–65.

Pellegrinelli, Lara. 2008. "Separated at 'Birth': Singing and the History of Jazz." In *Big Ears: Listening for Gender in Jazz Studies*, edited by Nichole T. Rustin and Sherrie Tucker, 31–47. Durham: Duke University Press.

Peretti, Burton W. 1992. *The Creation of Jazz: Music, Race, and Culture in Urban America*. Urbana: University of Illinois Press.

Porter, Lewis. 1989. "Jazz in American Education Today." *College Music Symposium* 29: 134–139.

Porter, Eric. 2002. *What Is This Thing Called Jazz? African American Musicians as Artists, Critics, and Activists*. Berkeley: University of California Press.

Povinelli, Elizabeth A. 2002. *The Cunning of Recognition: Indigenous Alterities and the Making of Australian Multiculturalism*. Durham: Duke University Press.

Powell, Walter W., and Paul J. DiMaggio, eds. 1991. *The New Institutionalism in Organizational Analysis*. Chicago: University of Chicago Press.

Prouty, Kenneth. 2004. "Canons in Harmony, or Canons in Conflict: A Cultural Perspective on the Curriculum and Pedagogy of Jazz Improvisation." *Research and Issues in Music Education* 2 (1): ssthomas.edu/rimeonline/vol2/prouty.htm.

———. 2005. "The History of Jazz Education: A Critical Reassessment." *Journal of Historical Research in Music Education* 26 (2): 79–100.

———. 2006. "Orality, Literacy, and Mediating Musical Experience: Rethinking Oral Tradition in the Learning of Jazz Improvisation." *Popular Music and Society* 29 (3): 317–334.

———. 2008 "The 'Finite' Art of Improvisation: Pedagogy and Power in Jazz Education." *Critical Studies in Improvisation* 4 (1).

———. 2011. *Knowing Jazz: Community, Pedagogy, and Canon in the Information Age.* Jackson: University Press of Mississippi.

Putnam, Robert. 1995. "Bowling Alone: America's Declining Social Capital." *Journal of Democracy* 6 (1): 65–78.

Rabinow, Paul. 1997. "The History of Systems of Thought." In *Michel Foucault: Ethics, Subjectivity, and Truth*, edited by Paul Rabinow, xi–xlii. New York: New Press.

Ramshaw, Sara. 2006. "Deconstructin(g) Jazz Improvisation: Derrida and the Law of the Singular Event." *Critical Studies in Improvisation* 2(1).

Ratliff, Ben. 2008. "A Jazz Lifeline to Academia Is Severed." *New York Times*, April 26.

Rimer, Sara, and Alan Finder. 2007. "Harvard to Aid Students High on Middle Class." *New York Times*, December 11.

Robbins, Joel, and Alan Rumsey. 2008. "Introduction: Cultural and Linguistic Anthropology and the Opacity of Other Minds." *Anthropological Quarterly* 81 (2): 407–420.

Rockhill, Kathleen. 1987. "Gender, Language and the Politics of Literacy." *British Journal of Sociology of Education* 8 (2): 153–167.

Rosaldo, Renato. 1989. "Imperialist Nostalgia." *Representations* 26: 107–122.

Rosenthal, David H. 1992. *Hard Bop: Jazz and Black Music, 1955–1965.* Oxford: Oxford University Press.

Rousseau, Jean-Jacques. 2000. *Confessions.* Translated by Angela Scholar. Oxford: Oxford University Press.

Rustin, Nichole T., and Sherrie Tucker, eds. 2008. *Big Ears: Listening for Gender in Jazz Studies.* Durham: Duke University Press Books.

Ryan, Marie-Laure. 1993. "Narrative in Real Time: Chronicle, Mimesis and Plot in Baseball Broadcast." *Narrative* 1 (2): 138–155.

Sahlins, Marshall. 1999. "What Is Anthropological Enlightenment: Some Lessons of the Twentieth Century." *Annual Review of Anthropology* 28: i–xxiii.

Sales, Grover. 1992. *Jazz: America's Classical Music.* New York: Da Capo Press.

Saperstein, Marc. 2003. "The Method of Doubts: Problematizing the Bible in Late Medieval Jewish Exegesis." In *With Reverence for the Word: Medieval Scriptural Exegesis in Judaism, Christianity, and Islam*, edited by Jane D. McAuliffe, Barry D. Walfish, and Joseph W. Goering, 133–56. Oxford: Oxford University Press.

Sawyer, Keith. 1996. "The Semiotics of Improvisation: The Pragmatics of Musical and Verbal Performance." *Semiotica* 108: 269–306.

———. 2003. *Group Creativity: Music, Theater, Collaboration.* New York: Psychology Press.

———. 2007. *Group Genius: The Creative Power of Collaboration.* New York: Basic Books.

Schieffelin, Bambi B. 1999. "Introducing Kaluli Literacy: A Chronology of Influences." In *Regimes of Languages: Ideologies, Polities, and Identities*, edited by Paul V. Kroskrity, 293–327. Santa Fe: School of American Research Press.

———. 2008. "Speaking Only Your Own Mind: Reflections on Talk, Gossip and Intentionality in Bosavi (PNG)." *Anthropological Quarterly* 81 (2): 431–441.

Schuller, Gunther. 1986. *Early Jazz: Its Roots and Musical Development.* Oxford: Oxford University Press.

———. 1991. *The Swing Era: The Development of Jazz, 1930–1945.* New York: Oxford University Press.

———. 1999. "Sonny Rollins and the Challenge of Thematic Improvisation." In *Musings: The Worlds of Gunther Schuller*, 86–97. New York: Da Capo Press.

Shannon, Jonathan H. 2003. "Emotion, Performance, and Temporality in Arab Music: Reflection on Tarab." *Cultural Anthropology* 18 (1): 72–98.

Shim, Eunmi. 2007. *Lennie Tristano: His Life in Music*. Ann Arbor: University of Michigan Press.

Shuman, Amy. 1986. *Storytelling Rights: The Uses of Oral and Written Texts by Urban Adolescents*. Cambridge: Cambridge University Press.

Silverstein, Michael. 1998. "The Improvisational Performance of Culture in Realtime Discursive Practice." In *Creativity in Performance*, edited by Keith Sawyer, 265–312. Greenwich, CT: Ablex.

———. 2004. "'Cultural' Concepts and the Language-Culture Nexus." *Current Anthropology* 45 (5): 621–645.

Silverstein, Michael, and Greg Urban, eds. 1996. *Natural Histories of Discourse*. Chicago: University of Chicago Press.

Singerman, Howard. 1999. *Art Subjects: Making Artists in the American University*. Berkeley: University of California Press.

Smith, Christopher. 1998. "A Sense of the Possible: Miles Davis and the Semiotics of Improvised Performance." In *In the Course of Performance: Studies in the World of Musical Improvisation*, edited by Bruno Nettl and Melinda Russell, 261–289. Chicago: University of Chicago Press.

Snead, James. 1981. "On Repetition in Black Culture." *Black American Literature Forum* 15 (4): 146–154.

Solis, Gabriel, and Bruno Nettl, eds. 2009. *Musical Improvisation: Art, Education, and Society*. Urbana: University of Illinois Press.

Stasch, Rupert. 2008. "Knowing Minds Is a Matter of Authority: Political Dimensions of Opacity Statements in Korowai Moral Psychology." *Anthropological Quarterly* 81 (2): 443–453.

Starrett, Gregory. 1995. "The Hexis of Interpretation: Islam and the Body in the Egyptian Popular School." *American Ethnologist* 22 (4): 953–969.

Stewart, Alex. 2007. *Making the Scene: Contemporary New York City Big Band Jazz*. Berkeley: University of California Press.

Strathern, Andrew. 1996. *Body Thoughts*. Ann Arbor: University of Michigan Press.

Strauss, Claudia. 1984. "Beyond 'Formal' versus 'Informal' Education: Uses of Psychological Theory in Anthropological Research." *Ethos* 12 (3): 195–222.

Street, Brian. 1984. *Literacy in Theory and Practice*. New York: Cambridge University Press.

———, ed. 1993. *Cross-Cultural Approaches to Literacy*. Cambridge: Cambridge University Press.

Stringham, Edward J. 1926. "'Jazz'—An Educational Problem." *Musical Quarterly* 12: 190–195.

Sudnow, David. 2001 [1978]. *Ways of the Hand: A Rewritten Account*. Cambridge: MIT Press.

Taylor, Charles. 1989. *Sources of the Self: The Making of the Modern Identity*. Cambridge MA: Harvard University Press.

———. 1992. *The Ethics of Authenticity*. Cambridge, MA: Harvard University Press.

Tekiner, Deniz. 2006. "Formalist Art Criticism and the Politics of Meaning." *Social Justice* 33 (2): 31–44.

Thomas, Rosalind. 1991. *Oral Tradition and Written Record in Classical Athens*. Cambridge: Cambridge University Press.

Torgovnick, Marianna. 1990. *Gone Primitive: Savage Intellects, Modern Lives*. Chicago: University of Chicago Press.

Townsend, Peter. 2000. *Jazz in American Culture*. Jackson: University Press of Mississippi.

Trager, Lillian. 1988. *The City Connection: Migration and Family Interdependence in the Philippines*. Ann Arbor: University of Michigan Press.

Turner, Victor. 1967. "Betwixt and Between: The Liminal Period in *Rites de Passage*." In *The Forest of Symbols: Aspects of Ndembu Ritual*, 93–111. Ithaca: Cornell University Press.

Urban, Greg. 1996. "Entextualization, Replication, and Power." In *Natural Histories of Discourse*, edited by Michael Silverstein and Greg Urban, 21–44. Chicago: University of Chicago Press.

———. 2001. *Metaculture: How Culture Moves through the World*. Minneapolis: University of Minnesota Press.

Vann, Elizabeth F. 2006. "The Limits of Authenticity in Vietnamese Consumer Markets." *American Anthropologist* 108 (2): 286–296.

Vargas, Joao H. C. 2008. "Exclusion, Openness, and Utopia in Black Male Performance at the World Stage Jazz Jam Sessions." In *Big Ears: Listening for Gender in Jazz Studies*, edited by Nichole T. Rustin and Sherrie Tucker, 320–347. Durham: Duke University Press.

Vincent, David. 1993. *Literacy and Popular Culture: England 1750–1914*. Cambridge: Cambridge University Press.

Walser, Robert. 1997. "'Out of Notes': Signification, Interpretation, and the Problem of Miles Davis." In *Keeping Score: Music, Disciplinarity, Culture*, edited by David Schwarz, Anahid Kassabian, and Lawrence Siegel, 147–168. Charlottesville: University Press of Virginia.

Watson, Kevin E. 2010. "The Effects of Aural versus Notated Instructional Materials on Achievement and Self-Efficacy in Jazz Improvisation." *Journal of Research in Music Education* 58 (3): 240–259.

Weber, Max. 1978a. "Bureaucracy." In *Economy and Society*, edited by Guenther Roth and Claus Wittich, 956–1005. Berkeley: University of California Press.

———. 1978b. "Charisma and Its Transformations." In *Economy and Society*, edited by Guenther Roth and Claus Wittich, 1111–1157. Berkeley: University of California Press.

———. 1978c. "The Routinization of Charisma." In *Economy and Society*, edited by Guenther Roth and Claus Wittich, 246–254. Berkeley: University of California Press.

———. 2001. *The Protestant Ethic and the Spirit of Capitalism*. Translated by Talcott Parsons. London: Routledge.

Weick, Karl E. 1998. "Improvisation as a Mindset for Organizational Analysis." *Organization Science* 9 (5): 543–555.

Weiner, Annette B. 1992. *Inalienable Possessions: The Paradox of Keeping While Giving*. Berkeley: University of California Press.

Whyte, William H. 2002. *The Organization Man*. Philadelphia: University of Pennsylvania Press.

Wilf, Eitan. 2010. "Swinging within the Iron Cage: Modernity, Creativity and Embodied Practice in American Postsecondary Jazz Education." *American Ethnologist* 37 (3): 563–582.

———. 2011. "Sincerity versus Self-Expression: Modern Creative Agency and the Materiality of Semiotic Forms." *Cultural Anthropology* 26 (3): 462–484.

———. 2012. "Rituals of Creativity: Tradition, Modernity, and the 'Acoustic Unconscious' in a U.S. Collegiate Jazz Music Program." *American Anthropologist* 114 (1): 32–44.

———. 2013. "Streamlining the Muse: Creative Agency and the Reconfiguration of Charismatic Education as Professional Training in Israeli Poetry-Writing Workshops." *Ethos* 41 (2): 127–149.

———. Forthcoming. "Modernity, Cultural Anesthesia, and Sensory Agency: Technologies of the Listening Self in a U.S. Collegiate Jazz Music Program." *Ethnos.*

Wilkinson, Christopher. 1994. "The Influence of West-African Pedagogy upon the Education of New Orleans Jazz Musicians." *Black Music Research Journal* 14 (1): 25–42.

Wilson, Olly. 1999. "The Heterogeneous Sound Ideal in African-American Music." In *Signifyin', Sanctifyin' & Slam Dunking: A Reader in African American Expressive Culture*, edited by Gena Caponi, 157–171. Amherst: University of Massachusetts Press.

Winkler, Peter. 1997. "Writing Ghost Notes: The Poetics and Politics of Transcription." In *Keeping Score: Music, Disciplinarity, Culture*, edited by David Schwarz, Anaid Kassabian, and Lawrence Siegel, 169–203. Charlottesville: University Press of Virginia.

Wittkower, Rudolf. 1973. "Genius: Individualism in Art and Artists." In *Dictionary of the History of Ideas: Studies of Selected Pivotal Ideas*, edited by Philip P. Wiener, 297–312. New York: Scribner's.

Woodmansee, Martha. 1996. "Genius and the Copyright." In *The Author, Art, and the Market: Rereading the History of Aesthetics*, 35–56. New York: Columbia University Press.

Woolard, Kathryn A. 1998. "Introduction: Language Ideology as a Field of Inquiry." In *Language Ideologies: Practice and Theory*, edited by Bambi B. Schieffelin, Kathryn A. Woolard, and Paul V. Kroskrity, 3–47. New York: Oxford University Press.

Young, Bob. 2006. "Branford Marsalis Sounds Off on All That Jazz." *Boston Herald*, September 11.

Young, Edward. 1759. *Conjectures on Original Composition.* London: Miller.

INDEX

abstract expressionism, 12

academic art programs: conservatory model and, 74; as contradiction in terms, 6; critics of as products of, 223; irreconcilable narratives about modernity and, 10, 11–12; rationalization of creative practice in, 221

academic jazz programs: academic bubble and, 84–87; accreditation-based versus experiential-performative expertise in, 222; as alternative sites for employment and training, 26, 48–51; ambivalence about, 5; as antithetical to creative agency, 127; as antithetical to jazz, 13–15, 18, 87; binary oppositions in, 14, 80–81, 222–23; blackness as marker of charisma in, 110; chord-scale theory in, 19, 142, 144; commodification of academia and, 70–72; community of musicians and, 234n16; compartmentalization of knowledge in, 92; competition within, 218–19; complexity of cultural reproduction in, 218; as complex social institution, 17; concerns about students' improvisational skills, 193; congruence between academic jazz and recorded solos and, 152; conservation versus market demand in, 74–75; consistency in criticisms of, 10–11; contentious beginning of, 28–29; content of, 7–8; as contradiction in terms, 6; creative cultivation of organizations, 228; cultivation of future audiences, 50; cultural loss and, 225; cultural position of jazz and, 28; cultural reproduction of jazz in, 226; differentiation of, 70; diversity training in, 107–8; emergence of, 4–5, 17, 26–27; enrollment rates in, 234n3; ensemble classes in, 205–6; epistemological crisis in, 198; essentialization of jazz in, 81; eye versus ear and, 178, 183, 184–85; faithfulness to jazz culture in, 14; in four-year colleges, 92; funding for jazz, 38; harmonic versus melodic emphasis of, 217; "in-breeding ideology" at, 95; increasing number of

257

academic jazz programs (*continued*)
programs in, 95; indigeneity in, 88; informal practices as well as formal instruction in, 218; institutional isomorphism in, 118; instructor recruitment, 14, 18, 97; instructors' authority in, 235–36n1; instructors' knowledge and skills at, 84–85; jazz's dependence on, 51; market demand and, 36, 68–69; mediating logic of, 103; musically incomplete musicians and, 225; named after producers of pedagogy material, 118; online courses in, 232n12; origin stories of, 33–35; pedagogical undoing of effects of, 18; play-along devices and rise of, 202–4; primordially unmediated jazz in, 112–14; professional versus experiential credentials of instructors in, 236n4; professional versus "real" jazz in, 112–13; proficiency of graduates from, 120; range of scholarship on, 232n6; rationality and Romantic creativity in, 13; rationalization of creative practice in, 221–23; as reconfigured jazz scenes, 48–52; as response to exclusion, 31; self-differentiation in, 173, 186–87; as site for anthropological fieldwork, 21–22; as site of cultural standardization, 89; storytelling in, 2, 226; student assessment in, 119; student evaluations in, 235–36n1; students in instructors' bands, 85; supervision of instructors in, 107–8; teachers teaching teachers in, 95–97; testable knowledge in, 14; training of educators in, 19; transformations of aurality, 223; tyranny of the eye in, 183; as velvet cage, 6; vocational training model, 36–37; white middle-class majority in, 20. *See also* Berklee College of Music; jazz learning; New School for Jazz and Contemporary Music; pedagogical strategies
Adderley, Cannonball, 96, 135, 160, 209–10
Adorno, Theodor, 237n9
Aebersold, Jamey, 91, 202–3, 236n1
African Americans and African heritage. *See* blacks and blackness
Agrama, Hussein Ali, 132–33
"Alex" (student), 42–43, 143, 206, 240n12
alienability and inalienability of creative agency, 130–34, 138

alienation, 11
American Jazz Museum (Kansas City), 27
Americans for the Arts, 113
anthropology: cultural continuity and loss in, 224–28; locations of fieldwork in, 21–22; play in, 241n2; production of selves and, 218; public rituals in, 57; visible versus invisible dimensions in, 223, 226–27
Aristotle, 174–75
arts and art: commodification of markers of higher education, 132; exclusionist definitions of, 73–74; folk, 159–60; high art and music literacy, 178; highbrow and lowbrow, 33, 64, 223; ignoring artist's context, 160, 239n11; inalienability of, 132; institutional infrastructure for, 79; Romantic notions of creative self, 170; scientification of, 68–69, 143; theory and sterility in, 79; timelessness of, 159; as transformative, 113–14
Asad, Talal, 174, 240n11
Attica Prison riots (1971), 161–62
aurality and orality: acoustic unconscious, 124–27; cultivating listening with chance objects, 199–202; cultivating listening on one's instrument, 195–99; great divide theories, 237n3; improvisation, 20; instrumental hierarchy, 185–86, 191–92; interactional games and, 20–21, 190–91; listening as scarce resource, 218; listening as valued skill, 191; versus literacy, 20, 79, 145, 177–79, 183–87, 190, 222–23, 227, 233n8, 237n3; oral tradition in music, 145; persistence of in academic jazz education, 227; versus printed instructional materials, 121, 122–23; singing, 191–92; symbiosis between musicians and instruments, 196–97, 198; transformations of, 223
authenticity: versus academic environment, 87; advertisers' use of jazz and, 113–14; blackness and, 12, 110; in blues, 103; versus coherent narrative, 156; indigeneity and, 88, 110; jazz masters' deification and, 156; listening-oriented, 193; in performance, 217–19; primordially unmediated jazz and, 113; Romantic self-realization and, 240n9; "the street" and, 104
authority: analysis of improvisation and, 152,

Faubus, Orval, 161
Feldman, Victor, 160
Finale (software), 205
folk music, jazz as, 159–60
formalism, in art criticism, 239n11
Foucault, Michel, 21, 192–95, 198, 218,
    241n2
Frankfurt School, 2
"Fred" (Berklee administrator), 34–36, 57, 66,
    72–75

games, interactional: analytical framework
    for, 192; chance objects and, 199–202,
    209, 241n5; cultivating listening on one's
    instrument, 195–99; "fresh milk" and,
    199–200; honking and whistling, 189–91;
    improvisational competence and, 217–18;
    jam sessions and, 240–41n1; play and
    games in social theory, 241n2; recognition
    of jazz performers and, 209–11; recogni-
    tion of jazz standards and, 211–17; as
    reflexive cultural work, 190; technologies
    of the self and, 194
Geertz, Clifford, 241n2
gender, 55–56, 78, 80, 83–84, 106–8
Gershwin, George, 233n5
Getz, Stan, 55
GI Bill, 34, 36
Gillespie, Dizzy, 46, 97, 109
Gioia, Ted, 39
Goodman, Benny, 233n5
Goodman, Jane E., 141–42
Great Migration, 44

habitus: practical mastery, 174–75
Hamilton, Chico, 49, 234n14
Hancock, Herbie, 2, 231n1
Hanna, Roland, 101
hard bop, 97
Harvard University, 25–26, 234–35n7
Hawkins, Coleman, 216
Heidegger, Martin, 201
Helmreich, Stephan, 22
Henderson, Joe, 212
Hill, Andrew, 71
hip-hop, 51, 73
Hobsbawm, Eric, 63
Holiday, Billie, 54, 217

Hubbard, Freddie, 165
Husserl, Edmund, 182

imagination, mimetic versus creative, 9–10
imitation: creativity and, 129–30, 133, 138; of
    improvisation, 115–17, 124–31, 133–38,
    232n8, 239n6; muscle memory and, 165;
    phenomenology of, 133; plagiarism and,
    130–31, 132
improvisation: aurality and, 20, 177–78; build-
    ing blocks of, 165; with chance objects,
    199–202, 209, 241n5; chord-scale theory
    and, 144, 146–48; classroom reproduc-
    tion of, 19, 124–27; clichéd patterns of,
    164; compartmentalized teaching of, 93;
    concern about students skills of, 193;
    context and, 146; as creation ex nihilo, 12;
    in the dark, 184–86; decontextualization
    of, 149–50; editorial playing, 20, 178, 183,
    198; embodied playing habits and, 176;
    European reception of jazz and, 233n1;
    evaluation of, 176; fictional versus actual
    commentary on, 150–51; funding for jazz
    and, 38–39; harmonic anticipation and,
    156; harmonic form in, 147; as imita-
    tion, 133; imitation of, 115–17, 124–31,
    133–38, 232n8, 239n6; immaculate
    solos and, 154–56; individuation of, 216;
    intentionality in, 150–54, 156, 157; in jazz
    canon, 127–28; jazz masters' decision-
    making processes, 19–20, 128, 140–41,
    238n7; key elements of, 145; learning the
    lyrics and, 216–17; listening skills and,
    191; versus mastery of printed music, 176;
    mastery required for, 197–98; mistakes
    in, 154–56; muscle memory and, 165–67;
    musicians' unique voice in, 173–74,
    210–11; oral-to-written tradition in teach-
    ing of, 145; organizational theory and,
    229; pedagogical strategies for, 18; perfor-
    mance as learning mode, 45; readiness for
    different situations in, 165–66; responding
    to other band members in, 197–98, 202,
    206–7; rhythm versus melody in, 179–80;
    Romantic notions of creative self and, 170;
    self-determination and, 158; simplicity
    in, 179–81, 183; storytelling with, 231n2;
    suspense and, 153, 154, 156; theory and,

master class and, 85; off-campus gigs and, 25–26; on paucity of rehearsal space, 206; on payment for performance, 233n10
pitch, flexible concept of, 238n4
plagiarism, 130–31, 132, 134
play-along devices, 90–91, 94, 145, 202–8, 236n2
poetry, financial security and, 234n13
political correctness, 107, 109
Ponomarev, Valery, 99–100
Porter, Lewis, 234n3
postbop, 97
Powell, Benny, 49
Powell, Bud, 5, 97
prestige discourses, 66–67
Princeton University, 234–35n7
printed instructional materials: aurality and, 121, 122–23, 227; Berklee Press and, 118, 143; chord-scale theory in, 144; clichéd patterns of improvisation in, 164; commercially successful method books, 89, 91; cultural legitimacy and, 118; defacement of objects associated with, 121–22; educators' distancing from, 237n4; erasure of musicians' unique sound in, 210; eye versus ear and, 178; "field people" and, 102–3; growing role of, 19; institutional authority and, 141; institutional environment and, 118; from oral to written tradition in jazz teaching and, 97, 145; versus performance, 122–23; with play-along devices, 202–3; publishing industry and, 117–18; students inability to swing and, 120–21; stylistic features not represented in, 118–21, 145, 210, 238n4; transcribed solos and, 46; ubiquity of, 117–21; Western classical notation system and, 118–20
Pro Tools (software), 205
Public Leveraging Arts, 38
purification and pollution, 79–80
Putnam, Robert, 205

race. *See* blacks and blackness
rationality: creativity and, 12–15, 20–21, 23–24, 78, 89, 113, 142, 157, 162, 170, 186–87, 218, 221–23, 228–29; hyper-rational social systems and, 94; as iron cage, 232n5; versus jazz's primordialism, 114. *See also* rule-governed behavior and creativity

religion: analysis of transcriptions as religious exegesis, 139–42, 155, 156; distancing from written word in, 237n4; exegetical Method of Doubts and, 155
rhythm: simplification of in improvisation, 179–80
rituals: of creativity, 127–30, 138; inhabitance of jazz masters' creativity, 129–31, 237n7; inhabitance of traditional texts, 131–32; invented traditions, 63; value of to anthropologists, 57
Roach, Max, 5
rock and roll, 73–74
Rockefeller, Nelson, 161
Rodney, Red, 160, 236n6
Rollins, Sonny, 97
Romanticism, 9, 170–72, 177, 239n7, 240n9
Rousseau, Jean-Jacques, 239n7
rule-governed behavior and creativity: ambivalence toward academic art programs and, 6–7, 127; anthropology and, 175; asymptotic approximation and, 138; chord-scale theory and, 157; epistemological hierarchy and, 179; imitation and, 131; inalienability of creative faculty and, 132; modern creative practice and, 12; phenomenological infrastructure of, 181–86; print pedagogy and, 19–20; self-differentiation and, 186
Russell, Bertrand, 142
Russell, George, 38

sacralization, 79
Sahlins, Marshall, 224–25, 226, 227
Santa Fe Institute, 22
"Sarah" (student), 189–91, 195–96, 198–201, 209–10
Schillinger, Joseph, 34, 142, 233nn5–6
Schneider, Maria, 50–51
Scofield, John, 95
Second Miles Davis Quintet, 97
self-determination, 162, 238n6
sexuality: blackness and, 110; creativity and, 106, 107; in jazz nostalgia, 83–84; public imaginary of jazz and, 106–7, 235n13; unmediated jazz and, 114
Share, Robert, 63
Sheldon, Jack, 120
Shorter, Wayne, 92, 146–47